# NORFOLK
## GOES TO WAR

NEIL R. STOREY

HALSGROVE

*Troops from 1st/1st Warwickshire Yeomanry carting fodder, Costessey December 1914.*

First published in Great Britain in 2014

Copyright © Neil Storey 2014

Title page:  *Mobilized Reserve soldiers leaving from Thorpe Station, Norwich bound for active service with 1ˢᵗ Battalion, The Norfolk Regiment 1914.*

British Library Cataloguing-in-Publication Data
A CIP record for this title is available from the British Library

ISBN 978 0 85704 235 4

**HALSGROVE**
Halsgrove House,
Ryelands Business Park,
Bagley Road, Wellington, Somerset TA21 9PZ
Tel: 01823 653777    Fax: 01823 216796
email: sales@halsgrove.com

Part of the Halsgrove group of companies
Information on all Halsgrove titles is available at: www.halsgrove.com

Printed and bound in China by Everbest Printing Co Ltd

*Soldiers of The Essex Regiment resting on the Cattle Market near The Shirehall, Norwich 1914.*

# Contents

*Signals section of 4<sup>th</sup> Battalion, The Norfolk Regiment 1914.*

# Acknowledgements

The National Archives; The Imperial War Museum, especially Peter Murton the research and information officer at IWM Duxford; The Commonwealth War Graves Commission; Kath Griffiths, Norfolk Library and Information Service Heritage Library; Dr. John Alban, Susan Maddock and Freda Wilkins-Jones at The Norfolk Record Office; Great Yarmouth Library (Local Studies); Alan Leventhall,  King's Lynn Library (Local Studies); Kate Thaxton, The Royal Norfolk Regimental Museum; Major Gary Walker, The Suffolk and Norfolk Yeomanry Collection; BBC Radio Norfolk; The Fleet Air Arm Museum, Yeovilton; Col. Stamford Cartwright, The Worcestershire Yeomanry; Eva Bredsdorff, Powysland Museum/Amgueddfa Powysland; The Welsh Regiment Museum; Ian Hook, The Essex Regiment Museum; Capt. J. M. Holtby, The Queen's Royal Lancers & Nottinghamshire Yeomanry Museum, Alan Popper, Lincolnshire Archives; Katherine Buckland, Redoubt Fortress & Military Museum; Alan Redman, West Sussex Record Office; Revd. Barry K. Furness, Smallburgh Benefice; Geoffrey Dixon; Major Graham Bandy; Dick Rayner; Martin Sercombe; Dr. Paul Davies and Andrew Fakes of Great Yarmouth Local History & Archaeological Society; Norfolk Family History Society; Peter Brooks; Peter Stibbons; Harry Barnard; Kevin Asplin; Helen Tovey, *Family Tree Magazine*; Raymond Rogers; Brenda Leedell; Dean Grady; Kay Reeve; the late John Slaughter; my loving family and my dear son Lawrence.

---

DEDICATION

For all my friends in the
Norfolk Family History Society

---

# Author's Foreword

Time flies. It certainly does not seem twenty years ago, *Norfolk at War,* my first real foray into the military history of my beloved county was first published. Nor does it seem possible that those grand gentlemen of the First World War with whom I marched on Armistice Day are now all gone. I travelled with some of them to France and Flanders and there they would stand in silent tribute to their fallen comrades on the soil where they fought all those years before, sometimes at the corner of some muddy foreign field where there was once a stretch of line that was fought for and men died for. Sometimes it would be in a market square upon rain-washed cobbles surrounded by buildings bedecked with the flags of the allies, or at the great memorials such as Thiepval Memorial to the Missing on the Somme, or the Menin Gate at Ypres with the standards of countless veterans groups on parade. At those memorial services well I remember seeing some of the last remaining survivors of the First World War struggle out of their wheelchairs to take just one pace to lay a wreath or stand for the Last Post, their bodies had become weak with age but such was their resolve and dignity and never ending sense of commitment to remember their comrades.

It is also hard to believe it was back in 2008 Halsgrove published my *Norfolk in the Great War,* during the research for which I had the privilege to have one of the last interviews with Henry Allingham, at the time the last surviving member of the Royal Naval Air Service and one of the very last surviving servicemen of the First World War. Henry died the following year aged 113. He had served at the RNAS Station on the South Denes at Great Yarmouth. Now on this centenary year I revisit a number of the topics covered in my previous books adding new photographs and research and a host of new material, with a special emphasis on the road to war, the outbreak and early war years with overviews of what happened afterwards.

I just hope I can do those who gave so much and those who never forgot their comrades during and after the Great War the justice they deserve, especially as they cannot speak for themselves any more. We, their descendents and friends have been trusted with their memories and legacy. This is my tribute to them.

*Newly uniformed recruits of 4th Battalion, The Norfolk Regiment on Chapelfield Gardens, Norwich 1914.*

*Members of 6th Battalion, The Norfolk Regiment (Cyclists) T.F. on manoeuvres 1912.* Image courtesy of Norfolk County Council Library and Information Service

*The Cheshire Yeomanry arrive on Church Plain, Loddon 1914.* Image courtesy of Norfolk County Council Library and Information Service

# 1 The Winds of War

At the dawn of the twentieth century the fighting forces of Great Britain were badly in need of reform and Norfolk men were at the vanguard of the improvements and innovations that would shape the new British Army and Royal Navy. For the Royal Navy it was Admiral Sir John 'Jackie' Fisher of Kilverston Hall, who, when created First Sea Lord, led the 'old guard push' to persuade the War Office and ultimately the government that investment would be worthwhile in the first all iron clad, all big gun, turbine driven battleship – HMS *Dreadnought*. Among his staunchest supporters was Admiral Sir Arthur Knyvet 'Tug' Wilson V.C. of Swaffham. A career naval officer, Wilson attained the rank of Admiral of the Fleet and made a significant contribution to the Royal Navy as a whole through his own innovations and support for the development of new weaponry for modern naval warfare, notably torpedoes and submarines.

The revolutionary HMS *Dreadnought* entered service in 1906. *Dreadnought* represented such a marked advance in naval technology that all other existing battleships were rendered obsolete. Her name came to be associated with an entire generation of battleships – the 'Dreadnoughts' and henceforward all surface navies would be measured by their dreadnought strength and Britannia literally ruled the waves! However, Kaiser Wilhelm II nurtured

*HMS* Dreadnought *and the Royal Navy Home Fleet off Cromer, 1906.*

a desire to construct a German navy capable of challenging the maritime dominance of the Royal Navy and entrusted the expansion of the German navy to his naval minister and close adviser Admiral Alfred von Tirpitz. Tirpitz expanded the German navy by championing four Fleet Acts between 1898 and 1912 and in the wake of Dreadnought set about building Germany's own version of the new generation of battleships. Thus began a naval race that was to become an aggressive thorn in the side of Anglo-German relations, particularly threatening British pre-eminence in colonial and trade spheres and, ultimately, a major contributing factor to the outbreak of war in 1914.

Britain had enjoyed the boom of the Industrial Revolution, factories, railways and increased mechanisation transformed the country but with better sanitation and health care the population rose and the migration from countryside to Norwich during the nineteenth century saw the massive expansion of the city population from 36,800 in 1801 to 111,733 in 1901. There were many jobs in the city at such great companies as J. J. Colman famous for their mustard, Norwich Union Fire and Life Insurance; there were breweries such as Steward & Patteson, Bullards, Morgans and Youngs, Crawshay & Youngs; the foundries and industry of Barnard, Bishop & Barnard, Laurence and Scott and Boulton & Paul. But above all Norwich was a centre of shoe manufacture with the massive 'super factories' of Howlett & White, Sexton & Everards, James Southall & Co. and Edwards & Holmes dominating the scene. There were also a number of smaller firms which in total employed nearly 8,000 citizens in the shoe trade alone.

*Admiral Sir John 'Jackie' Fisher, 1st Baron Fisher of Kilverstone 'father of the Dreadnought'.*

Even in a city of so many jobs there were still those who could not find work; the problem was often far more acute in the countryside too. Agriculture was still the largest source of employment across the county and the working conditions for the agricultural labourer were improving after George Edwards founded the Eastern Counties Agricultural Labourers & Small Holders Union (later known as the National Union of Agricultural and Allied Workers) at North Walsham in 1906, and became its general secretary. But life and living was still 'tight' in the winter time when there was very little work to be had on the land. Many men turned their hand to whatever they could to tide them over until spring sowing, some even walked to 'go on the boats' and sailed as hands on the fishing trawlers

*Some of the agricultural labourers who had been given assisted passage to start new lives in Canada leaving Stalham Station 1908.*

out of Yarmouth. Those who had managed to earn a living in the country worked hard, from sun up to sun down, but they too often suffered a life living in sub-standard cottages – very charming and 'rustic' to look at in old photographs but often draughty, damp and leaky, especially if there was a hole in the thatch above *your* bed. To support those in need in the city there was the Norwich Distress Committee who could pay a 'dole.' Surprisingly in a city of over 100,000 the applications for dole received by the committee in 1908-9 numbered just 2,734. Families who had not managed to make a go of it or dared to take up the challenge of a new start in a 'land of opportunity' could look to emigrate. Organisations such as the Norwich Distress Committee put up posters appealing for unskilled labourers, navvies, domestic servants and all willing workers to go (with the assistance of the Committee) to 'Canada: Britain's nearest and greatest colony.' If you were a tenant farmer you might also be tempted by offers of 160 acres free to the man and his family who sought a fresh start in the New World. Under a variety of local and national initiatives hundreds of families from the city and county, with children aged upwards of 11 months, were sent or given assisted passage from Norfolk to Canada, Australia and New Zealand. This was, however, an expensive venture. To send a party of 53 men, women and children from Norwich to Toronto in 1906 cost over £400.

*Soldiers from the North Heigham area of Norwich serving with 2ⁿᵈ Battalion, The Norfolk Regiment, India 1912.*

Other young men sought a way to find a new life and regular employment, to escape the often hand-to-mouth experience of living and working in the countryside or to escape the tenements of the city, to seek adventure and see the world. Other fit young men walked to their nearest barracks and joined the Regular Army, a fact borne out on the service records of Norfolk men who, upon enlistment, state their previous trade as labourer. These men formed the core of the fighting men of the British Army. Regular soldiers would have a very active life – sports and games, military training and exercises all rounded a soldier's training. Regular battalions of The Norfolk Regiment served both at home and abroad, usually garrisoning India much as they had done in the nineteenth century. But these soldiers reaped the benefits of organisations established in the nineteenth century to improve the service life of the soldier in mind, body and soul, such as temperance associations. These aimed to keep soldiers sober and improve army education. Christian societies in turn worked towards troops 'keeping the faith'. Indeed, the British soldier in India could live very well, even Other Ranks could take their families out there and afford to have servants.

During the South African War (1899-1902), The Norfolk Regiment supplied both Regular and Volunteer infantry battalions for service but for the British army as a whole it was a steep learning curve to come to grips with the ways of war employed by the Boers. General concerns over the short-falls in fitness, education and training of military personnel had also become all too apparent among the volunteer forces. Richard Burdon Haldane, Secretary of State for War 1905 to 1912, had the duty of implementing the Esher Report's recommendations to reform the British Army.

The children who were maturing to man and womanhood in the early twentieth century, had been a generation that had benefitted from the 1870 Foster Education Act having been schooled in the three 'R's of Reading, wRiting and aRithmetic. They could look to a greater variety of employment oppor-tunities than any generation before. Cross country transport and international shipping could mean the world, or at least the great British Empire, was their oyster. But these children were different; they had not only been schooled in education, they had been educated in patriotism. Schools would often have flag poles and begin and end each day with a flag ceremony; the children would give thanks to the monarch in their prayers and with the Empire at its zenith the children's text books and lessons would regularly include overt and subtle references to it. Children's illustrated story papers such as *The Boy's Own Paper* and *Union Jack* were filled with tales of brave and patriotic young folk while school prize books hammered home this ethos with volumes swathed in suitably dramatic pictorial covers. Authors as G. A. Henty, Captain F. S. Brereton and Rudyard Kipling told stories of derring do from English history and the exploits of the men who built and fought to defend the far flung outposts of the British Empire.

From 1902 there was even Empire Day every 24th May (held on the birthday of the late Queen and Empress); an event consisting of costumed parades, speeches and much flag waving in both the physical and metaphorical sense. It was created with the express intention to 'remind children that they formed part of the British Empire, and that they might think with others in lands across the sea, what it meant to be sons and daughters of such a glorious Empire'. It reinforced the idea that the strength of the Empire depended upon them and they must never forget it. Patriotism, sense of duty and loyalty to the monarch pervaded every child's education.

Some of the children left destitute and alone by family or fate found a new start in Norfolk. The old Norfolk County School set up in the 1870s to serve the educational needs of the 'sons of farmers and artisans' was turned into a home for orphans and destitute boys under the charge of Dr Thomas Barnardo in March 1903. The cost of furnishing the institution for 300 boys and the necessary staff was covered by Fenwick S Watts Esq. in memory of his father. Formally opened by the Earl of Leicester on 17 April 1906, the school maintained the name of its last owner – Watt's Naval Training College – and was used for the training of selected Barnardo's boys for a life at sea in the Royal Navy or Mercan-tile Marine. Orphan and destitute boys between 11 and 14 years of age were admitted for a two year course of general education followed, upon attaining the age of 14, by a two year course of naval training. Most of these lads then progressed to Royal Naval Training Establishment HMS *Ganges*, at Shotley, Suffolk.

The greater affluence of the new middle class in the 19th century also saw the unprecedented expansion and creation of Grammar Schools and new public schools. Public schools were the heart-lands of the new generation of young men being prepared through education and tutored to aspire to lead as managers, business directors and captains of industry and, above all, to become ultra patriotic military leaders fit to be officers *and* gentlemen. Haldane began by creating his seed bed of future military leaders by creating the Officers Training Corps in 1907. The movement had two divisions: 'Senior' based in the universities and 'Junior' working in the schools but both working with the express aim of providing as many officers as possible for the Special Reserve and the new Territorial Force. Gresham's School at Holt embraced the Officers Training Corps scheme and membership of the OTC was soon compulsory at the school. Some of the masters became instructors and the school raised a band to smartly lead the boys on parade. Soon they were off on manoeuvres across the school field and surrounding heathland, camping and attending central OTC camps with other schools. Haldane's vision matured in 1914 and in the first seven months of the war, the OTC provided over 20,000 commissioned officers; many of them joining their regiments straight from school.

Boys from less affluent backgrounds did not miss out either. They had the chance to learn the skills required to be a loyal and adventurous Britons in the Boy Scout movement founded by another national hero Robert Baden Powell in 1907; the first Scout units in Norfolk emerged from 1909. During this period the patriotic ethos was omnipotent in public life and a number of cadet corps were also created at a local level. In 1911 one of the first achievements of the newly formed Norfolk and Norwich Branch of the Navy League was the creation of the Norwich Sea Cadet Corps. In 1912 a subscription raised the necessary money to buy the old Lowestoft trawler *Elsie* and fit her out as a training brig renamed *Lord Nelson*. The Cadet Norfolk Artillery was also formed in 1911, received official recognition in April 1913, and was affiliated to 1st East Anglian Brigade Royal Field Artillery (TF).

*Members of 6th Battalion, The Norfolk Regiment (Cyclists) T.F. on parade at the summer training camp at Boughton Park, Kettering, Northamptonshire, September 1913.*

The lion's share of Haldane's reforms were concerned with the massive task of reorganizing the British Army, including the creation of a British Expeditionary Force (BEF) and the Territorial Force. Under the reforms, officially introduced on 1 April 1908, The Norfolk Regiment was allocated three battalions in the new Territorial Force. These new battalions were initially created out of the old Norfolk Volunteer Battalions; the 4th Battalion drawing its men from the 1st and 2nd V.B.s and the 5th Battalion from the 3rd and 4th V.B.s respectively. The Norfolk Regiment was also granted the honour of raising one of the much heralded eleven Cyclist Battalions (Eight English, two Scottish and one Welsh) included in the scheme; thus our final Battalion was designated 6th Battalion (Cyclists) T. F. The Norfolk Regiment receiving a battalion of military cyclists was not overly surprising as its commanding officer, Lt-Col Bernard Henry Leathes Prior, was not only a charismatic and a very 'hands-on' leader who had served in the South African War, with Major W.H Besant he had established, and later commanded, the Norfolk Volunteer Infantry Brigade Cyclists and wrote one of the first training manuals for bicycle-mounted soldiers entitled *The Military Cyclist: Notes on the Work of the Individual Soldier* in 1907.

The new Norfolk Territorial Battalions were made up of eight companies, each of which consisted of about 4 officers and a hundred men. Although a few came from outside, most of them were Norfolk men and just about all parts of the county were represented. The allocation of men to each company depended largely upon in which part of the county they lived or worked. This suited most recruits who were more than happy to serve with their relations, friends and acquaintances and it made the battalion a close knit community. In fact amongst all ranks the battalion was riddled with complicated family ties of uncles, nephews, brothers and cousins serving side by side and throughout the various companies. This rank structure reflected society at the time: the officers were from the local gentry or the directors of larger local industries, the NCOs works foremen and ex-servicemen and the Other Ranks comprised of domestic staff, labourers, gardeners and estate workers.

The new Norfolk Territorial Force battalions had their first major parade at a grand review on Mousehold Heath on the occasion of the visit of HM King Edward VII to Norwich on 25 October 1909. On the day 11,000 city children were marshalled on to the heath in front of Britannia Barracks to sing to the King, and thousands more came to wave flags and watch the spectacle with over 3000 troops parading including Yeomanry, Artillery, Infantry, Cyclists, Army Service and Medical Corps under the overall command of Brigadier General J H Campbell, the commander of the East Anglian Division. Lining parties and a parade contingent were also provided by the members of the Royal Norfolk Veterans Association. The RNVA (founded 1898) was one of the very first ex-serviceman's welfare associations in the country and comprised Norfolk men who had served in the Royal Navy and many various branches and regiments of the British Army in campaigns going back to the 1840s. Their smart turnout, polished boots and fine array of bright medal ribbons and shiny medals were remembered by all who saw this parade and later a bronze medal was struck by the veterans to commemorate the event. But the highlight of the occasion for the military was the presentation of colours by the King to the K.O.R.R. Norfolk Yeomanry, the 4th and 5th Territorial Battalions of The Norfolk Regiment. This magnificent occasion was concluded with a general march past by all units. The King then retired for luncheon in the Officer's Mess at the Chapel Field Drill Hall. The whole event was one of the earliest occasions in Norwich to be captured on moving film.

By 1909, the War Office had recognized that in the event of a major European war, the existing medical arrangements for Britain's armed forces would be wholly inadequate. Some form of supplementary aid in addition to the Territorial Force Medical Service would be required to provide transport and care for the thousands of casualties returned from a British Expeditionary Force fighting on the Continent. The problem was training and maintaining such a force in peacetime when the demands upon the extant army medical services were not heavy but it was solved in the same manner with a call for an all-volunteer scheme, specifically *Scheme for the Organisation of Voluntary Aid in England and Wales* issued on 16 August 1909. The British Red Cross Society and Order of St John (although at that time working as separate Voluntary Aid Societies) immediately began to establish so-called Voluntary Aid Detachments (VADs) to recruit and train local volunteers for the task and very soon VAD detachments were being established across Norfolk.

With these massive changes to the military came new uniforms, equipment and the first field service operations and regulations manuals that provided the army with its first standard official manuals that clearly stated, in detail, staff responsibilities and procedures as diverse as fighting troops and their

*Some of the members of F Company, 5th Battalion, The Norfolk Regiment of to Territorial camp from Sheringham Station, July 1910.*

*Sandringham Voluntary Aid Detachment c1912.*

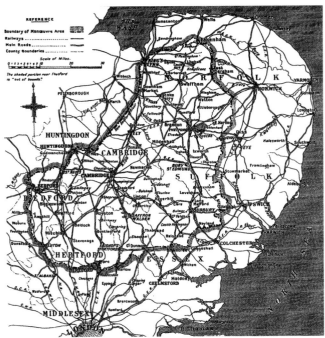

*Map showing the 'Great Manoeuvres' September 1912.*

characteristics, intercommunication and orders, movements by land and sea, protection, the battle, siege operations and night operations, quarters, camps and bivouacs. All this would ultimately shape the way the British Army was organized and how it conducted operations during the First World War. The practical application of the official operational guidelines were adopted and tested on numerous occasions during exercises and larger manoeuvres but the greatest of all these, conducted when the new reforms had 'found their feet' were the 'Great Manoeuvres' of September 1912.

These manoeuvres were different, conducted across a great swathe of East Anglia their scale was unprecedented in Great Britain. They almost did not take place at all however, after torrential rainfall caused extensive flooding and drowned a number of camps that had been set up prior to commencement. The troops from 1st and 2nd Coldstream Guards and 2nd and 3rd Grenadier Guards arrived at Swaffham on Saturday 24 August. The weather experienced during the morning had made it impossible for the troops to occupy the meadows where their tents had been pitched and 1st Coldstreams were immediately sent back by train (to await an improvement in the weather), one battalion was left on the camp ground and the rest of the men, around 2,000 in number, had to be found billets around the town of Swaffham in all manner of accommodation from Assembly Rooms to stables and barns.

The special correspondent dispatched by *The Times* to cover the manoeuvres recorded 'As I stand by the side of a Norfolk turnpike, this inimitable infantry swung by, wet to the skin, perhaps chilled to the marrow, chanting a roundelay to prove it takes more than weather to fathom the bottom of the *esprit* of British infantry…' In hindsight his words are an eerie premonition of phrases that were to feature prominently in the newspaper reportage of the war on the Western Front in 1914.

On 12 September *The Times* correspondent wrote 'Today, thank goodness, a change has come. The bitter north wind has dropped, the mists have rolled away off the Norfolk Broads and the kindly sun has dried the wringing khaki of the gallant men who were moved yesterday into standing camp to relieve them of the rigors of the cheerless bivouac.' With the weather improved the manoeuvres went ahead as planned. The general idea of the exercise was that the coast line of East Anglia represented the frontier between an imaginary 'Red Enemy' under the command of Lieutenant General Sir Douglas Haig and 'Blue England' commanded by Lieutenant General Sir James Grierson. The scenario was that the Red enemy had crossed the frontier between Wells and Hunstanton and was moving southward when operations began. Blue England had ordered a general mobilization and was urgent to prevent the entry of Red troops into London. In order to confine troops within reasonable limits an area of ten miles broad was declared as 'impassable' from the Wash to Somersham. Each force consisted of a cavalry division, two infantry divisions, army troops, two aeroplane flights and

*The flooded Guards camp at Swaffham, August 1912.*

*Drummers of 2ⁿᵈ Battalion, The Grenadier Guards in their emergency billet at the Assembly Rooms, Swaffham August 1912.*

each side also had an airship (The airships were named *Gamma* and *Delta*). To monitor and referee the manoeuvres the Chief Umpire was General Sir John French, and with his Staff he based himself in Cambridge. He was later joined by the King and other international military dignitaries and delegations.

The forces were nearly equal in size. The Staff of the Red Army were Aldershot command who were accustomed to working together. In contrast, the Blue Staff were drawn from all commands except Aldershot. Red cavalry and infantry were all regular Aldershot divisions. Conversely the Blue, had two brigades drawn from Household Cavalry, Scots Greys, Yeomanry and Cyclists while the Blue infantry came from the Southern Command (3rd Division) and Eastern Command (4th Division) and Territorial Force. All ranks and services included, the total number of troops involved across East Anglia amounted to nearly 50,000.

The public had already had their appetites whetted during the Aldershot Command Training before the commencement of the main manoeuvres. The special correspondent from *The Times* had been sent to Thetford and submitted his report dramatically headlined: 'A Battle at Dawn', it concludes 'The Aldershot Army has become a flank guard and has already had a brush with the advance guard of the Swaffham enemy. The menace from this direction is so great that the second army has detached a brigade of infantry to help the flank guard. At sundown the river Wissey, a tributary of the Ouse, separated the outposts of the opposing forces, and early tomorrow an issue of great importance will be decided. The announcement here that Sir Douglas Haig's army is marching by night to the drifts will disclose nothing to the enemy, as by the time this despatch is public, the battle will be lost and won.'

On the eve before the main manoeuvres the Red cavalry was at Barnham and Euston with patrols on the line of the river Lark as far south as Bury St Edmunds. The rest of the Red army was halted for the night in the areas of Stoke Ferry, Methwold, Mundford, Sandford, Watton and Swaffham, with Red communications running through Wells and an advance base at East Dereham. At 6am on 16 September 1912, it was declared 'commencement of hostilities' and both sides went into action knowing time was critical to success or failure. Both local and national papers avidly followed the manoeuvres and public interest grew apace with each 'action' particularly if the readers recognised somewhere in their locality.

Country folks stood on the streets and by the fields and watched in amazement; many had undoubtedly seen the local volunteers or the new Territorials on their weekend manoeuvres or Field Days but they really had never seen

*Officers and men of 2ⁿᵈ Battalion, Coldstream Guards marching out to do battle across Breckland during the 'Great Manoeuvres' September 1912.*

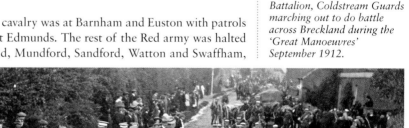

anything on this scale before. It was the last of the gentlemanly experience of warfare. Yes, lessons had been learned since the Boer war; kit and weaponry had evolved but still the senior officers rode their horses in front of their men and marker flags were carried to show the progress of the advancing troops in action. Such flags were to play a fateful role in the battles of the Great War when it came and the fate of many a young soldier could depend on whether some report, accurate or not, had been received of marker flags being seen in enemy trenches during an attack.

During the manoeuvres it soon became abundantly clear Haig had not realised the importance of the spotter aircraft. Grierson, the victor, had hidden his troops from observation and Haig had failed to ascertain the movements or deployment of the Blue forces. In contrast, Grierson had almost perfect knowledge of the movements of Haig's troops.  In the final analysis of the manoeuvres in spite of the efforts of the umpires and judges to make the contest appear more even, Haig was simply out-gener-alled by Grierson. There would be another manoeuvres in 1913 but they were nowhere near the scale of those conducted in 1912. In 1914 the British Army went to war. General Grierson died of an aneurism of the heart shortly after the outbreak of war on 17 August 1914 and General Haig went on to command the British Expeditionary Force on the Western Front from 1915 until the conclusion of hostilities in 1918.

In the immediate aftermath of the great manoeuvres and with much militarism in the air, national hero Field Marshal Lord Roberts VC, known affectionately to the British public and old soldiers alike

*Field Marshal Lord Roberts V.C. addressing a packed St Andrew's Hall, Norwich in his capacity as President of the National Service League, 23 September 1912.*

as 'Bobs', toured the country speaking at large gatherings in prominent buildings in his capacity as President of the National Service League. The League was a pressure group founded in February 1902 'to alert the country to the inadequacy of the British Army to fight a major war and to propose the solution of compulsory training', specifically four years military training for home defence for every man aged between eighteen and thirty. Such militarism was not universally popular but by the time Roberts came to Norwich on 23 September 1912 the League claimed it had over 21,500 members and claimed a further 30,000 'adherents' across Great Britain.

Robert's visit to Norwich aroused great public interest and was held in long remembrance by those who attended the evening meeting in St Andrew's Hall. After a speech by the chairman, The Earl of Leicester, Lord Roberts stood up to speak and was greeted with prolonged cheers. In his speech he explained his anxiety over of the nation's military preparedness:

Roberts detailed the rising concern he had for the 'increase of the naval power of foreign states' especially that there was 'a German Navy of sufficient strength and of suitable formation to be able to hold its own against the greatest maritime power.' He then voiced his concerns for the British Army:

'It is only when there is a prospect of war that any interest is taken in the army by the general public and then only in a hysterical and excitable fashion. No enquiry is even then made by the public as to whether the men who are sent off to fight, and perhaps to die, are thoroughly qualified for their perilous duties; whether they are numerically strong enough or sufficiently trained as soldiers to cope with the enemy troops they may have to meet; whether they are properly equipped or whether their arms are all that they should be. But when disasters occur from want of numbers, insufficient training or inferior weapons the army and its commanders are as unfairly as they are unstintingly condemned by the same public.

'It is as short sighted as it is unpatriotic but it will never be otherwise until the army is looked upon as part and parcel of the nation, as something belonging to the people themselves, the interests of which are identical with their own, until, in fact, we become 'A Nation in Arms.''

Roberts concluded: 'It is the citizen army and not the regular army upon which we have to depend for the safety of our homes. Are we going to be mad enough to allow this important, this sacred duty to be entrusted to men unfitted for it? Should the invasion of England ever take place, the troops our defending force would have to meet would be composed of picked men, the most experienced and the most highly trained the enemy possesses. To have any chance of holding our own against such men we must, without delay, adopt the system of compulsory training. The only system which is fair upon all, high and low, rich and poor, and the only system by which our citizen soldiers are given the required amount of discipline and training.'

In 1913 the smaller scale Army Manoeuvres were held in the Midlands during September, and through the summer Territorial Force units held their camps in good weather. The canvas tents remained dry, kit inspections were carried out in the open, soldiers trained on grassy land, dug their trenches into dry soil, troops went on route marches, Yeomanry rode out and the cyclists raced around country lanes on manoeuvres. For the families, friends and sweethearts that came to see the 'Field Days' the scene was impressive and the white summer dresses and blouses of wives and sweethearts who were permitted to come and watch punctuate the background of many photographs taken at this time.

The last peacetime showcase for the Territorial Force in Norfolk came in July 1914 when the Norfolk and Suffolk Brigade held their two week camp on the Holkham Estate. The Brigade on this camp comprised the 4th and 5th Battalions Norfolk Regiment, 5th Suffolks, 2nd East Anglian Brigade Royal Army Medical Corps (T.F.), Norfolk and Suffolk Company of the Army Service Corps (T.F.). During the week they worked together in field operations and played in sporting competitions in the evenings. The culmination of the camp was a parade of over 2000 Territorials who marched past the Earl of Leicester, Lord Lieutenant of Norfolk, and Major General E S Inglefield CB DSO, the General Officer Commanding the East Anglian Division, in extended column of companies, with colours flying and bayonets fixed.

Once the parade had marched past the troops formed a square and were addressed by the Lord Lieutenant who expressed his great pleasure at what he had seen, not only on the parade but throughout the week's camp, stating: 'You marched past well and if each battalion is called upon for more serious work it will do its duty to uphold the honour of its county and country.' For many men it would seem like they were never out of khaki again because they found OHMS envelopes warning of the embodiment of the Territorial Force waiting for them when they returned home. Some would recall those last camps as truly idyllic, and almost innocent. Although the men had trained well, indeed the British Army was one of the best trained armies in the world but nothing could have prepared them for the coming cataclysm of the most modern war yet known.

*The last great parade of the The Norfolk and Suffolk Brigade of the Territorial Force. Over 2000 Territorials march past the Earl of Leicester, President of the County Territorial Association and Major General E S Inglefield CB DSO, the General Officer Commanding the East Anglian Division, Holkham July 1914.*

# 2 **When War Was Declared**

From July in that glorious summer of 1914 it was not a question of if there was going to be war with Germany, but when. With Europe edging ever closer to the precipice of war it was time to take a holiday while one could, the weather was excellent and the coastal resorts were enjoying a bumper season, among them was Clementine Churchill, wife of First Lord of the Admiralty, Winston Churchill, who had taken their children for a bucket-and-spade holiday on the Norfolk coast staying at Pear Tree Cottage at Overstrand, near Cromer. While still working unrelentingly to bring the Royal Navy up to the highest state of readiness for war, Winston joined them at weekends. He would sometimes arrive by the Admiralty yacht *Enchantress* which would be anchored off Overstrand and Mr Churchill would come ashore in a steam pinnace. The visits would often be reported in the local newspapers along with Mrs Churchill's shopping expeditions to Cromer. While there it was recalled how Winston Churchill would mobilise all the children on the beach to build giant sandcastles and man their defences against the incoming sea. All too soon the weekends would be over and he would leave early for London by the Monday morning express.

In the last days of July Churchill left his family by the seaside and hurried back to London to postpone the dispersal of the First and Second Fleets and the demobilisation of the Third – an act initiated after a phone call from the nearby Sea Marge Hotel (there was no telephone at Pear Tree Cottage). By the end of the month he was able to report to the King:

*The Rt. Hon. Winston Churchill, First Lord of the Admiralty, 1914.*

31 July 1914
Admiralty

12.30 a.m.

SECRET

Sir,

Your Majesty is informed of the diplomatic, so I confine myself to the military aspect.   The First Fleet is now in the open seas. The Second Fleet will assemble tomorrow at Portland. All 'precautionary' measures have (so far) behaved magnificently. The four old battleships will reach the Humber tomorrow. All the flotillas have reached their stations …

The following night, acting on his own responsibility, Churchill instigated the summons to all Reservists for the full mobilisation of the Fleet. He wrote to his 'Clemmie' at Cromer:

SECRET
Not to be left about but locked up or burned

My darling,

There is still hope although the clouds are blacker & blacker. Germany is realising I think how great are the forces against her & is trying tardily to restrain her idiot ally. We are working to soothe Russia. But everybody is preparing swiftly for war. And at any moment now the stroke may fall. We are ready…

Two days later Germany declared war on Russia and on 3 August her forces invaded Belgium. Britain's ultimatum to Germany, demanding respect for Belgian neutrality, expired at midnight (German time) the following night. At that instant Churchill flashed the fateful signal to all HM Ships and Naval Establishments:

4 August 1914
Admiralty
11 p.m.

Commence hostilities against Germany

In *Twenty-One Years* Randolph Churchill recorded his memories, as a boy of three, of the coming of the war:

We were staying at the seaside ... There was a lot of excitement and my father had to go to London. One day we were told that war had come. We looked out to sea expecting that German ships would soon come into view but nothing happened, except that my father could not come down from London. We children were all disappointed – no Germans and no Papa.

In the county of Norfolk, over the weekend of Saturday 1 and Sunday 2 August 1914, a palpable military presence manifested as soldiers were posted to guard key areas such as railway stations, utilities, wireless stations and military installations, among them the Yarmouth Coastguard Station which had been taken over as the headquarters of the Flying Corps Staff. The people of the nation and the county knew they were on the brink of war. First to be called were the men of the Royal Naval Reserve, most of whom lived in the towns and hamlets along the coast. The Admiralty order calling up all classes of naval reserves reached some towns as early as 4 o'clock on the morning of Sunday 2 August. In *Norwich War Record* (1920), Herbert Leeds recalled the day, 'Motor cars sped into the neighbouring villages, and a cutter went down into The Wash carrying instructions to those who were with the fishing fleet. There were about sixty Naval Reservists in King's Lynn, and by one o'clock forty-eight out of the sixty presented themselves in uniform at Lynn Custom House. They left by train in the afternoon for Chatham and were given an enthusiastic send off.'

*Mobilised Royal Navy Reservists draw quite a crowd in front of the Custom House, King's Lynn, 2 August 1914.*

At Great Yarmouth the Naval Reservists reported to the Custom House throughout the morning and gathered on the Quay in the afternoon and made their way to Southtown Station headed by a red ensign carried on a boat hook. Many were accompanied by their wives and in some instances the departing men carried their youngsters shoulder high as they were cheered along the way by crowds mostly made up of holiday visitors. As they passed the river steam boats moored at the Town Hall quay they were given a farewell salvo from their steam whistles.

The permanent staff of the Norfolk & Suffolk Territorial Infantry Brigade had set up an office in the Royal Hotel at Great Yarmouth and the Brigadier and his staff proceeded there immediately after the Holkham Camp. The adjutants of the various companies made arrangements to place themselves in close contact with their respective headquarters and kept a weather eye on the post offices who had extended the hours of their telegraph service in the event of urgent announcements or orders being transmitted.

The *Yarmouth Mercury* picks up the story:

*On Monday (3 August) it was difficult to realise that we were on the verge of war. Visitors poured into the town in thousands, indeed the day from this point of view probably equalled previous records. It is true the majority as they passed up Regent Street stopped to read the placards outside the press office and eagerly bought up the various editions of the evening papers but they were out for a holiday and apparently for the most part were determined to enjoy themselves for the time being. As one looked upon the gay throng making merry one could not but recall the oft quoted French saying as to Englishmen taking their pleasures sadly. Could a Frenchman have seen them he would have been astonished that under the circumstances there could be so much hilarity and jollity. Amid all the fun which prevailed on the Drive a note of solemnity however obtruded itself upon the gay and laughing crowd as it passed up and down This was due to the presence of a khaki clad member of the Royal Garrison Artillery with bayonet fixed rifle on sentry go in front of the old Coastguard Station now the headquarters of the Flying Corps staff. All day long there was quite a crowd leaning over the wall watching the sentry as he paced cease-lessly backwards and forwards or interested in the movements of members of the Flying Corps who were on watch with telescope at the upper windows of the building.*

*Late birds who were out between eleven and twelve on the Monday night were surprised and in the case of the more timid somewhat alarmed by all the public lights of the town being extinguished. We have been informed that the reason was that a small unit of our Navy which had been lying in the roadstead desired to established communication with the authorities ashore and this done by means of flashing with a small hand lamp, the lights on the Parade made it difficult to read the message. It was at first thought that only the Parade lamps needed to be extinguished but either because it was necessary or more probably because it was not quite understood what was required, all the public lamps in the town were put out. This incident gave rise to all sorts of rumours the next day and it was asserted that not only would there be no public illuminations on the Tuesday night but that the supply of gas and electricity to the shops on the front would also be cut off.*

*On Monday too, the local batteries of the Territorial artillery who had proceeded to Colchester on Saturday for their annual training, received orders to return home and reached Yarmouth shortly after 10.00pm on Tuesday . On Tuesday there were also signs about the town that thing were coming to a climax. The Territorials were mobilised and while some were sent to do duty at various spots along the coast northward, a squad was sent to the Post Office and a guard placed at the Regent Street entrance. This unusual spectacle and the continuous passing up and down the street by cyclist troops, was a source of great interest to the public. During the day there was an undercurrent of repressed excitement as ominous news filtered through which seemed to leave little room for doubt that England would have to take up arms. The board outside the Daily Press office, upon which from time to time a brief summary of more important news is exhibited was eagerly scanned by hundreds of people. Late in the evening all uncertainty as to what part England would play in the Titanic struggle was removed and the tension of the previous days was somewhat relaxed and gave place to a generally shared feeling that terrible as it was to contemplate the effect of such a step, it was humanely speaking inevitable.*

*Meantime with all these happenings it was a matter of no little surprise that the large numbers of visitors in our town spending their holidays should take things so quietly. It was anticipated the majority would have cut their holidays short and hurried home, if not because of the possibility of the railway service being restricted and travelling rendered difficult with the object of husbanding their resources to meet eventualities. But there was nothing in the nature of a rush home and the sea front has continued to present all its usual holiday aspect and the places of entertainment have so far been well patronised.*

*There are those in the town who have no direct financial interest in the summer season however who have been inclined to show some resentment at the apparent unconcern of our visitors to the present situation. 'Why,' they ask, 'should we as a town be called upon to provide all these strangers with food which we may be sorely in need of later ourselves.'*

*This situation was created by the run on foods on the outbreak of war as people began to hoard and food prices became inflated. On Tuesday and Wednesday several of the principal grocery and provision stores in Yarmouth closed their doors against the public temporarily to enable them to execute the large number of orders sent in. In not a few cases the proprietors declined to fulfil all the requests on their orders as it was obvious they were of a 'panic' description.*

Despite official warnings against hoarding provision merchants had a massive increase in sales of tinned food and comments were made in the press about how the prices were creeping up and unnecessary shortages being caused. Some towns were better prepared than others; foremost was Sheringham UDC who took direct action calling together all the provision dealers to ascertain what stocks they had on hand, what arrangement they had in place to replenish and obtained a promise from the traders that prices would not be raised more than absolutely necessary. At the same meeting a general Emergency Committee was formed 'to deal with any matters that might crop up unexpectedly'.

It was also on 3 August that the first public appeal on behalf of The Norwich Branch of the British Red Cross Society was published in the *Eastern Daily Press* asking for volunteers to come forward for the war emergency:

*To the Editor – Sir- Will you allow me to make this appeal through your paper. In view of the very serious war news will all those holding any first aid or home nursing certificates and who are willing to give their services in case of need kindly send their names to me without delay. I shall be glad if retired fully trained nurses will kindly do same*

*Christabel E. N. Burton-Fanning*
*Vice-President Norwich Division*
*Red Cross Society*
*1 St Faith's Lane Norwich.*

On 4 August Sir Edward Grey, the Secretary of Foreign Affairs wired to the British ambassador in Berlin asking for a reply from Germany before midnight. In anticipation of mobilization of the Territorial Force Lieut-Col. E. E. le Mottee, commander of 1st East Anglian Brigade Royal Field Artillery applied to J. J. Colman Ltd for the use of their recreation ground connected with the Carrow Works for the purpose of providing accommodation for the men when embodied. Permission was readily given and the club house offered for sleeping accommodation and other purposes.

During the day of 4 August more soldiers were placed on guard at main post offices in larger towns across the county and throughout the evening crowds had gradually massed in front of the telegraph and newspaper offices as the ultimatum deadline approached. Along the coast as the evening light faded many lingered on the sea front 'where the lights of warcraft were discernible'. In the early evening almost 300 men from The Norwich Division of The National Reserve (Army) paraded at the Agricultural Hall and from them were selected those who had served in mounted units for the mobilization section. They divided by class of Reservist: those from the first class were sent direct to their old regiments, second class went to Territorial units and third class sent for Home Defence. At 11.00pm the streets were heard to ring with cheers, patriotic songs, the drink flowed, streamers were thrown and flags were waved. The message had been received that war had been declared against Germany.

On the morning of 5 August 1914 the men of the Territorial Force were mobilized and ordered to proceed to their headquarters immediately. In North Norfolk three United Automobile Services motor coaches were pressed into service leaving at a late hour on Tuesday night to collect the men of the 5th Battalion's North Norfolk company to Cromer for the early hours of Wednesday morning. Those arriving at particularly early hours were given the chance to get what sleep they could on mattresses and straw provided by A. H. Fox Ltd at the Parish Hall. As the men formed up in the market places to leave to leave their towns, civic dignitaries and local clerics often gave a short address before the townsfolk waved off 'their brave boys' from their local detachments. In Norwich the road area in front of the 2nd East Anglian Field Ambulance headquarters, Bethel Street, was soon clogged up with RAMC Territorials who were marched to the Technical and Old Middle Schools in St George's to await movement instructions. The Norfolk Yeomanry mustered at the Drill Hall on the Cattle Market. They made a smart sight on their parade at 4pm. The men who had come from outside the city would be accommodated in the Technical Institute but those who were local, and provided they reported at 8am the following morning at the Drill Hall, were permitted to go home and sleep in their own beds.

More National Reserves received the call-up and appeared to form a constant stream along Riverside Road and Gurney Road on their way to Britannia Barracks to rejoin the colours. The territorial infantry boys of 4th Battalion, The Norfolk Regiment were embodied at the Chapelfield Drill Hall in Norwich. Sentries were posted there all day with fixed bayonets to ensure no one except those connected with military matters entered the building and as the day progressed Companies from outlying areas arrived in the city by train and marched up to the Drill Hall to report, drawing large cheering crowds along the way. Upon arrival the men were placed in ranks and medical inspection was carried out and the men of the Battalion were billeted at the City of Norwich Schools on Newmarket Road.

The companies of 5th Battalion, The Norfolk Regiment mustered at their Battalion Headquarters in East Dereham. At Aylsham the local Territorials paraded in the Market Place and adjourned to

*Men of 4th Battalion, The Norfolk Regiment waiting to be billeted at the City of Norwich Schools on Newmarket Road, 5 August 1914.*

the Town Hall where Captain Purdy addressed his men urging upon them the importance of making themselves fit in every way, and not to grumble if they should be called upon to ensure hardships. He asked them to take as their motto 'For God and the King'. The men replied with cheers. Captain Purdy then formed the men up in the Market Place where the vicar, Canon Hoare, offered up a prayer and the men marched in high spirits to the GER Station headed by the band and a number of local men fell in behind to join up and go with their pals.

The Yarmouth men of B Company took with them some 30 recruits in civvies. At Cromer the men of F Company, under the command of Capt H. N. Bridgewater marched from the Parish Hall to the GER station to entrain for Dereham. The *Norfolk Chronicle* reported 'All of them were in the best of spirits, and were singing with great heartiness their company song 'Roll the Chariot Along'. It was estimated by the *Lynn News* that a crowd of some 2,000 saw the Downham boys off at the station and its vicinity, especially around the crossing gates upon which boys climbed to wave off older brothers and many a local lass mopped a tear as she waved her sweetheart goodbye.

At King's Lynn despite the pelting rain the men of the Lynn Companies of 5th and 6th Battalions were given a rousing send off. The men of the 5th Battalion fell in at the Armoury on London Road and marched in batches to the St James's Hall. Here they were fully equipped and to each man was given a Soldiers Pay Book – for use on active service – and ammunition was brought up from the magazine under special guard. When all the men had assembled Rev. A. H. Hayes, Rector of All Saints addressed them after they had been drawn up to attention by Capt. Arthur Pattrick. After the special address and prayers the dismiss was given and he shook hands with members of the company one by one, wishing all God speed.

At the station the crowds thronged the departing soldiers. The Lynn boys met up with the Downham and district platoons and Hunstanton men of the 5th Battalion leaving together on the 12.30 train for East Dereham. As the train moved out to the accompaniment of cheering crowds and waving hands a young man of the 5th waved a union flag out from the window and the train blew its whistle several times, even after it had passed out of sight.

At Downham crowds of family members and well wishers gathered to watch their local Territorials (Downham Section of B Company, 5th Battalion, The Norfolk Regiment) and batches of Reservists march to the railway station for entraining. The *Lynn News* recorded: 'The excitement began when the main body of Territorials left and their departure was witnessed by an immense crowd. It is estimated that at least 2,000 people were at the station or in its vicinity and the platforms were so crowded that people had difficulty in entering and leaving the trains. Numbers of people climbed on to the railway crossing gates and there were immense numbers in the vicinity of the station. When the Territorials left it was amid rousing cheers.'

At different times during the day reservists in similar batches arrived in the town ready to join their trains and as parties were formed there were processions to the station by the Hilgay Excelsior band under the conductorship of Bandmaster Long. At 1.30pm a large crowd assembled in the Market Place around contingents who were intending to leave and the Rev. E. T. Leslie the senior curate of

*Men of the Lynn Company, 5th Battalion, The Norfolk Regiment ready to leave from King's Lynn Station, 5 August 1914.*

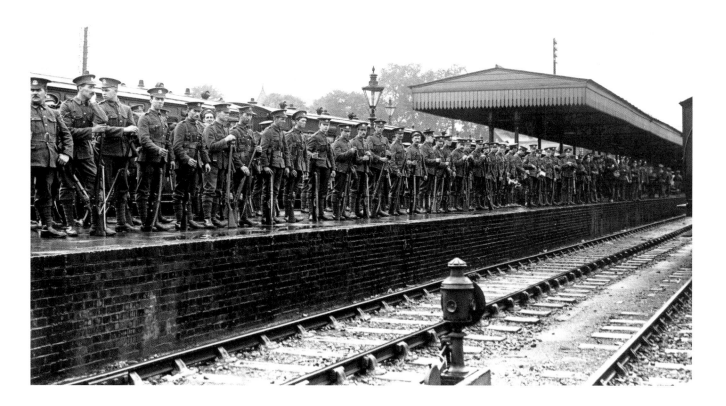

*The people of Downham Market give a fine send off to their local lads of the Downham Section of B Company, 5th Battalion, The Norfolk Regiment, 5 August 1914.*

Hitching (doing duty for the Rev. Capron who was on holiday) conducted a short service of intercession. After the offering of appropriate prayers and the singing of hymns the reverend gentleman, addressing the Reservists, impressed upon them the importance of the duties committed to them and, amid resounding cheers, wished them God speed. On his call too, hearty cheers were given for the King and the forces.

Throughout the morning of 5 August the companies of the 5th Battalion poured in to Battalion Headquarters at East Dereham from Cromer, Yarmouth, Lynn, Swaffham, Downham, Sandringham and Fakenham. Because of the sheer numbers involved as the men arrived they were sent to muster in the Market Place. As the men mustered a union flag was hoisted over two businesses in the Market Place and the troops broke into loud cheers and sang 'Rule Britannia'. Each man in the battalion had to pass through the Assembly Rooms and were examined to ensure fitness and freedom from infestations and contagious diseases by Drs Belding (the Medical Officer for Health for the Dereham Urban District), Duigan and Howlett. The Drill Hall certainly could not accommodate all 800 men of the battalion so the maltings belonging to Messrs F. D. G. Smith were requisitioned for the men, with the officers accommodated on the top floor of Hobbies Ltd warehouse. The place of assembly for the battalion was the Corn Hall with the Masonic Hall in Norwich Street used for stores and Assembly Rooms retained for military purposes. By nightfall on 5 August, 800 men of 5th Battalion, The Norfolk Regiment were accommodated in the town.

*Companies of 5th Battalion, The Norfolk Regiment muster in East Dereham Market Place, 5 August 1914*

The 6th (Cyclist) Battalion were on their annual training camp with the 6th Suffolk Cyclists at the Pakefield Rifle Range near Lowestoft when news of standby for mobilization came from the War Office and camp was broken on 3 August. By 9pm on 4 August the cyclists were described as on a 'war footing'. On August 5th at King's Lynn the 'C' Company Cyclists formed up at their headquarters on Purfleet Quay. Rev A. H. Hayes prayed with them and then gave a short address before the men left for the station. As the members of the Cyclist Battalion paraded in the station yard and were just about ready for entraining the Mayor stepped forward bareheaded and addressed them. He said 'We all wish you God speed and quick return. This is not the time for speechmaking but for action and I hope you will all do your duty to your King.' Three hearty cheers for his Majesty were given on the call of the Mayor. The 6th (Cyclist) Battalion was mobilized from its headquarters and Drill Hall on the Cattle Market in Norwich. They knew that under the scheme of Home Defence prevailing in 1914 the observation and patrol of the British Coast had been entrusted to certain cycle and mounted corps of the Territorial Force. The men of the 6th had been ready and keen to proceed to their war station on 'active service' from 1100 hours but were kept waiting until after 1800 hours when the final order to proceed arrived. Very shortly after the men were ready to depart. The *Eastern Daily Press* reported 'Each man had a formidable equipment to carry that made the civilians gasp as the Territorials vaulted into the saddles of their cycles. This included a haversack, water bottle, heavy valise, great coat, waterproof cape, a supply of ammunition (100 rounds) and rifle, the whole weighing from 20 to 30 lbs. The men, as they were making the final preparations for leaving, were in the highest spirits. They sang favourite melodies with vigour and shook hands cordially with friends who came to have a last word with them. And with a final whiff of their cigarettes and pipes which afforded them so much solace, and with a few smart exercises in drill, and with a fine burst of cheering they stepped gaily out of the Drill Hall. Girls rushed forward with merry laughter just to pat their military friends on the back, and to receive a warm glance of recognition as a reward. Umbrellas were waved in the air, handkerchiefs were flourished and all was done to make the Territorials feel that they were carrying away with them the best wishes of the people of the ancient city.' As the Cyclists rode off, smartly spaced to regulation distance they really did cut a dash. Tradesmen came quickly to their shop doors to see and people stopped, cheered and waved as the Cyclists turned the bend into Crown Road, passed across Prince of Wales Road past the bustling Territorial Association Headquarters on Tombland and on to Magdalen Street and out of the city to their 'war station' at North Walsham where they were to make their headquarters in the Board School and began to establish patrol sections dispersed along the coast.

On Thursday 6 August when Sections A and B of the Reservists entrained for service from Thorpe Station, Norwich to join 1st Battalion, The Norfolk Regiment, the *Eastern Daily Press* recorded:

*These are all men with about nine years service, all of them seemingly in the prime of life and pink of soldierly condition. There were about 500 of them, many drawn from Norfolk, but by no means all, for one came from as far away as Newcastle. The train was timed to leave at a quarter to three. Long before that hour a crowd, mostly consisting of poor and sorrowful looking women, many of them carrying children or pushing a perambulator, gathered on the platform. Hundreds of other people joined them, attracted from the throngs of spectacle hunters who now daily beset Thorpe station. The men, without any sort of musical embellishment for their march stepped briskly from Britannia Barracks and along the Riverside Road. Inside the station they passed between two crowded lines with difficulty preserved by the police and many an affecting incident was witnessed, the women having forced themselves to the front for the sake of a last farewell. The train started out at three, the men returning lustily a cheer sent up from the crowd behind the barriers.*

On the same day a general parade of A Squadron, The Norfolk Yeomanry took place on the Norwich Cattle Market to allot horses to the troops. Mr. R. E. Parker of Easton Hall was busily engaged in inspecting and purchasing horses. Comparatively few were rejected and among some of the mounts were some very superior animals. Once selected and allotted the horses were stabled at Fiddy's and Caley's (St Stephen's Back Street). The following day, Friday 7 August, The Norfolk Yeomanry were despatched to home war stations. B Squadron entrained at North Walsham. Their departure was witnessed by a great number of townspeople, including the Earl of Kimberley, and the officers and men, who were in the best of spirits, were given a hearty send off.

An impressive scene was witnessed in Fakenham Market Place when crowds of enthusiastic people assembled to watch the departure of C Squadron. Wymondham Troop were first to leave, followed by the Hunstanton Troop, then the Fakenham Troop and finally Petygard Troop. Special dismissal prayers and the blessing were said to each troop by Fakenham rector, the Rev. A. J. Seggar and Rev. A. F. Fenn, rector of Stibbard. As each troop left they were accorded a rousing send off and the singing of the National Anthem.

At Norwich there were three detachments departing at three widely separated times and on each occasion there was an enthusiastic demonstration of the public, particularly so at 4.50 when the approaches to the platform were thronged. The onlookers mounted on window sills, baggage barrows and anything for the sake of a view and they roused a lusty cheer as the train moved out.

At the time of the outbreak of the war there were only eighty motor vehicles in the entire British Army, all other transportation of guns, munitions, equipment, supplies and fuel relied on horse power. With the mobilization and the expansion of the army horses would be required in unprecedented numbers, and an immediate call for an additional 25,000 was made in the first six months of the war. The responsibility for this massive task was the sole responsibility of the Army Remounts Service and a National Emergency Impressment Order was issued under Section 115 of the Army Act whereby the names of locally appointed purchasing officers were empowered to impress horses, vehicles and equipment for the war effort details of which were published at the request of the War Office in the local press:

To horse-owners, farmers and others concerned the authorities wish to give notice that the following gentlemen are the sole persons authorised to act as purchasing officers and to impress horses, vehicles and equipment for His Majesty's Government:-

*Horses, carts and wagons impressed for military service under the Army Act in East Dereham Market Place, August 1914.*

Norwich and District: Collecting Station, Norwich – Mr. A. Collison; co-purchasers Messrs. H. Beard and R. E. Parker.

North East Norfolk Collecting Stations, Aylsham and North Walsham – Colonel Kerrison; co-purchaser, Mr. W. Case.

West Norfolk: Collecting Stations, Fakenham and East Dereham – Mr. H. Overman; co-purchaser, Mr. John Wharton.

King's Lynn and District: Collecting Station, King's Lynn – Rev. F. ffolkes; co-purchaser, Mr. R. Bullard.

Attleborough and District: Collecting Stations, Attleborough, Kenninghall and Wymondham – Mr. Roger Allen; co-purchasers Messrs. P. Ashburnham and F. Gaze.

Swaffham and District: Collecting Stations, Swaffham and Brandon – Messrs. B. Birkbeck and F. Knight

Soon market places and village greens were filling up with lines of horses, piles of tack and commandeered carts from farms and businesses in the locality as local yeomanry units and territorials were allotted their mounts watched by large crowds curious of onlookers. Many motor vehicles were also commandeered and because their use was far more important than their appearance there was a time before the pots of green paint were brought out, when troops were to be seen conveyed in brightly painted delivery trucks! Despite willing compliance from businesses across the county to give up some of their horses as the days passed it soon became apparent there were simply not enough horses for sale or voluntary requisition – for many farmers it was the height of harvest time; a story repeated across the country. Harvest or not the army needed horses and soon cars carrying officers and perhaps a farrier sergeant with a keen eye were bouncing along the streets of city and town, rural roads and rutted country lanes in search of suitable horses and wagons to be requisitioned. Rule of thumb was applied that a small farm should only require one horse. Many farmers complained bitterly at this imposition but a horse would only be returned upon submission of a written deposition that clearly showed hardship had been caused by the loss of a working animal. Nationally, a total of 165,000 horses were drafted into service. Very few were returned after hardship plea or war service.

*Members of The Essex Regiment transport section and their impressed horses in front of the Black Swan, Horsham St. Faiths 1914.*

# 3 Spy Scares

The day immediately after the outbreak of war saw a massive mobilization, movement and deployment of military forces across the entire country. Desiring troops to gel as units without the temptations of regular visits home and considering the impact on morale for soldiers 'going to war stations' even if they actually remained in Britain, most Territorial or Yeomanry units were deployed away from their home county. By the weekend of Saturday 8 and Sunday 9 August 1914 Norfolk was, like many other parts of the country, feeling a palpable military presence descend upon it as troops marched through the streets, occupied all manner of buildings and billets while white bell-tented encampments sprang up across estate grounds and parkland, especially along the coastline where there were fears of invasion and spies.

Anglo-German political and military relations had not been good for the majority of the ten years before the First World War and fears and mistrust of the German nation had been compounded in popular literature, as in *Riddle of the Sands*(1903) where Erskine Childers weaves a tale of two young amateur sailors who battle the secret forces of mighty Germany. Their navigational skills prove as important as their powers of deduction in uncovering the sinister plot that looms over the international community. Other titles such as *The Invasion of 1910* (1906) and *Spies of the Kaiser* (1909) both by William le Queux ably demonstrate the tenor of such literature which reached its zenith in the early years of the war with John Buchan's *The Thirty-Nine Steps* (1915).

But then for some there was no smoke without fire. Spies could be anywhere, especially when in July 1908, *The Times* reported how the Secretary of State for War was asked in Parliament whether he could say anything concerning 'a staff ride through England organised by a foreign power' and whether he had 'received any official information or reports from chief constables in the Eastern Counties as to espionage in England by foreign nations.' In 1909 Haldane set up and personally chaired a subcommittee of the Committee of Imperial Defence to consider 'the nature and extent of the foreign espionage that is at present taking place in the country.' In a report presented to this committee by Colonel James Edmonds head of MO5, which ran the 'Special Section' of the War Office, twelve cases of 'alleged reconnaissance work by Germans' – among them the report from a Norfolk inn-keeper who had 'two foreigners, stoutish, well-set-up men' who had called at his establishment. Another informant reported 'individuals, unmistakably foreigners' who were 'too absorbed and businesslike for ordinary tourists' in the North Walsham area.

Within hours of war being declared in 1914 anti-German outbursts saw some families purge their homes of German products: clocks, printed pictures, toys, especially trains and teddies were destroyed. Some German businesses, or even if the name above the shop appeared to be German, or selling a large number of overtly German products, suffered instances of damage and graffiti; even the King of Prussia pub on Ipswich Road in Norwich had its sign defaced and windows smashed and when repairs had been affected it re-opened as the King George V. Indeed the King himself was somewhat concerned about the clear German lineage of his surname and changed it to Windsor!

On 8 August 1914 the Defence of the Realm Act (DORA) was passed, its powers were wide ranging but above all the media and public imagination was caught by the clauses of the act which covered national security and the role they as good citizens could play in this crucial time of war:

(a)     to prevent persons communicating with the enemy or obtaining information for that purpose or any purpose calculated to jeopardise the success of the operations of any of His Majesty's forces or the forces of his allies or to assist the enemy; or

(b)     to secure the safety of His Majesty's forces and ships and the safety of any means of communication and of railways, ports, and harbours; or

(c)     to prevent the spread of false reports or reports likely to cause disaffection to His Majesty or to interfere with the success of His Majesty's forces by land or sea or to prejudice His Majesty's relations with foreign powers; or

*Soldiers of 2ⁿᵈ Battalion, The Essex Regiment marching along the East Promenade, Cromer, during the weekend of 8-9 August 1914.*

## Scaremonger Par Excellence

William le Queux claimed his books, although fiction, were based on secret knowledge he had obtained through his work in international intelligence. His pulp novels were enormously popular and responded to an anti-German mood that pervaded Britain in the first decade of the 20th century and gained a certain credence in the minds of many among the populace. In *Spies of the Kaiser* (1909), a book with such loaded chapter titles as 'The Peril of England,' 'The Back Door of England' and 'How the Germans are Preparing for Invasion' le Queux's heroes pursue German agents across the North Norfolk countryside and eventually track down the lair of the enemy spies to a perfectly respectable house just outside Roughton where once inside they discovered...

> *'Pinned down to the large deal table before the window was a huge map of the district from Weybourne towards Yarmouth, about five feet square, made up of various sections of the six-inch ordnance map, and literally covered with annotations and amplifications in German, written in red ink. Upon strings stretched across one end of the room were a number of photographic films and prints in process of drying, while strewn about the place were rough military sketches – the result of the labours of many months – a couple of cameras, measuring tapes, a heliograph apparatus, a portfolio full of carefully drawn plans with German explanations beneath, and a tin box, which, when opened, we found to contain a number of neatly written reports and memoranda in German, all ready for transmission to Berlin!'*

Which le Queux goes on to detail:

### EAST COAST OF ENGLAND—DISTRICT VI

Memoranda by Captain Wilhelm Stolberg, 114th Regiment Westphalian Cuirassiers, on special duty February, 1906 – December, 1908.

**WEYBOURNE – Norfolk – England.** (Section coloured red upon large scale map. Photographs Series B, 221 to 386.)

In Sheringham and Cromer comprised in this District are resident forty-six German subjects, mostly hotel servants, waiters, and tradesmen, who have each been allotted their task on "the Day."

ARMS: – a store of arms is in a house at Kelling Heath, where on receipt of the signal all will secretly assemble, and at a given hour surprise and hold up the coastguard at all stations in their district, cut all telegraph and telephones shown upon the large map to be destroyed, wire [79] in pre-arranged cipher to their comrades at Happisburgh to seize the German cable there, and take every precaution to prevent any fact whatsoever leaking out concerning the presence of our ships.

MEN: – Every man is a trained soldier, and has taken the oath of loyalty to your Imperial Majesty. Their leader is Lieutenant Bischoffsheim, living in Tucker Street, Cromer, in the guise of a baker.

EXPLOSIVES FOR BRIDGES: – These have been stored at Sandy Hill, close to Weybourne Station, marked on map.

LANDING PLACE: – Weybourne is the easiest and safest along the whole coast. The coast-guard station, on the east, has a wire to Harwich, which will be cut before our ships are in sight. In Weybourne village there is a small telegraph office, but this will at the same time be seized by our people occupying an inn in the vicinity, a place which will be recognised by the display of a Union Jack.

WIRES: – Eight important wires run through here, five of which must be cut, as well as the trunk telephone. Direct communication with Beccles is obtained.

BEACH: – Hard, and an excellent road runs from the sea to the highway south. For soundings, see notes upon British soundings. Admiralty Chart No. 1630 accompanying.

FORGE: – There is one at the end of the village.

PROVISIONS: – Grocers' shops in village are small, therefore do not contain much stock. There are plenty of sheep and oxen in the district towards Gunton. (See accompanying lists of amount of live stock upon each farm.)

MOTOR-CARS: – (List of owners and addresses attached)...

It is hardly surprising given such detail, hyperbole and popularity of le Queux's works that such a vehement belief and fear of spies emerged and transformed into a veritable paranoid spy scare during the opening months of the First World War.

(d)      to secure the navigation of vessels in accordance with directions given by or under the authority of the Admiralty; or

(e)      otherwise to prevent assistance being given to the enemy or the successful prosecution of the war being endangered.

Combine this with The Aliens Registration Act (1914) that made the registration of all aliens over the age of 16 with the police mandatory and you have a green light for every patriotic Britain to root out 'enemy aliens', German sympathisers and spies. Under these draconian charters the police and military authorities had their work cut out for them.

At King's Lynn the *Lynn News* diary recorded: *Men of the 6th Sussex Regiment have come to look after Lynn and the unprecedented signs of military occupation of the port begin to be manifest. Some points such as the Cut Bridges are guarded by men with loaded rifles and fixed bayonets and already I have heard of a case of a motorist getting his tyre cut because he ignored the sentinel's challenge. The Cut is watched as never before and soldiers have taken possession of the pilot's conning tower. Boy Scouts flit here and there, looking grave beyond their years and some of the mild mannered policemen who ever kissed the book carry revolvers.*

While along the coast the *Norfolk Chronicle* recorded the arrival of troops, including the men of 2nd Battalion, The Essex Regiment at a well known coastal resort: *Cromer has the appearance of a military garrison. Troops trains arrived all day Saturday and by dusk soldiers appeared to be everywhere – officers were in the hotels and the men were quartered wherever cover could be found for them – in the Town Hall and other public buildings on the pier and almost every available field. There were nearly 6000 officers and men in all. Their arrival created great excitement but a hearty reception was accorded the men with presents of refreshments and smokes from residents and visitors. Their presence brought down many people from Norwich and the country districts on Sunday. Many Germans, most of whom have been employed at local hotels were arrested at the weekend and came up at a court martial on Sunday. Most of them were subsequently released but four were taken by the military when they left Cromer on Monday 10th.*

*Commonwealth War Graves headstone for Private Frederick William Toll, 2nd Battalion, The Essex Regiment. The first man to die in Norfolk during the First World War.*

The first tragedy of the war in Norfolk occurred on 8 August 1914 with the death of East Ham born Private Frederick William Toll, 2nd Battalion, The Essex Regiment while the Battalion were in Cromer. He is buried in Cromer Cemetery on Holt Road.

The *Eastern Daily Press* carried on the story of the arrival of 2nd Battalion, The Essex Regiment and the 'spies' in their charge when they arrived at Norwich: *Their arrival caused considerable interest and excitement. They brought with them four prisoners. The troops marched from Thorpe Station along Prince of Wales Road and London Street to the Market Place where they piled their arms. For several hours the square offered an animated scene. A large crowd collected on the outskirts and eagerly sought to get into conversation with the soldiers. Taking advantage of the halt many of them made hasty calls at the adjacent public houses and returned quickly with bottles of mineral water and handy eatables. The services of several local hairdressers were obtained and chairs were lent from business premises, the unique sight was soon witnessed of soldiers having their hair cut in the open Market Place. The demand made upon the barbers was very rapid, for as soon as one man was out of the chair another was in it. Everyone appeared in the best of humour and spirits and good-natured chaff was everywhere prevalent.*

*The entire 2nd Battalion, The Essex Regiment crammed into Norwich Market Place, 10 August 1914.*

The 2nd Battalion, The Essex Regiment and the German 'spies' they 'captured' and kept under guard at a stall drew hoards of intrigued citizens to Norwich Market Place, 10 August 1914.

'The German prisoners were allowed to rest themselves on a stall almost immediately beside the Wellington statue. All four of them were well dressed and seemed to accept their position with perfect coolness. Except for the fact that they were the only civilians amid the soldiery and that a guard surrounded them, there was nothing to attract the attention of the crowd to their presence. Many persons, however, on learning who they were made strategic movements to get as close a view as possible. The prisoners were seen frequently talking with their guard and therefore could presumably speak English with ease. One of the soldiers handed an illustrated paper to one of them and he quickly became engrossed with its war contents. A well-set tall and erect member of the little group appeared to derive a keen interest from the scene around him. He frequently gazed at the crowd and those who were aware of his identity returned the recognition with interested keenness. To the soldiers he showed particular amiability and was free with his cigarette case. The other prisoners seemed less interested in the situation and chatted mainly among themselves.

The four prisoners left the city by an early afternoon train for Liverpool Street. Their progress from the Market Place to Thorpe Station was watched with tremendous interest. A big crowd followed the men who were under military escort. While seated in the train and waiting for their departure they were anxious to see an evening paper. They told our representative they had been engaged in a hotel as waiters for the past five weeks. Their English seemed good.'

The German 'spies' being taken under military escort to Thorpe Station, Norwich, followed by a large crowd on the afternoon of 10 August 1914.

Around the same time an urgent order had been received at Yarmouth affecting aliens. No alien was allowed to land from a vessel arriving at Yarmouth, whether passenger or member of a crew, without the permission of the aliens officer, which in the instance of Yarmouth was the inspector of the Custom House. No alien enemy was to be permitted on shore and only subject to certain stipulations could alien friends land at Yarmouth, which was designated 'a prohibited port'. Similar regulations applied in regard to the departure of aliens on outgoing ships. All vessels arriving at Yarmouth were instructed to hand in immediately a list of their passengers and crews. Within hours of the order being issued the first action under the order saw a couple of Germans that landed from the *Belle* steamer. They explained they had only been out of Yarmouth on a trip but they were handed over to the police to investigate their statement.

In late August 1914 the Norwich City Police Chief Constable published a statement in response to scaremongering over the number of aliens in the city:

*'The total numbers of aliens in Norwich is under 200 and of these those from Germany and Austria number fewer than a score; most of these have lived in the city many years. In addition there are a small number of foreign birth who are naturalised British subjects. The greatest number of foreigners in Norwich are Italian ice-cream makers and organ grinders. Many visitors to the city have to undergo registration. Among them have been Americans, Russians, Frenchmen, Poles, Swedes, Roumanians, Swiss, Japanese, Chinese, Dutch Belgians, Spanish and Norwegians.*

*All aliens must register their names and addresses and certain other particulars with the Chief Constable and those who have not done so should lose no time in complying with the request and so avoid prosecution. The Aliens Restriction Order imposes special obligations upon alien enemies i.e. Germans and Austrians. They have to get a special permit from the Chief Constable to be allowed to still reside here and are prohibited from moving further than five miles from their homes without permission. Even then they are not allowed to be absent from home for a longer period than four days. They are also prohibited without a special authorisation by the Chief Constable from possessing – Any firearms, ammunition or explosives; any petroleum spirit, naphtha, benzol petroleum or other inflammable liquid in quantities exceeding 3 gallons; any apparatus or contrivance intended for or capable of being used for a signalling apparatus, either visual or otherwise; any carrier or homing pigeons; any motor, motor-cycle or aircraft; any cipher code or other means of conducting secret correspondence; telephone installation; camera or any other photographic apparatus; military or naval map, chart or handbook.*

*The only disability imposed upon the other aliens is that they should give notice to the Chief Constable of any change of residence. The Aliens Restriction Order does not apply to all parts of England but only to certain scheduled areas of which Norwich is one. This area includes in addition to the county borough of Yarmouth, three urban districts, viz, Cromer, North Walsham and Sheringham and the rural districts of Aylsham, Blofield, East and West Flegg, Erpingham, Loddon, Clavering and Smallburgh.*

*Residents in above areas should keep their eyes and ears well open and if they find any of the above being contravened they should at once inform the police or military authorities.'*

One of the first of numerous instances of suspicious characters and potential spies reported to the authorities in Norfolk during the war was reported in the *Dereham and Fakenham Times* on Saturday 22 August 1914: '*On Tuesday morning a very smart caravan of the type used by holidaymakers drawn by two stout horses had been noticed on the coast and very early in the morning was observed at Weybourne at the time an aeroplane alighted to leave a message ... approaching noon a young violinist made his appearance in Blakeney and the excellent music he played induced a musician who is a summer resident to solicit permission to examine the violin. The examination revealed some uncommon features and the violinists answers to searching questions addressed to him being unsatisfactory the gentleman felt it his duty to convey certain suspicions he had formed to the authorities, who were soon on the track of the musician and likewise the caravan, which was found in the neighbourhood of Morston. Inside were found two men and a woman. A search revealed sufficient to cause the detention of the entire party. The musician and a second man were detained at Morston and an escort of our Territorials conveyed the caravan and the remainder of the party to Holt... on the heels of this came the news that on the same day a motor car containing three persons, which had been carefully noted had been bagged between Sheringham and Weybourne.'*

Other cases soon followed such as the one on the evening of Thursday 20 August in the vicinity of the Royal Naval Air Station on the South Denes, Great Yarmouth described in the *Yarmouth Mercury* as an incident : '*which would seem to indicate the possibility that the town has received the attention of a spy and also served to illustrate the vigilance of those to whom is entrusted the duty of protecting the buildings and their contents. One of the sentries on duty detected a man approaching the station and challenged him. He received no reply from the man, who at once made off and the sentry fired in his direction. In the darkness the individual quickly disappeared. A number of men from the Royal Garrison Artillery Barracks were turned out as quickly as possible and a thorough a search made of the Denes but no trace of anyone could be found.'*

*Yarmouth Mercury* published the story of another incident on 5 September 1914 :

> *On Monday evening the Marine Parade was filled with excitement. Someone observed the flashing of a lamp from the top bedroom window of a well known hotel. It was Morse code signalling without a doubt and he at once hurried with the news to the Air Station. Three other people also saw the flashes and told the Navy men and the police were also informed. The sailors hurried up the steps three at a time, detectives also disappeared into the hotel. Outside a gaping, wondering crowd collected and rumour was as busy as its many tongues could possibly make it. 'A German signalling to a mine layer' – it could be nothing less than that. Indeed, some thought the German fleet was in the offing or somewhere similar. But though the crowd waited long there was no further development and if a spy was captured he must have been spirited away by a back door unknown to the spectators. Subsequently it transpired that a boy was amusing himself with an electric flash lamp spelling out Morse talk, quite unaware of the commotion he had caused among the promenaders below.*

The *Mercury* did however proceed to offer an overview and attempt to calm the growing hysteria in the same edition:

> *Stories of spies caught sketching, signalling etc at Gorleston have for some time past been very prevalent but in each case, so far, every 'incident' of its kind has ended in smoke and certain well-known people, to say nothing of other visitors of years standing to the parish, who were supposed to have been marched off to captivity are still mingling with the free. Meanwhile our military squads of cyclists, infantry etc are spending busy times in Yarmouth and district to the discomfort of 'suspects' who are promptly held up and escorted to the police station under armed guards. Last weekend witnessed some activity in this direction, when a shipping agent staying on the cliffs found his bungalows 'invested' and searched for evidence of a suspicious character which was not, however, found. On Sunday a Jewish minister staying on Lowestoft Road found his rooms raided in a similar manner, cameras, photo plates etc being the special objects of attention in each case, while in both cases the persons concerned experienced the discomforts of temporary arrest until enquiries had been made elsewhere into their movements.*
> *During the same morning no little surprise was created by the appearance of another armed guard marching a 'prisoner' down Lowestoft Road and through the High Street to the Police Station. Nearly everyone recognised the 'capture' as Ernie LeGrice, a photographer in the employ of Miss A. O. Yardley, which increased the interest aroused. Mr. Le Grice had gone with his bag of photographic material to take a picture of a family of visitors at a boarding house before they left Gorleston when he was 'caught with the gear' by the 'Terriers' and marched back to the station, where the morning was spent in convincing the soldiers of their mistake. Various other cases have been recounted of the suspicious movements of strangers in our midst which have occupied the attention of civic, naval and military authorities. On one occasion two officers of one naval craft lying in the harbour followed a man home who had, it was alleged, been sketching in the harbour but nothing came of this official visit to Lower Cliff Road.*
> *That suspicious signalling had been going on at night from a house on top of the cliffs was a conviction with some people, who saw for themselves 'those twinkling lights facing the sea. This scare had been investigated and discounted but was revived last Sunday by some more people who saw the 'signals' while out on the cliffs. They in turn were later on convinced that they were in error and that the 'signals' were nothing more than the bright rays of an electric lamp in a room thickly screened by the trees outside but momentarily exposed by the breeze-stirred leafy branches in these well wooded grounds.*

*Another 'spy' being brought to the authorities under military escort at Gorleston 1914.*

As outing of 'enemy' aliens heightened it became nothing less than a witchhunt.  A stern warning came from Blofield Petty Sessions where a number of cases of motorists travelling without their driving licenses were brought before the Blofield Sessions in mid-October. Commenting to one man who claimed his license 'was run out' and thought a friend's would do Major Jary told him bluntly from the Bench: 'you could be liable to be shot as a spy.'

The Chairman Colonel H. H. Gilbert, endorsed Jary's words, stating: 'These are times when magistrates must take notice of these things. The country is honeycombed with spies.' The defendant was fined the maximum £5 and £2.2s.6d costs, or 28 days. The fine was paid and several of the other defendants were also fined.

Long naturalised Germans or their descendents also came under attack, even those doing their bit for the British King and Country. In Norwich, for example, in October 1914 Jacob Lanzer (39) a man of German nationality serving as a Private in the 5th Battalion, The Essex Regiment was brought before the Magistrates charged with failing to register himself as an alien upon changing his address. Deputy Chief Constable Lockett said the prisoner had told him he was born in Bavaria. He had registered at Brentford and professed ignorance of the requirement to register again on removing to Norfolk. It was stated that the man had been in the Essex Regiment for 17 years, having attested as an Englishman. He had married an Englishwoman and had nine children. When not with his regiment Lanzer worked at Hoffman's Ball Bearing Co. at Chelmsford, which Mr. Lockett pointed out to the court, was originally a German company but now was an English company. An officer of the regiment confirmed Lanzer's length of service in the Essex Regiment, adding he bore a good character and possessed the efficiency medal. The Essex police also confirmed they knew of his whereabouts. Lanzer professed ignorance of the law and added he felt it was very hard to be called a German after having lived in England practically all his life, having come here as a child. He was discharged on undertaking to register at once.

The spy scares on the North Norfolk coast even reached the pages of *The Times* on 19 October 1914:

*To The Editor of The Times*

*Sir, I was glad to read your article to-day in The Times on German espionage and preparation for this war. Here is an instance. About three years ago I was staying in Norfolk and I asked a friend of mine if the Germans had ever found out a place called Weybourne on the coast, where Nelson said was the place to land an invading force for England. My Friend answered: "Found it out; the Germans have bought land there and built a hotel.' About 10 days ago I was motoring along the coast there and was stopped several times by the cycle corps guarding the coast. I happened to ask one of the men how much coast they looked after and he told me from Hunstanton to Weybourne. I said, "There is a hotel at Weybourne which belongs to the Germans." And he replied, "I don't know about that: but a short time ago we made a raid on the hotel and found several Germans in it.' I send you this in case it may be of interest to know preparations have been made in this county just as in France and Belgium.*

*Yours faithfully,*

*J. B. Stracey-Clitherow*
*Hotham Hall, Brough, East Yorkshire Oct 15.*

During that same month Mrs Montgomery Coates of Sheringham became the prime mover in the preparation of a petition to the Home Secretary asking him to make more stringent regulations in connection with enemy aliens which contended:

That the existence of aliens in our midst constitutes a serious menace to national safety.

That this menace especially affects the East Coast in the County of Norfolk.

That in our opinion the measures taken to minimise the danger of espionage are inefficient.

That we have every reason to believe that there are now in Sheringham many aliens of German and Austrian origin and who have now in some cases assumed English names.

That until there has been a strict investigation, even though it necessitates a house-to house visitation, the neighbourhood will not be clear of spies.

We hope that severe measures will be at once put into force with the result that all subjects will be removed at least 50 miles distant from the coast.

Mrs Montgomery Coates stated she had already received over 1000 signatures including – H.M. Upcher, W. J. Ernley-Sumpter, T. M. Critchley Salmonson, Edgar C. Rolfe, Hester M. Henderson and M. H. Bridgewater and it was announced shortly after that the Home Office issued instructions making practically the whole of the East Coast a prohibited area for Germans and Austrians.

Some voices of calm and reason were published too, as in *The Cromer and North Norfolk Post* on 30 October 1914:

'Many ridiculous tales have been circulated about German spies in North Norfolk. Recently we have heard that a whole party of Germans had been arrested near Sheringham, but on investigation found there was no truth whatever in the report although one lady assured us that she saw the arrest. The following letter, which appeared in *The Times* will interest many of the readers.'

*Sir,*

*My attention has been called to the letter by Mr J. B. Stracey-Clitherow in your issue of 19ᵗʰ inst. The letter only shows how tales grow in the telling. May I state the facts? About 10 years ago Mr. Crundall, an Englishman and the brother of Sir W. Crundall Mayor of Dover, purchased an estate of about 1,000 acres at Kelling Heath, Norfolk, with the intention of developing a holiday resort – laying out a golf course, building houses, bungalows etc. He also built a small hotel in this property, close to Weybourne Station. The scheme was not successful and the property was sold. I am now the owner of the hotel, which I use as a seaside residence and which is now called Weybourne Court.*

*No German has ever owned the place but now for the grain of truth! In August last the house was in the charge of a caretaker. About 2 o'clock one morning the coastguard on duty saw a light in the turret of the house apparently signalling to sea and another light on the hill behind. It is stated that a line projected through these two lights indicated the point at sea where the sea is deepest near the shore. A party of troops was at once rushed off to search the house, which is 1 ¼ miles away from the sea.*

*They found nobody but there were a few match ends, evidently recently used. Since then troops about 150 in number have been billeted in the house.*

*Yours faithfully*

*J. G. Gordon-Munn*
*Heigham Hall,*
*Norwich Oct. 21.*

Despite the voices of reason the spy scares ran on unabated across the county and accusations and rumours of being an enemy alien when people were nothing of the sort could end in public disclaimers and threats of legal action. In Great Yarmouth, an old and respected townsman named Mr Fred Flanders, of the Motor Cycle Garage, Regent Road, was caused much annoyance by the suggestions 'that have been recently freely circulated' that he was a German and he saw to it the allegation was refuted in the *Yarmouth Mercury*, Mr. Flanders having 'been able most definitely to give the lie to the allegations by the production of his birth certificate. Further, he is in a position to prove that not only his father but his grandfather before him were born in England.' Frank Leigh of Gorleston had to go further and publish a formal disclaimer in the paper on 21 November:

**£10 REWARD.**

─────────────

**Whereas** malicious and unfounded reports have been circulated that Edward Gane Inge, Pharmacist of North Walsham and Mundesley is of alien nationality and has been arrested as a spy of the King's Enemies:

**And Whereas** the said Edward Gane Inge was born at Winchester of English parents, has never resided out of England, and is now serving as a Corporal in Queen Mary's Own Surrey Yeomanry, stationed at Old Park Farm Camp, Canterbury, and such reports are calculated to damage his businesses at North Walsham and Mundesley which have been left by him, whilst serving his Country, under the charge of fully qualified Managers.

**Notice is hereby given** that the sum of Ten Pounds will be paid to any person able to prove to me, the undersigned, who originated the unfounded and malicious reports above referred to.

**Notice is further given** that proceedings will be taken against any person or persons circulating or repeating the same or similar statements after the publication of this Notice.

Dated this 13th day of November, 1914,

**H. W. T. Empson,**
North Walsham,
Solicitor for the said Edward Gane Inge.

*A poster appeal to stop rumours about a North Norfolk pharmacist, November 1914.*

*A Disclaimer*

To The Editor

*Dear Sir – I shall be greatly obliged if you will kindly publish the following for me:-*
*I am at present suffering much annoyance owing to the fact that certain persons in this neighbourhood are persistently circulating reports that I am of German nationality in spite of the fact that they must be aware that by this time all enemy aliens have been removed from the district.*
*These reports I wish most emphatically to deny, being a British subject born in Essex.*
*I have given instructions for inquiries to be made and legal action to be taken against any person or persons who continue to spread such reports.*
*In order to avoid any annoyance in the future, either to myself or my family, I have taken steps in due legal form to drop from this date my present surname of 'Ehrke' and assume my other family name of Leigh in its place and I might point out that the fact that I can make this change is in itself a proof of nationality as this course is not at present open to an alien.*

*I am, Yours faithfully,*

*Frank L. Leigh*

Eventually The Lord Lieutenant of Norfolk issued a statement to the press of reassurance that he had received from the Chief Constable regarding spies and aliens:

To the Editor

*Sir – I will be much obliged if you will publish the enclosed letter I have received from the Chief*

Constable as regards alien enemies in Norfolk.

Yours faithfully,

Leicester
The Rt. Hon. The Earl of Leicester
Holkham Hall, Norfolk
The Norfolk Club, Norwich 14 November 1914

Copy

Dear Lord Leicester

In reply to you letter of 9th inst. relative to the communication you have received from Mr Edmund Reeve enclosing a press cutting of the remarks by his Honour Judge Mulligan KC, I had seen this report in the paper and intended to write to his Honour direct, but on reflection, thought it would be preferable to await your letter on the matter which from the press report I expected to get. The actual facts are these and in order to deal with the questions that you have raised, I will take them seriatim:

1. The prohibition of Germans is a dead letter so far as Norfolk is concerned. I find from my returns that whereas there were 176 aliens of German and Austrian nationality alone registered in this county before the war commenced (at that time police only registered those who were known to them and that without the aliens' knowledge) they are at the present time 32 persons of alien enemy nationality in this country, made up as follows:

Germans – 4 Males, 17 females
Austrians 1 male, 10 females

**BEWARE OF SPIES.**

**DON'T** TALK. THE ENEMY HAS EARS EVERYWHERE.

**DON'T** imagine that everyone who SPEAKS ENGLISH is to be trusted, and that every UNIFORM covers a FRIEND.

**DON'T** exchange confidences with CASUAL COMPANIONS or when travelling at home or abroad.

**DON'T** trust STRANGERS who write to you, who offer gifts or hospitality, or who tell you their secrets.

**DON'T** carry about with you or show MAPS, PLANS, ORDERS, or any naval or military document.

**DON'T** hesitate to PREVENT and to REPORT at once any leakage of information or any suspicious action.

**DON'T** mention naval or military matters in your LETTERS. They have a habit of getting into print to the advantage of the enemy.

**DON'T** imagine that private DIARIES or NOTE BOOKS will keep secrets. They sometimes get lost or stolen.

**DON'T** leave written SCRAPS OF PAPER about. BURN them. They might tell tales.

**DON'T** forget that a CHANCE WORD or a SCRAP OF PAPER may help your enemy and SLAY YOUR FRIEND.

Poster warning the public of the spy danger, 1916.

Of this number one male German is a pauper in a workhouse – a very old man- whilst the other three German males have been found to be perfectly harmless after thorough investigation.

The Austrian male has been vouched for by the members of the club at Hunstanton, of which he is steward and his case has been fully investigated. The female aliens have all been under full inquiry. About half the number consist of English women married to Germans and in convents. The others are governesses and domestics vouched for by responsible persons.

2. John Jacob Lichters,* referred to in the Press reports is now under consideration by the military authorities in accordance with the powers conferred upon them. This man on medical grounds is not liable for military service and consequently is not eligible for internment in a concentration camp on action by police. Removal from his home would have deprived him of his means of earning a livelihood, a result not desired by the authorities.

Every inquiry has been made in reference to him and my file of papers go to show that prominent residents in Sheringham have vouched for him.

3. Lodging houses permitted to be kept by Germans on coasts – the man Lichters is the only case now in Norfolk, the other aliens having left the locality by police orders some time since.

4. Law disregarded throughout the county. I can only say that the intricate instructions issued to police have been faithfully carried out to the best of the ability of all officers concerned and I must assert that everything possible has been done under those instructions, by police, who are the responsible authority.

---

*Author's Note
John Jacob Lichters, described at the North Walsham Magistrates Court as a German, 'and owes his allegiance to the Kaiser' attempted to sue 'subjects of the King because they declined when the war broke out to go and reside in the house of this German at Sheringham on the North Sea and thereby broke contract.' In other words they let him down with their holiday booking and he was suing them for recompense. The Magistrate decided that during the war such a German had no rights in this country according to the common law of England and commented: 'It is painful to see that lodging houses are permitted to be kept by Germans along our coasts. It seems the prohibition of Germans from our coasts is a dead letter so far as Norfolk is concerned. I think you should call the attention of the Lord Lieutenant to these cases, with a view to his taking action on them in his place in Parliament.'

*5. Houses occupied by aliens in Cromer and Overstrand. The houses have been built some years by their owners who formerly had a perfect right to reside there if desired.*

*All these houses have been visited by the military and police on various occasions and every inquiry has been made in reference to their owners, the results of which are filed in my office should anyone wish to have specific information. Most of them are unoccupied and have been for some considerable time.*

*Naturalised aliens claim the 'Civis Romanus sum' privilege and no action can be taken against them under existing regulations unless they give cause for suspicion.*

*6. In conclusion, I would like to observe that confidence in the military and police authorities is essential at the present time and would be better for all parties concerned. Both authorities are working in conjunction and have all matters in hand.*

*With a vue to preventing the circulation of irresponsible statements and of avoiding the unpleasant necessity which has arisen in one or two cases in other parts of the country, of taking proceedings against any person under the Defence of the Realm Regulations for the dissemination of false or alarming reports, I should with your approval be glad if you will insert this letter in the press in the interests of the public and in fairness to authorities.*

*Yours very truly*

*Egbert Napier, Major*
*Chief Constable of Norfolk.*

In some parts of Norfolk such as Weybourne and Gorleston the spy fever did not abate. The *Yarmouth Mercury* of 5 December 1914 ran the account:

*Gorleston, is still somewhat 'nervy' as a result of the somewhat prolonged attack of spy fever, and the various alarms which almost daily crop up set the parish buzzing with wonderful stories of strange men and women being spotted in the early hours of the morning coming from empty houses with glazed turrets in the roofs, etc., all of which include the signalling with lights seawards in the 'black hours' but still enquiries and investigations have laid low these phantoms of the dreaded spy. On Tuesday evening (3 November 1914 – evening after the bombardment) the vicinity of the High Street and Priory Street was the scene of great excitement when it was reported that a spy had been captured in Mr. Philip Wright's grocery establishment. Crowds of people gathered to see armed sailors and officers practically take charge of the premises, which were searched. As a result the police were called in and report was persistent that a man had been arrested. So far as we have been able to make out, the commotion all arose over the antics of two errand boys who got down the grocer's cellar and began playing with the electric light. The cellar built in the side of the hill of the High Street overlooks the riverside and the flashing lights were spotted by the signaller on one of the torpedo craft, who saw something of a code message blinking from the small cellar windows. It subsequently turned out that one of the boys possessed a book in which a relative had copied some code signalling words and upon which he was harmlessly practicing in what he thought to be the security of the cellar, when he was suddenly surrounded, captured and nearly frightened out of his wits.*

The spy scares rumbled on into 1915 and flared up occasionally throughout the First World War but by May 1915 the hysteria was dying down and Norfolk coastal residents had, frankly, had enough. Ironically one of the cases was brought against none other than William le Queux!. *The Cromer Post* of 7 May 1915 reporting:

*Damaging Statements Withdrawn*

*Dear Sir*

*Many of the residents in Sheringham and the neighbourhood were considerably perturbed by the following statement which occurred in the May number of the 'Royal Magazine' in an article entitled 'The Spy Peril'*

*'For the past five years the East Coast has swarmed with spies. My assistant, a clever Russian, who has posed as a German on many occasions of late, and who speaks German as a German, I sent to Sheringham in Norfolk in January last. He actually lived there in a boarding house on the sea front kept by a German and sat up half the night with this enemy alien denouncing the British, the boarding-house keeper declaring to his supposed compatriot that when the enemy made a raid he had arranged to give them certain assistance.*

*What was done concerning him you ask. Why nothing. At the time of writing he was still carrying on his boarding house. Why? Because the military and civil authorities in Norfolk had quarrelled over espionage and the measures which the one took the other reversed.'*

*This statement as is proved by the letter written by their solicitors on behalf of the proprietors of the 'Royal Magazine' printed on p1 is nothing more or less than a piece of jingoistic imagination but it is a statement which unless widely contradicted is likely to do an immense amount of harm.*

*Firstly it is calculated to bring into disrepute the authority responsible for the carrying out of the Alien Restriction Order and secondly, it is more likely to have a serious effect on Sheringham, a place already hard hit by the war as a holiday resort.*

*I think it is only right that all concerned should know the true facts which are as follows:*

*The Russian referred to, so far from being employed by Mr William Le Queux was an ex-Scotland Yard detective employed by the Norfolk County Police and paid by them! Under their orders he made a tour of the Norfolk coast for the purpose of ascertaining whether there was any danger from the presence of aliens and he made a report to the police that, in his opinion, no such danger was likely to arise.*

*The detective did, as a matter of fact, stay with the German boarding-house proprietor referred to in the article, who at once reported the presence of this Russian to the police considering his a suspicious character.*

*The police and military authorities in Norfolk are acting with the utmost harmony in all matters arising out of proceedings for carrying into effect the Aliens Restriction Orders.*

*It is beyond a doubt that any person reading this article and believing it to be true would at once assume that Sheringham had been selected as a suitable place for a raid by the enemy, when such action was possible, whereas, for reasons into which it would perhaps not be advisable to enter, it is extremely improbable that the enemy would deliberately choose Sheringham as a landing place.*

*Sheringham has suffered quite enough already through irresponsible journalists who seem to have this particular part of the coast on the brain and who let their imagination run wild without stopping to think what harm they may be doing.*

*Yours faithfully*

*Edgar C. Rolfe*
*Clerk to the Sheringham Urban District Council*
*6 May 1915.*

With pressure put on the police to deal with potential enemy aliens, spies and suspicious characters, chase up registrations and a host of other tasks war generates, coupled with the fact that many

*City of Norwich Police Special Constable's appointment certificate for Ernest Williams, December 1914.*

policemen were ex-soldiers and had been called to the colours, the ranks of those who maintained law and order in Norfolk were in desperate need of increase. Mr J. A. Porter, the Lord Mayor of Norwich, had summoned a meeting at St Andrew's Hall on 4 September 1914, a poignant date chosen deliberately because it was exactly one month after the declaration of war, with a view to alleviate the situation. The evening was met with 'enthusiastic fervour' which culminated in 419 of the men of Norwich joining the Special Constabulary. They were sworn in batches before local magistrates, and many more followed later who were sworn before the City Magistrates at the Guildhall.

By the end of 1914 680 specials had been 'sworn in' and at its height 714 war emergency 'specials' were on the beat in Norwich. The only down side for these men was, initially, they didn't look much like constables – yes they had truncheons and handcuffs but these had to be shared, passed from specials going on and off duty and their 'uniform' was only an arm band and their civvy clothes. A lapel badge arrived soon after but caps did not arrive until in January 1916 and it was only in the following August they eventually got their 'full pride of blue uniform'. In the opening months of the war nationally 6,000 properties were searched, 120,000 reported cases of 'suspicious activity' investigated and many migrants and those who had fled the war from the continent, some 9,000 of them all told, were interned. A total of 24,522 German civilian internees were held in British detention camps during the First World War.

*Parade of City of Norwich Special Constabulary in Norwich Market Place 1918.*

# 4 Invasion Defences

From the outbreak of hostilities in August 1914 one of the major fears to be addressed by both military and civil authorities was the danger of invasion.

Civil authorities had no directives as to their course of action in the event of invasion but Local Emergency Committees were set up in each parish across the county under the direction of the Lord Lieutenant. The chief duty of the Emergency Committees was that of planning with the local military authorities the necessary measures to be adopted in the locality for facilitating the operations of HM forces and the hindrance of the enemy and provision of the organisation necessary to carry out those measures – such as digging trenches, the construction of road blocks, and obtaining lists of motorised vehicles that could be used to assist in the event of an evacuations or in response to the needs of the military. The manpower provided for this scheme, as well as other related measures such as the provision of tools and labour for the military, or for example the removal or destruction of horses and harness or rendering vehicles unserviceable in the event of imminent invasion, was drawn from and allotted to trustworthy local volunteers or special constables. In Norwich a Civilian Emergency Corps was formed for the same purpose, originally consisting of 1,600 volunteers each one of them had an allocated duty and a unique numbered white metal lapel badge surmounted by the heraldic arms of the City. The committees also ensured they had a clear invasion warning system; in Norwich a visual telegraph was erected on top of Norwich Castle to communicate with the one on Strumpshaw Hill, while that in turn was visible from Yarmouth church tower.

*Lapel badge of the Norwich Civilian Emergency Corps.*

*Members of the Norwich Civilian Emergency Corps marching up Aylsham Road, 1914.*

In addition a secret Observer scheme was established by the Lord Lieutenants of counties under direct threat of invasion immediately after the outbreak of hostilities and was fully organised and working by December 1914. Staffed by specially selected upstanding members of the community who would not be liable for call up, their duties were to observe and report back any rumours of invasion or spy threats they took seriously or believed should receive serious investigation by the police or the military as a priority. A rare surviving document is the list of Observers for the North East Norfolk area:

CONFIDENTIAL

List of Observers in District 4.

Remarks: Each Observer will in future be known by the number placed opposite his name and should it be necessary to communicate any intelligence to any other observer will be by number and not by name.

| NAME | ADDRESS | NUMBER |
|---|---|---|
| Ch. OB. Fairfax Davies | North Walsham | 30401 |
| Dr. Dent | Cromer | 30402 |
| Major Collison | Cromer | 30403 |
| Rev. Sir F. Sullivan Bart | Southrepps Rectory | 30404 |
| S. G. Baker | Roughton | 30405 |
| Rev. A. C. Davies | Antingham Rectory | 30406 |
| Rev. S. Page | Trimingham Rectory | 30407 |
| J. H. Palmer | Mundesley | 30408 |
| Rev. Dr. Watson | Knapton | 30409 |
| E. Woodyatt | Trunch | 30410 |
| G. Cobon | Paston | 30411 |
| B. Cubitt | Witton | 30412 |
| Rev. T. C. H. Nash | North Walsham | 30413 |
| A. J. Denny | North Walsham | 30414 |
| L. Bircham | North Walsham | 30415 |
| Rev. G. Stook | East Ruston Rectory | 30416 |
| G. Cole | East Ruston | 30417 |
| J. Durrell | East Ruston | 30418 |
| Robert Gurney | Ingham Old Hall | 30419 |
| Rev. M. C. H. Bird | Brunstead Rectory | 30420 |
| Rev. W. M. C. McAllister | Hempstead Rectory | 30421 |
| H. Thompson | Coastguard Station, Happisburgh | 30422 |
| Dr. Cutting | Stalham | 30423 |
| J. A. Daniels | Stalham | 30424 |
| C. Cordswell | Catfield | 30425 |
| W. J. Neave | Neatishead | 30426 |
| G. A. Dale | Ludham | 30427 |
| Rev. A. G. T. Cross | Hickling Vicarage | 30428 |
| G. O. Cubitt | Palling | 30429 |
| W. Exton | Smallburgh Workhouse | 30430 |

*Naval personnel and Boy Scouts at Gorleston.*

Boy Scouts had also loyally 'done their bit' as messenger runners or bicycled despatch riders from the earliest days of the war and were soon employed at coastguard stations but as the cold winter began to bite something had to be done about their clothing so the County Commissioner, The Earl of Albemarle, wrote a letter to be published in local newspapers on 1 October in which he stated 108 scouts in the county were recognised by the Admiralty as doing duty on the Norfolk coast watching for invaders and in various ways assisting the coastguards. Their pay was one shilling a day but he took trouble to point out 'These boys are not clothed in a manner fitted to withstand the cold and inclement weather of a winter on the Norfolk coast. As the patrols are constantly being changed we find it impossible to supply the whole of them with underclothing but contributions in money or oil skin coats and sou'westers (boys and youth size) will be thankfully received and should be sent to Colonel Barclay at Hanworth Hall.'

In another letter published in the *Cromer Post*, Mr. C. Anson Parker, Scoutmaster of 1st Cromer Scouts, described some of the duties of the Scouts working with coastguards:

*'Patrols of eight scouts are posted to all the important signal stations along the East Coast and in Norfolk we have Scouts attached to most of the stations between Lynn in the north and*

*Gorleston in the south. Their work consists of patrolling roads and stretches of beaches, fatigue work, like cleaning up on all the stations, message carrying and any amount of odd jobs according to the wishes of the chief officer of the station to which they are attached.*

*The eight lads at Cromer were given temporary accommodation in a loose box at North Lodge stable, kindly lent by Mr Douro Hoare, the owner and Sir Fowell Buxton, the tenant. One lad is always on duty at the station, while the others patrol the roads from Cromer to Weybourne and from Cromer to Mundesley.*

*They cycle out to these two places taking note of what is going on around them and then they return by the beach, riding where the sand is firm enough but it generally means walking most of the journey.'*

With regard to the civil population, it was recognised that although the military authorities considered it preferable that people stayed where they were except in case of heavy bombardment, this really would not be practical – a planned and organised evacuation was infinitely more preferable to a mass exodus in panic so posters and handbills were prepared showing the roads which would be closed or open to the public. Special constables were charged with picketing the roads and maintaining order. Evacuation procedures were published for areas along the coast, typical of them is this example delivered to every household in Mundesley and district during December 1914, issued by Mr. J. H. Farmer of 'Fairfield,' Mundesley, Chief Special Emergency Constable for Mundesley, Knapton, Paston, Trimingham and Trunch:

*The following directions are issued now in order (1) to familiarise the public with the possibility of having to leave their homes at short notice in the event of  Military Operations commencing and orders being given to act and (2) to safeguard the inhabitants from the disasters which would certainly follow a precipitate, unprepared fight with its consequent hampering of the movements of our troops.*

*Though a hostile attack is merely a possibility – certainly not a probability – the public are advised in their own interest to prepare for it.*

*If orders are given to leave the villages the public are advised, on leaving, to cut off their gas and water, to lock up their houses and to take warm clothing and a little food with them. Unnecessary articles should be left at home.*

*As trains will not be at the service of the public, those people who are unable to walk or who do not possess vehicles or other transport of their own, should arrange for seats in farm carts or other vehicles to be reserved for them. Owners of such vehicles are expected to reserve seats in them for the aged, the women and children.*

*The military hope to be able to give some hours notice to quit.*

*The main roads will only be available for the military, and troops must not on any account be hampered by the presence of civilians, carts or animals on these roads.*

*The route that will be free for civilians use and not likely to be required by the military is through Trunch, Bradfield, Antingham, Felmingham, Skeyton and Mayton Bridges (i.e. the Old Norwich Turnpike Road), but circumstances might arise causing the public to be ordered to make for Honing in one case or for Roughton in another.*

*Live stock and forage are not to be removed or destroyed except by military or police orders.*

*When military operations are threatened and orders have been given by the military to the constables to act, traction engines, motors, cycles, vehicles and harness are to be removed or rendered useless or destroyed.*

*Nothing of use to the enemy should be allowed to fall into his hands.*

*Reasonable compensation will be paid for all property destroyed or damage done by owners to their property by order of the military.*

*Further information may be obtained from Emergency Constables, a list of whom is posted up in each village.*

In the 'front line' town of Great Yarmouth the 'Directions to the Public in the event of Bombardment or Invasion' were issued to householders in February 1915 with the instruction 'Keep this in a prominent place' emblazoned in bold across the top.

The general line of evacuation of the civil population, horned stock and transport beyond 10 miles from the East Coast was approved by General Sir Horace Smith-Dorrien from 1st Army Central Force, Cambridge as follows:

| | |
|---|---|
| No.1 Acle | To Norwich. No stock to be moved. |
| No.2 Aylsham | Towards King's Lynn and Terrington |
| No. 3 Dereham | Swaffham and Downham Market |
| No. 4 Docking | To King's Lynn and Terrington |
| No.5 Downham | To March |
| No. 6 Harling | To Thetford and Newmarket |
| No.7 Holt | Rudham, Hillington, King's Lynn and Terrington |
| No.8 Loddon | North of Loddon, Brooke to Norwich. South of that line to New Buckenham, Harlind and Thetford |
| No.9 North Walsham | To Norwich |
| No.10 Norwich | East of Norwich to Norwich. Rest to Hingham and Watton |
| No.11 Pulham | To Harling, Thetford and Newmarket |
| No. 12 Swaffham | To Downham Market and March |
| No. 13 Terrington | If necessary, to Wisbeach or Spalding way. |
| No.14 Walsingham | To King's Lynn and Terrington |
| No. 15 Wymondham | To Hingham, Watton, Mundford and Littleford |
| No. 16 Norwich | To remain. But those removing to go via Hingham, Watton and Mundford |
| No.17 Yarmouth | If the landing is in Norfolk to go via Suffolk. If the landing is in Suffolk go via Acle to Norwich |
| No. 18 King's Lynn | Through Terrington to Wisbech or Spalding way. |

Fears of invasion saw the establishment of local invasion committees in towns and villages across the country and very soon groups of men, normally led by a local retired ex-army officer gathered together to form units specifically for the defence of their town or village. Although this was not part of the official Emergency Committee directives such groups were usually created with the knowledge of the committee, and there were often men who were members of both. Examples of such early units could be found in Holt, Swaffham and Great Yarmouth. The military authorities and government were not entirely comfortable with the idea of unregulated bands of armed men no matter how patriotic they may be, and very soon began organising an official national volunteer scheme. On 19 November 1914 the War Office officially recognised the new 'corps' and placed the raised units under the control of the Central Association of Volunteer Training Corps in England and Wales

In the case of Norwich it was Mr W. E. Keefe who began the correspondence in the *Eastern Daily Press* and supported by Malcom Caley (of the chocolate manufacturing family) in November 1914. The corps was established at a meeting held in the Assembly Room of the Agricultural Hall on 4 December with Mr Francis Hornor, Sheriff of Norwich, presiding. A total of 276 names of volunteers were collected and an appeal for more was launched and after an agreed approach, the well respected Lt Colonel Leathes Prior VD accepted the post of the unit's first commandant, but volunteers remained democratic, the men came from all walks of life, a committee was set up and every subsequent officer began as a member of the rank and file.

*The first parade of the Norwich Volunteer Training Corps, 15 December 1914.*

Joining regulations were clear; membership was restricted to 'able' men over 38 years of age (it was later raised by the War Office to 41) who were not eligible for service in the Regular or Territorial Forces. The first parade of the Norwich Volunteer Training Corps (VTC) took place at the Chapel Field Drill Hall on 15 December 1914, where it was announced 550 men had enrolled to date, the names of new members published day by day by favour of the *Eastern Daily Press*. By January 1915, there were twenty-eight squads drilling three times a week in various public buildings around the city and afternoon drills on Thursdays and Saturdays on the Earlham Road Recreation Ground.

One who was there at the time in Norwich was W. G. Clarke who recalled: 'Inspired by a sense of duty, and a desire not to be compelled to remain hapless in case of an invasion of East Anglia grey-bearded veterans vied with active men of middle age in learning the mysteries of drill. Bricklayers jostled doctors; clergymen, solicitors, architects and men who had given long years service to the city rubbed shoulders with penurious patriots.'

Initially the men did not have uniforms except a red armband marked 'G R' (Georgious Rex – King George V) but still they took their training seriously and turned out in their civilian clothes, regularly assembling in local market places or playing fields and proceeded on route marches. Some units near

*A parade of the Cyclist Company of The Great Yarmouth Volunteer Corps 1914.*

schools with OTC units were able to draw upon their armouries for rifles, other units had to wait for their weapons which when they did eventually arrive were usually found to be of Victorian vintage, many of them having seen action during the Boer War. In any society there will be the sceptics or those who simply find some satisfaction in their derisory comments and soon some were referring to the volunteers as 'The Cripple's Brigade', certainly a bit harsh when one considers the average age of a VTC volunteer was 44, but that said the recruiting booklets were at pains to point out 'First-class Life and Accident insurance offices are quite willing that service in the Volunteers shall not invalidate their policies.' Uniforms were eventually sanctioned on the understanding that they should not look like those worn by the Regular or Territorial army units, so Volunteer uniforms although of a similar cut made a by a variety of suppliers, some local, the major difference was that the material used was grey-green in colour.

In April 1916 control of the V.T.C.s passed to the Central Association of Volunteer Regiments, indeed more or less the same organisation, but the remit was to reorganise the V.T.C. units as local Volunteer Regiments, all volunteers would be 'sworn in' and members would have to pass a standard of health and physique and as a consequence some of the oldest or unfit men were retired or discharged. Compulsory enlistment had been introduced in January 1916; men of suitable service age but found unfit for active service abroad would often be given a choice of being placed with home garrison units, which could mean they would be sent anywhere in Britain, or they could remain at home on the condition they joined their local volunteers. But this still meant many had to buy their own uniform until October 1916 when Army Council Instructions announced that each of the Voluntary Infantry Battalions was entitled to claim 200 sets of infantry equipment.

*The 1ˢᵗ (City of Norwich) Battalion, Norfolk Volunteers being inspected by the Earl of Leicester, accompanied by Lt Col. Leathes Prior VD, 26 September 1915.*

Uniformed or not the volunteers entered into the spirit of their duties from the word go, such as conducting patrols and providing sentries for the likes of bridges, tunnels, utility works and even important stretches of railway – from nine or ten in the evening until six in the morning they kept their vigil in case of sabotage, suspicious characters being seen or even to warn of landings and invasion. Mobile sections and companies evolved mounted on bicycles for scouting, message carrying and rapid deployment. Many units were deployed under requests and orders from the War Office to construct anti-invasions defences.

The War Office and Admiralty were both keen to utilise the services of the Volunteers and detachments from across the county were employed in such duties as guarding, constructing defensive earthworks and assisting ground crew with the movement of aircraft on airfields such as Bacton or, eventually, airships at Pulham. The City of Norwich boys (and some from Norfolk Volunteer Battalions such as Attleborough) got to Pulham by a special train chartered by the Admiralty and would march to the air station headed by their band where locals often came out to give them a wave and a cheer as they passed by. The work, however, was hard as they were initially helping to prepare the ground for the construction of the air station. They grubbed up hedges and filled ditches; initially the men even had to take their own tools! Much of the work of digging the cutting for the permanent way of the railway that connected the site with the line at Pulham Market was carried out by the Volunteers.

*The Wymondham Company of The Norfolk Volunteers proudly wearing their new uniforms and cap badges, 1918. Locally they were known as 'The Wymondham 'Old and Bold'.*

*Volunteer Force discharge certificate awarded to Cpl. William Crick of 1ˢᵗ Volunteer Battalion, The Norfolk Regiment.*

*Members of the Norfolk National Reserve at Crosskeys Bridge c.1914.*

In October 1916 army rank badges were adopted and in December of that same year the first army khaki uniforms were issued to the Volunteers. In July 1918 the Volunteers became Volunteer Battalions of their local line regiments. They were permitted to wear khaki uniforms the same as those of the army and their county regiment badges but with no battle honours or the badge of the Royal Arms supported by the lion and unicorn in brass for other ranks and bronze for officers.

After the Armistice in November 1918 the Volunteers units were gradually stood down and were finally disbanded in 1919. Oft forgotten by history and sadly, no matter what they did the old sobriquet of 'England's Last Hope' seemed to stick to the Volunteers; a nick-name, with others, which was to be applied again to their next incarnation as Local Defence Volunteers in 1940.

The anti-invasion forces deployed in or to the Norfolk coast by the military were either Home Defence Battalions of the National Reserve for foot patrols or guarding fixed positions such as bridges, airfields, military camps or buildings or mounted members of the Territorial Force on either horseback or bicycles. The coastline from Wells to Gorleston was patrolled by 1/6th Battalion, The Norfolk Regiment (Cyclists), 1/6ᵗʰ Battalion, The Royal Sussex Regiment (Cyclists) and 1/25th (County of London) Cyclist Battalion, The London Regiment.

*Some of the 1/6ᵗʰ Battalion, The Royal Sussex Regiment (Cyclists) with one of their motor patrol cars 1914.*

*Some of the Bridgend boys serving in the 1/1ˢᵗ Galmorgan Yeomanry at Aylsham, 1915.*

The horse mounted troops for quick response in the event of invasion were provided from the Yeomanry. In East Anglia they were all part of the 1ˢᵗ and 2ⁿᵈ Mounted Divisions. A number of the Yeomanry units based in North Norfolk were from Wales, some of them such as the 1/1ˢᵗ Glamorgan Yeomanry at Aylsham even had a choir and were remembered for their performances in the town and at Cromer.

*A Squadron, 1/1ˢᵗ Montgomeryshire Yeomanry at Blickling Hall, 1915.*

## 1st Mounted Division 1914-15

Formed in August 1914, for the home defence from the existing mounted brigades each of three regiments of Yeomanry from the Territorial Force.

### Commanding Generals
Major General E. Alderson (5 August to 28 September 1914)
Lieutenant General R. Broadwood (September 1914 to November 1916)

### Eastern Mounted Brigade
1/1st Loyal Suffolk Hussars
1/1ˢᵗ Norfolk Yeomanry
1/1ˢᵗ Essex Yeomanry
Essex Battery Royal Horse Artillery

In September 1915 the brigade was dismounted and moved via Egypt to Gallipoli, attached to 54ᵗʰ Division.

### 1st South Midland Mounted Brigade
1/1ˢᵗ Warwickshire Yeomanry
1/1ˢᵗ Royal Gloucestershire Hussars
1/1ˢᵗ Queen's Worcestershire Hussars
Warwickshire Battery Royal Horse Artillery

The Brigade moved to the 2ⁿᵈ Mounted Division in September 1914, and was replaced in the Division by the South Wales Mounted Brigade.

### 2nd South Midland Mounted Brigade
1/1ˢᵗ Berkshire Yeomanry
1/1ˢᵗ Royal Buckinghamshire Hussars
1/1ˢᵗ Queen's Own Oxfordshire Hussars
Berkshire Battery Royal Horse Artillery

The Brigade moved to the 2nd Mounted Division in September 1914 and was replaced in the Division by the Welsh Border Mounted Brigade.

### Notts and Derby Mounted Brigade
1/1st Sherwood Rangers Yeomanry 1/1st South Nottinghamshire Hussars

1/1ˢᵗ Derbyshire Yeomanry
1/1ˢᵗ Nottinghamshire Royal Horse Artillery

The Brigade moved to the 2ⁿᵈ Mounted Division in August 1914 and was replaced in the Division by the North Midland Mounted Brigade.

### South Wales Mounted Brigade
1/1ˢᵗ Pembroke Yeomanry
1/1ˢᵗ Montgomeryshire Yeomanry
1/1ˢᵗ Glamorgan Yeomanry
Glamorgan Battery Royal Horse Artillery

The Brigade joined the Division in September 1914 to replace the South Midland Brigade and was itself replaced in the Division by the 2/1st Eastern Mounted Brigade. In November 1915 the Brigade units were dismounted and moved to Egypt in March 1916.

### Welsh Border Mounted Brigade
1/1ˢᵗ Shropshire Yeomanry
1/1ˢᵗ Cheshire Yeomanry
1/1ˢᵗ Denbighshire Hussars
Shropshire Battery Royal Horse Artillery

The Brigade joined the Division in September 1914 to replace the 2nd South Midland Brigade, in November 1915 the regiments were dismounted and moved to Egypt in March 1916.

### North Midland Brigade
1/1ˢᵗ Staffordshire Yeomanry
1/1ˢᵗ Lincolnshire Yeomanry
1/1ˢᵗ Welsh Horse (joined and left early 1915)
1/1ˢᵗ East Riding Yeomanry (joined May 1915)
Leicestershire Battery Royal Horse Artillery

The Brigade joined the Division in September 1914 to replace the Notts and Derbys Brigade.

**2/1st South Wales Mounted Brigade**
2/1st Pembroke Yeomanry
2/1st Montgomeryshire Yeomanry
2/1st Glamorgan Yeomanry

The Brigade replaced the Eastern Brigade in October 1915.

**2/1st North Midland Brigade**
2/1st Staffordshire Yeomanry
2/1st Leicestershire Yeomanry
2/1st Lincolnshire Yeomanry

The 2/1st North Midland Brigade Replaced the North Midland Brigade in October 1915

**Cyclist Units**
1/6th (Cyclist) Battalion, The Norfolk Regiment
1/6th (Cyclist) Battalion, The Suffolk Regiment
1/6th (Cyclist) Battalion, The Royal Sussex Regiment
1/25th (County of London) Cyclist Battalion,
The London Regiment

## 2nd Mounted Division 1914-15

At the outbreak of war the 2nd Mounted Division was assigned to defence of the Norfolk coast. In March 1915 it formed a second-line duplicate of itself, the 2/2 Mounted Division. Leaving the 2/2nd on coastal defence, it then fought at Gallipoli from April to December 1915, under the command of Major General William Peyton, before being disbanded in January 1916.

**1st South Midland Mounted Brigade**
1/1st Royal Gloucestershire Hussars
1/1st Warwickshire Yeomanry
1/1st Queen's Own Worcestershire Hussars

**2nd South Midland Mounted Brigade**
1/1st Berkshire Yeomanry
1/1st Royal Buckinghamshire Yeomanry
1/1st Queen's Own Dorset Yeomanry

**London Mounted Brigade**
1/1st City of London Yeomanry
1/1st County of London Yeomanry
1/3rd County of London Yeomanry

**Notts & Derby Mounted Brigade**
1/1st Nottinghamshire Yeomanry (Sherwood Rangers)
1/1st Nottinghamshire Yeomanry (South Notts Hussars)
1/1st Derbyshire Yeomanry
1/1st Nottinghamshire Battery R.H.A. (left in April 1915 for the Imperial Mounted Division)

**Yeomanry Mounted Brigade**
1/1st Hertfordshire Yeomanry
1/2nd County of London Yeomanry

The following extract from the history of 25th (City of London) Cyclist Battalion relates the story of the 2/25th London Cyclists who arrived in Norfolk for their tour of coastal defence duties in April 1915 and presents a vivid insight into the life and events experienced by the troops engaged in anti-invasion duties on the North Norfolk Coast:

'On the 19th, the companies from Brighton went to Lewes and the whole unit left the county town in two trains for Norfolk. Four companies and headquarters went direct to Holt and the other half battalion to Sheringham. This course was rendered necessary owing to the lack of billeting facilities in Holt, where the Sussex Cyclists were still installed. The transport, in the meantime, had proceeded by road from the South Coast, under Captain E. H. Barton.

The battalion took over all coast duties, from the retiring battalion, two days later, on a line from Runton Gap (inclusive) to Snettisham, just south of Hunstanton, and came under Brigadier-General Fryer, Commanding the 2/1st South Wales Mounted Brigade.

It then found itself in an area quite different to that of the South Coast. Instead of sea fronts with rows of houses bordering on esplanades, it found a lonely coastline with occasional small villages or isolated farmhouses. It included Weybourne, with a beach having deep water at all states of the tide and low hills a short distance inland. These, if occupied by the enemy, would permit of a landing on the beach without molestation. An old rhyme, current in Norfolk from ancient times, ran thus:

'He who would old England win
Must at Weybourne beach begin'

The hint was not disregarded by the C. O. when making his dispositions to guard the coast. There were innumerable small creeks running in from the sea. In other sections of the area and close to Hunstanton there was a War Signal station where, if all accounts were true, wonderful things were done intercepting German wireless messages. At any rate, this point had to be guarded closely, night and day. Finally, just over twenty miles due south of the coast was Norwich, a busy, populous city with railways and factories, a big prize for an enemy if he could secure it. At that date a brigade of Yeomanry and a few guns were the only troops between the cyclists and the city. The good people of Norfolk were quite alive to the fact that 'there was a war on' and, consequently, were far more hospitable and interested in the cyclists than the South Coast population had been.

The look-out stations taken over from the Sussex Cyclists extended from Sheringham eastwards to Hunstanton and then south to Snettisham. Originally two companies with the M. G. section, were accommodated in the wooden huts in the Fairfield at Holt, the battalion headquarters; Hunstanton and Weybourne Hope each had one company, and Weybourne Springs and Wells two companies. This disposition was subsequently changed.

The battalion made a further acquaintance with Zeppelins on 30 April, when four which had raided Ipswich and Bury St Edmunds were reported, on their return, to be passing out to sea over Wells. This was only the first of many similar reports of a like nature, nor was it unusual to hear sounds of firing out at sea. The actual coastal duties were not so onerous as on the South Coast and, as a result, more time was available for training. It was the general rule for field training to be carried out, from May onwards, three days a week, affecting practically all the men who were not actually on duty. Musketry was practiced on Cawston Range.

The battalion, being less scattered than previously, it was possible on Whit Monday to hold a sports meeting in a field near Weybourne Springs Hotel. This, the first event of its kind since the formation of the unit, proved a great success especially as it brought members of different companies more closely together. In this connection in must be remembered that, since leaving London the previous November, the battalion had never been together as a whole and the majority of men knew no one outside the sixty or so others comprising their own company. On the South Coast the position was even more peculiar in this respect. In the case of one company at least, the men were divided into two halves in November. These were on duty on alternate days, continually, till the following Easter, with the result that, except during the few minutes employed in changing over look-out stations, the men of one half company had had no interaction whatever with those of the other. On the East Coast, things were rather better, in that, for a large portion of the time, half the battalion was stationed at Holt with two companies at Weybourne Hope hutments and only two other outlying companies at Brancaster Staithe and Wells respectively.

A slight alteration in duties took place at the end of May, when a company of the Royal Defence Corps assumed responsibility for the I.O.S. at Hunstanton, thus allowing the company stationed there to be transferred to Brancaster Staithe. The look-out station at Snettisham, however, was retained.

The men now commenced to reap the benefit of coast service. For the most part, the ensuing summer was a good one and for those companies stationed away from Holt it meant a very fair proportion of bathing parties – a dangerous form of exercise at Weybourne for those unable to swim. For the company stationed at Brancaster, there was a limited amount of boating and sailing available on the local waters, while shooting on the surrounding marshes was also not unknown.

Reference has been made to the depth of water at Weybourne. Locally, it is said that in places the six fathom mark is only six fathoms out at high tide; in other words, the beach slopes at 45°. One summer night a loud, grating sound showed us that the S.S. *Rosalie* of between 2,000 and 3,000 tons register, had run her bows well up the shingle, though her stern remained afloat. Torpedoed on her maiden voyage, she had been beached to save sinking. Subsequently she settled and later still broke her back.

In July orders to transfer to ordnance factories any men suitable for making munitions were received almost daily. In the same month, Provisional Battalions (formed of returned wounded soldiers and Territorials who had not taken on the obligation for foreign service) came into existence and the section of coastline from West Runton to Cley was handed over to them.

On a Saturday evening in September 1915 reports came from the Provisional Battalion stationed at Weybourne that the Germans were landing on the beach. The message, in accordance with standing instructions, was phoned on to all superior commanders and, as a result, the Yeomanry came rushing to Holt and the orders were received for the cyclist battalion, who turned out as soon as the alarm was given, to proceed at once to Weybourne. No sounds of firing could be heard, but the battalion moved off at about 3.00am passing through the Yeomen, who lined each side of the road, only to find, on arrival at Weybourne, that all was quiet. Subsequently the G.O.C. arrived and had a somewhat heated interview with the O.C. Provisional Battalion. The cyclists and Yeomanry were ordered to return to their billets, but all Sunday, troops, infantry and guns were moving on the railway through Holt to the coast and back again; ample evidence that the message as to an enemy landing had been taken seriously by Higher Command.

The following month (October) orders were received to construct strong points in various positions on the low cliffs. This meant excavations and lining with timber, a class of work to which most cyclists were not accustomed. They were fortunate, however, in having the Adjutant, Captain Latham, a professional Civil Engineer; under his direction the works were put in hand and were partially completed when War Office instructions were received to send all available men and also all officers with machine gun training, to the first line for service in East Africa. All coast duties, except Brancaster Section, were handed over to a Provisional Battalion and the M.O. proceeded to select all those with the unit fit for foreign service, and 375 rank and file left to join the 1st Battalion.

The first detachment of 75, under 2nd Lieut. Downs, left on 1 December 1915 and the remainder, with Lieut. H. G. Smith and 2nd. Lieut. Chamberlain, four days later. It was still dark when the parade formed up on the Fairfield and marched to the station headed by the glee party of 'H' Company, which had often cheered the battalion on the march with its part songs, to the tune of 'The Ten Blue

*Members of 2/25th City of London Cyclists digging trenches on Kelling Heath, 1915.*

Bottles'. The 300 moved through the sleeping town and, just as day broke, the special train departed leaving the officers and the majority of the N.C.Os to lament the break-up of the battalion, but confident that the men they had trained would prove their mettle.'

By the end of 1914 first line defence trenches to repel invaders had been dug across the Sheringham Golf Links; indeed, between Weybourne and Salthouse eleven defensive positions overlooked the beach, manned by four companies. There were thirty trenches running from Gallow Hill to Weybourne Mill and in strategic areas in the countryside between Sheringham and Holt with further trench systems dug around Sea Palling and around Yarmouth and Gorleston. Second and third line trenches to back these up were also dug near Aylsham and between Hunworth and Briston; as a further anti-invasion measure the marshes at Salthouse were allowed to flood.

Heavy Batteries consisting of six 60-pounders of the Royal Field Artillery were stationed at Weybourne and Mundesley. There were also two 4.7-inch guns on travelling carriages stationed at Cromer and a single in an entrenchment on Gorleston cliffs. Two 15-pounders were manned at Salthouse and further guns of the same calibre were set up in small emplacements at Eccles, Newport and Caister. This artillery could have hardly sunk a battleship but rather was intended as the heavy armour to harry an invasion force as it disembarked. There was also an armoured train (one of just two in the entire country) consisting of four armoured wagons armed with two 12-pounder guns and two machines guns, which ran along the M&GN branch line to Mundesley with occasional trips as far afield as Yarmouth and Lowestoft.

Some of the earliest fixed defences constructed in Britain during the First World War were built in Norfolk. Begun in 1916/17 the first major generation of these fixed defences were constructed from concrete blocks with heavy steel doors and loopholes with steel shutters behind that could be raised or dropped as necessary; circular in design with a flat roof this design gave raise to their nickname of 'pillboxes' – a name which has stuck to such defences ever since, no matter what their shape. Built to supplement the existing trench lines along the Norfolk coast, pillboxes were erected by companies of Royal Engineers at selected points on the coast and a short distance inland in an extended line from Stiffkey and Weybourne to Sea Palling and at almost every river crossing along the line of the river Ant from Bradfield to Wayford Bridge. Many of the river crossing defence pillboxes were constructed with their loopholes placed at different levels and built in pairs, often staggered on either side of a road on the inland side of the crossing for mutual support. The next generation of pillbox was hexagonal and made of poured concrete – these had 18 inch thick walls, half inch thick steel doors and steel lined loop holes; in many ways these pillboxes were the prototypes of what were to become the standard pillbox erected during the invasion scares of the Second World War. These hexagonal pillboxes were constructed further down the coast just outside Great Yarmouth on the Acle New Road, at Haddiscoe and St Olaves and into Suffolk. They were built with the intention of containing an invasion force which had already landed. The army continued to rehearse procedures to combat an enemy landing as late as June 1918 and the programme of fixed emplacement construction ran on after the cessation of hostilities when the costal defences were finally stood down and disbanded. They never fired a shot

*One of the pillboxes built along the River Ant.*

in anger but the silent sentinels of the Norfolk coast maintain their vigil; today many have been lost, are in a bad state of repair or are heavily overgrown but still they remain a reminder of the very real fears of invasion during the First World War.

# 5 Bombardments and the War at Sea

Despite the county of Norfolk having a seaboard of nearly 100 miles from Hopton-on-Sea to The Wash and having a long and rich maritime history, the story of the war at sea off the county during the First World War and the bombardments it suffered from the battleships of the Imperial German Navy are often forgotten, as is the bloody U-Boat campaign conducted against British minesweepers and fishing vessels. Indeed many people don't realise these things happened at all. Perhaps this is because the press coverage for these incidents during the war was heavily censored, often minimal or even subject to complete news blackouts because they were bad for morale. In many cases the stories in the following chapter only appear in official records and publications and are revealed here to a wider audience for the first time.

During the August of 1914 real concerns were voiced over the future of the fishing trade during the war. About eighty-five drifters returned to Yarmouth from their Scottish herring voyage and some of them had met torpedo boats and destroyers on patrol duty on their way home. There were still a number of boats at Wick and other northern ports some of which were thought to be likely to remain while others would only venture on the passage back by hugging our own coast. It was reported that 60 per cent of the Scottish crews had been called up as Naval Reservists, so that the prospects of a big Scots fleet visiting Yarmouth in the autumn were not very hopeful. From Yarmouth boats as many as 35 per cent of the men were claimed to be similarly called up and how the fleet could undertake the herring voyage from Yarmouth was put into doubt in view of the Admiralty request that all fishing boats should be withdrawn from the North Sea. The shipment of cured herrings was also suspended owing to the traders running to and from the Mediterranean ports having cancelled their sailings. The fishing trade was therefore faced with a serious position and it was remarked, with some concern, that Yarmouth shipbrokers due to cessation of Continental trade were finding themselves with little or nothing to do.

Meanwhile over at Gorleston four destroyers had been engaged to watch the outlying portion of the coast. Patrolling all night with lights out they would return to the harbour each morning and coal their craft from the collier in the harbour. The stokers and seamen aboard the destroyers were at work practically all night and day, and with the night work being of a particularly nerve-racking character they were soon feeling the effects of this continuous watchfulness. It then occurred to the Port and Haven Commissioners and Harbourmaster Captain J. G. Bammant, that something might be done to relieve the men on the destroyers. The workmen in the employ of the Harbour Commissioners were approached with the result that fifty volunteers became volunteer coal heavers who would fill up the necessary bags of coal in readiness for the craft when they arrived in the mornings.

The first reaction to the war at sea had come on the morning of 5 August 1914 when the German schooner *Fiducia* from Hamburg was seized at Yarmouth. She had been discharging her cargo of oil cake on the west side of the river at J. H. Bunn, no doubt as hundreds of German boats like her had done in peacetime. But now we were at war and to the complete bemusement of her master, Captain Mohr, and her crew the vessel was formally boarded by a naval officer and Custom House official and taken through the bridge to berth at Stonecutter's Quay where she became the 'centre of great interest on the part of thousands of visitors and townspeople'.

On the evening of Sunday 9 August a good deal of excitement occurred among the large crowds of promenaders on the Parade at Great Yarmouth when a destroyer was observed coming through the Yarmouth Roads from the North Sea with another war prize in tow in the shape of a German three-masted schooner *Theodor*, of Basel, Germany. The two vessels proceeded to the Harbour's mouth where anchor were dropped until the tide was suitable for entering the river. *Theodor* was eventually berthed at one of Messrs Palgrave Brown & Sons wharves in Southtown at midnight. She had been laden with about 300 tons of locust beans and came from Faro on the African coast bound for King's Lynn. Her German crew of seven hands were taken off, made prisoners of war and held at the Barracks. In the morning they were marched back down to their vessel under an armed guard to take possession of their clothes and then returned to the Barracks to await removal to a detention centre.

A terrible blow was dealt to the Royal Navy when the armoured Cruisers *Aboukir, Hogue* and *Cressy*, then engaged keeping North Sea waters south of Dogger Bank clear of German torpedo craft and mine layers, were all sunk by the German submarine U.9 under the Command of Kapitänleutnant Otto Weddigen on Tuesday 22 September 1914. Distressing scenes were witnessed in Lynn when the Admiralty announcement of the loss of the three cruisers was made known. Most of the Royal Naval Reserve men who had such a send off from Lynn on that memorable Sunday at the opening of the war had been posted to various warships and several from the town were known to be on either the *Aboukir*, the *Cressy* or the *Hogue*. The men were predominantly from the North End, most were not young but were married men, mostly in their 30s with wives and families and were well-known among the fisher folk and other sections of the townspeople and it was remarked on how a tension hung over the whole town as the news of survivors or those who had been killed or posted missing reached their relatives by official telegram.

In some cases wives and other friends received their telegrams on Tuesday night announcing the safety of individual men while news of others came later. But the uncertainly as to the well-being of survivors and the suspense generally cast a gloom over the town during the whole week, in the North End in particular. Most affecting was the sight of the womenfolk calling anxiously at the Custom House for hoped for information.

On the evening after the sinking a number of Lynn men were already reported missing; among them was Thomas Martin Allen of Checker Street, a Royal Navy Reservist, last seen bravely signalling to the other cruisers from the sinking *Aboukir*; his body was never recovered. Eleven Lynn men were lost in the action:

Thomas Martin Allen, Seaman, R.N.R, Checker Street (married) – *Aboukir*

Philip Barnard (36), Seaman, R.N.R, Pilot Street – *Hogue*

Frederick Bowman (34), Seaman, R.N.R, Armes Yard, High Street (married with three children) – HMS *Aboukir*

George Bunn (27), Seaman, R.N.R, Devonshire's Yard, North Street (married with two children) – HMS *Cressy*

John Farr (30), Seaman, R.N.R, 21 South Street (married with three children) – HMS *Aboukir*

William Fysh, Seaman, R.N.R, North-End Yard (married) – HMS *Aboukir*

Henry Edmund Horsley (41), Seaman, R.N.R, 17 Lansdowne Street – HMS *Cressy*

George Rodgers, Leading Seaman, R.N.R, Chapel Street (married with two children) – HMS *Aboukir*

John Rose (38), Seaman, R.N.R, Whitening Yard, North Street (married with nine children) – HMS *Cressy*

Charles Scott (22), Seaman, R.N.R, 5 Pilot Street – HMS *Aboukir*

Walter Waudby (31), Able Seaman, R.N.R, 2 Long Row, Highgate (married with four children) – HMS *Hogue*

*King's Lynn civic dignitaries with some of the returned local Royal Navy Reservist survivors of the sinking of* Aboukir, Hogue *and* Cressy *1914.*

Sailors from Great Yarmouth and other parts of Norfolk were also involved and lost in the sinkings. One survivor was Mr William Read of 20 Belsize Road, Thorpe Hamlet, Norwich, a member of the Royal Fleet Reserve serving aboard H.M.S. *Hogue* who was returned home to recuperate. His experiences were published in *The Cromer and North Norfolk Post* where the report began:

*'Except for his nerves being somewhat shaky, he is in good health and spirits. Despite his desperate experience, he remains undaunted. 'I don't want another time like the last adventure' he briskly remarked 'but I am quite eager, as I am sure my fellow survivors are to serve with destroyers so we can perhaps get a chance to get a little of our own back.' He has furnished a graphic account of his experiences. After describing how the Hogue with her sister ships the Aboukir and the Cressy, who were in the early morning of 23 September on patrol duty and mentioning the fact that he was asleep with the third watch below, when at about half past six o'clock they were suddenly aroused by an order to clear the lower deck, he proceeds:*

*'In a twinkling of an eye we were up. We slipped a few clothes on and rushed to the deck. We noticed the Aboukir heeling over to starboard we received orders to lower our boats for rescue purposes. The Aboukir had no boats for use, as they had been damaged during a storm a day or two previously. The launch was the first of our boats to go to the Aboukir's assistance. Then we prepared to get out*
*the picket boat and throw overboard two lifebuoys and all articles that might help to save life. While on the foc'sle I felt the Hogue heave slightly to one side. I felt sure that we had been struck by a mine or a torpedo. A dense volume of smoke poured up from the funnels which meant that the coal bunkers were blown up. A few seconds after the Hogue gave a second big bump, a more severe shock than the first. Every man was perfectly cool and the remark was simply made 'We have got it as well.' After she was first struck the Hogue only slightly heeled over and if a second torpedo had not struck her I think she might have recovered herself. But after the second blow she went on to sink rapidly. In fact only five minutes before she was completely gone.*

*When the order was given 'Each man for himself' I jumped over the side of the Hogue as the water was washing her decks. I was wearing a flannel shirt, trousers, collar, belt and pants. At this time I could see that the Aboukir was sinking fast and many of her crew swimming about. A cutter with some of the Aboukir's crew had just got alongside the Hogue as the latter received her first damage. In consequence of this the cutter shoved away from the Hogue. I am a strong swimmer and after I was in the water and found I could not get to our picket boat I tried to make for the Cressy. Many others of the Hogue's crew were doing the same. A number of the Aboukir's crew were saved through catching up with the lifebuoys and other things were had previously thrown over from the Hogue. But the Hogue's crew went into the water from the other side, and therefore had nothing to catch at.*

*Having got about half way between the Hogue and the Cressy I suddenly heard gun firing from the Cressy. Then the water seemed to tightly grip me and instantly I saw part of the bows and periscope of a submarine come up swiftly out of the water. I saw some of the Cressy's crew point to the craft. Then the submarine went down and I saw hands waving and heard shouts of joy coming from the Cressy. With such strength as I had left I raised my arm above the water and waved too. Others swimming about did same. I am perfectly certain the Cressy's guns sank that craft. I am also certain that I saw the periscope of three or four more submariners but only the one I have referred to was sunk so far as I am aware.*

*Just after I again felt a sensation of being severely gripped by the waters and saw the Cressy heel over. I at once concluded that she had been torpedoed as the Aboukir and Hogue had been.*

*I heard the sound of the contact of two torpedoes. None of the three ships caught fire but sank through the water rushing in. Seeing that the Cressy was being struck, I turned to swim away from her and saw the Hogue's launch in the distance. I made for her but she was pulling to the opposite direction. I hailed her but I could not have been seen or heard. I came to the conclusion that it was no good exhausting such strength as I had left by hard swimming so I made up my mind to try and keep afloat with as little effort as possible hoping that a piece of wreckage might possibly come in my direction. In the meantime I was watching the Cressy go down. Her crew acted magnificently. After she began to heel over I saw her Marine standing at attention on the quarter deck. In sinking she heeled to starboard and then turned completely upside down. Some of her crew simply kept walking up one side of her as the other side went down until they finally reached her keel. I saw about thirty men sitting on her keel. I lost sight of them in time so I suppose they must have floated off somewhere.*

*Eventually the Hogue's launch came my way and I used all the remaining strength I had to reach her. I got alongside her and had just enough strength to get hold of her gunwale but had not the power to grip it. A Maltese messman saw my condition and grasped my wrist. He held me until I had mustered a little strength and then assisted me into the boat. I had been for over two hours in the water. I was not injured in any way but was exhausted. The boat picked up a few more men and as no others were to be seen we made for the direction of a sail which proved to be that of a Lowestoft trawler J.C.C. LT. 639. Her skipper Mr Jacobs was making for us. From the launch we went on board the trawler whose crew proved themselves as true heroes. They removed almost every bit of clothing they possessed and gave it to we who were quite or partially naked. Hot tea was made they fried some fish they had just caught, which they served out as fast as they could. I cannot speak too highly of their conduct. The boat had previously cut away all her fishing gear so as to be 'free for rescue work.'*

*Destroyers afterwards came to the trawlers assistance, HMS Lowestoft made signals for us to come to her but as soon as we were alongside her the Commodore gave orders for us to cast off as he had observed a submarine. The Lowestoft headed off at full speed. We had gone in the launch to the Lowestoft, but as the latter could not take us the Trawler started to tow us away. The Lowestoft steamed round looking for the submarine, but being unable to find it, again signalled us to make for her. This we did and while we were being taken on board the Lowestoft five destroyers kept guard around. After other survivors had been taken aboard the Lowestoft steamed for Harwich which we reached about seven o'clock in the evening. On landing we were taken to Shotley Barracks where we were treated with ultimate kindness and sympathy.'*

The men on the minesweepers faced acute danger every day they were on patrol. The risks taken by these brave men in the nerve-shaking business of clearing the North Sea of the murderous menace scattered by the Germans in it waters was tremendous. Hundreds of vessels were employed in this duty and it was calculated that as many as 6,000 men formed their crews. The men were mainly fishermen and included many men from Yarmouth and Lowestoft, although not all the boats were steamers, there were firemen and stokers as well as deck hands. Crews numbered about ten to twelve men in every vessel along with the officers. The boats would go out for several weeks at a stretch with a period of rest in port once a month working in groups under the supervision and protection of warships.

The plucky crews worked in trawlers and drifters hired by the Admiralty. The trawlers worked in pairs with specially constructed trawling gear comprising hundreds of yards of steel wire which formed the trawl. The wire was weighted to lie deep and as it was dragged through the water it caught the moorings of any mines below the surface. Sometimes the mines exploded but more often it was necessary to pull them to the surface where the nearest warship could destroy them.

The drifters used nets, a number of these being fastened together and spread out by the boats. In this way a broad sweep could be made and a wide expanse of water cleared very quickly. Many German mines were insecurely moored and when they drifted together in bad weather a bunch could easily explode when they bumped against one another. It was in these circumstances that they were most dangerous and nearly all the mishaps to minesweepers occurred in this manner. Hundreds of mines were cleared in the opening months of the war, they did their best but the Imperial German Navy kept up the mine laying offensive and some met their mark.

The first major loss of local men aboard a fishing drifter occurred when the North Shields herring fishing boat *Lily* had just shot her nets when she struck a mine off the East Coast on Wednesday 7 October 1914. The Yarmouth fishing boats *Fioandi* and *Oakland* came to her aid. *Fioandi* recovered the body of Yarmouth fisherman Frank Self (64) while Harry Blowers the plucky Skipper of the *Oakland* rescued three survivors: Daniel Dunham and Mr Shillings of Lowestoft and William Nichols of Great Yarmouth. Two of the latter were suffering from minor injuries and shock but the third (Daniel Dunham) was seriously hurt. One crewman was in his bunk filling his pipe at the time the boat struck the mine and was blown clean through the deck. The *Fioandi* and *Oakland* put into the Tyne in the evening and landed the survivors who were taken to Tynemouth Victoria Jubilee Infirmary. The body of the dead fisherman was also brought ashore.

The four members of the crew lost on the *Lily* tells a tragic tale of local losses:

George Robert Chester Cockell, driver of the *Lily* had lived at 40, High Street, Gorleston. His wife was left with one child and was within weeks of the birth of a second. Mrs Blake of 10, Norman Lane, Cobholm, was prostrated with grief at the loss of her son William and tearfully remarked that his father, who was on board one of the lightships, did not know his son had gone to sea. The boy had been apprenticed to the coopering trade in Cobholm but joined the *Lily* to go minesweeping. It had been his first trip to sea and he had only recently written to his mother to say he had 'got with a very good crew' and was then 'quite safe'. Mrs Leonard, of 14, Napoleon Place, Great Yarmouth, the widow of the third victim, was left with four little children. Her husband had not told her until she received a letter home that he was engaged on a mine sweeper.

The funeral service for Frank Self was held in the Mission for Deep Sea Fishermen at the New Quay. Some difficulty had been experienced in tracing relatives of Mr Self and there were none present at his funeral but it was attended by many members of the local fishing community and over 130 fishermen who escorted the coffin to Preston Cemetery, North Shields. A tragic postscript to the story was that brave Skipper Blowers who rescued the three survivors had a number of his own crew leave him after they saw what befell the *Lily*. He had to bring his boat home shorthanded, though he was not a well man himself. Despite being attended by a doctor he died on 20 October, just a few days after his return, leaving a wife and three young children under five.

The enemy vessels seized at Great Yarmouth in August 1914 were small fry in comparison to a vessel initially described as a 'mystery ship' brought into the Yarmouth Roads and anchored with a Royal Navy cruiser and torpedo boat destroyer lying nearby on 19 October. The vessel was observed to be riding high out of the water and appeared to be very light. Her hull was painted white with a band of green. She had two masts and the Red Cross flag was flying on her mainmast. No name could be read from the shore on her stern, above which from a flagstaff the German colours were flying – the first time such a flag had been seen in the Yarmouth Roads since the declaration of war. Many people went to the seafront to catch a glimpse of her but not much could be seen from the shore as she was some distance between Wellington Pier and the harbour mouth. Public curiosity was very keen regarding her and all sorts of ingenious theories were current about her, ranging from a mine layer to a petrol supply ship. A few days later it was revealed the 'mystery ship' was in fact the *Ophelia* a Hamburg steamer of 1153 tons gross which was said to have been in pre-war days a well-known trader to London but had been requisitioned, officially at least, as a hospital ship.

It was later revealed after a number of German torpedo boats were destroyed during the Battle of Texel on 17 October and the *Ophelia* had been sent to supposedly search for survivors. Suspicions were aroused when British intelligence learned that *Ophelia* was using a wireless radio set, which was at that time unusual for a hospital ship, to communicate with the German wireless base at Norddeich station. She was also using coded wireless transmissions; a practice forbidden on hospital ships under the Hague Convention. Boarded and seized for the violation the *Ophelia* lay off Yarmouth under the supervision of a destroyer until Thursday 12 November when it escorted her to Gravesend where the crew, Captain Ritter, two other officers, about 20 sailors and a number of civilians were landed and the *Ophelia* was formally seized by the Admiralty as 'a prize of war'.

## The Bombardments

There had been fears and even totally unfounded rumours since the outbreak of war that the coastal towns such as Sheringham and Yarmouth had been shelled by German battleships and left in ruins. Concern was such that First Sea Lord Winston Churchill announced in the House of Commons that no actual fighting had taken place out at sea. In the reality the German Fleet had been 300 miles from the Norfolk shore. The Admiralty sought to calm the situation and issued a notice to the municipal authorities in all coastal towns to pay no heed to such communications and that visitors and the general public were advised to take no notice of rumours spread about that it was unsafe to visit seaside resorts. The Sheringham and Cromer Urban Councils also issued special notices to the public instructing them to ignore the misleading reports and rumours but on 3 November 1914 Imperial German battleships shelled Great Yarmouth. Other coastal towns such as Scarborough, Hartlepool, Whitby would subsequently suffer similar and worse bombardments in December but it was Great Yarmouth and Gorleston that suffered the very first.

Shortly after 7.00am on the misty morning of 3 November Commodore Reginald York Tyrwhitt commander of the 'Harwich Striking Force' (composed of the Third and Tenth Destroyer Flotillas and the Eighth Submarine Flotilla) was surprised by a wholly unexpected signal. It came from Commander Ballard of the Lowestoft based mine-sweeping gunboat *Halcyon* which had been working near Smith's Knoll and stated it had been engaged with a superior enemy; at that same time the enemy vessels had begun to fire salvoes of shells towards Great Yarmouth.

*Commodore Reginald York Tyrwhitt*

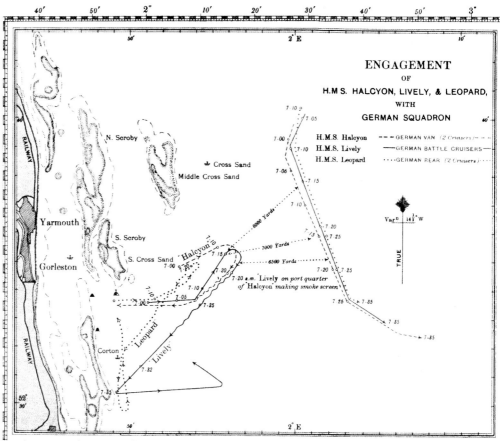

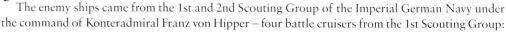

The enemy ships came from the 1st and 2nd Scouting Group of the Imperial German Navy under the command of Konteradmiral Franz von Hipper – four battle cruisers from the 1st Scouting Group:

*Seydlitz*, under Kapitan zur See von Egidy, the Flag Ship of von Hipper.
*Moltke*, KzS von Levetzow
*Von der Tann*, KzS Hahn, Flag of KA Tapken
*Blucher*, Freggattenkapitan Erdmann

and four light cruisers of the 2nd Scouting Group:

*Stralsund*, KzS Harder (SO of 2nd SG)
*Strassburg*, Fk Retzman
*Graudenz*, Fk Pullen
*Kolberg*, KzS Widenmann

*Konteradmiral Franz von Hipper.*

Corbett's *Naval Operations* states: '*They had left the Bight the previous evening under orders to make a demonstration against the English coast. Making the Cross Sands light-vessel about daybreak, they surprised the Halcyon some four miles south of it, steering north-easterly. Two miles south-west of her was the Torpedo Boat Destroyer Lively (Lieutenant Baillie-Grohman), patrolling to the eastward, and astern, near the Scroby Buoy, was another Torpedo Boat Destroyer, the Leopard (Lieutenant V. S. Butler). On seeing the leading ships of the enemy coming out of the morning mist the Halcyon turned towards them and made the challenge. It was greeted with salvoes of 11" and other guns, and she at once turned away to the south-west. Seeing her acute danger Lieutenant Baillie-Grohman, who also had altered course towards the enemy, dashed across her stern and boldly turned down on a parallel course with her and set up a smoke screen between her and the enemy. For about a quarter of an hour the two ships were under heavy fire, but thanks to continual changes of course and the smoke screen neither was seriously hit when, at about 7.40 the enemy, who had been steaming parallel to and about ten miles from the coast, firing heavily on Yarmouth, without, however, actually hitting the town, ceased fire and made off eastward. The Leopard, who all through had been under heavy fire, now turned to search down the coast while the Lively held after the enemy till she lost them in the mist.*'

A member of the crew from the *Leopard* was interviewed by a reporter shortly after the action:

'*It was a marvellous escape. The firing opened without the slightest warning and although we were stationary and broadside on the Germans could not hit us. One of their big boats fired its complete broadside at us in salvoes and although the shells came near, two passing over the stern and one between the funnel and the wireless, we were untouched.*

*The skipper took command in his pyjamas. I remember thinking he would find it pretty cold in that rig, but he didn't seem to mind, although he warned us it was going to be a tight thing, as it was not possible for us to move. There was not sufficient pressure in the boilers to move us. We thought our number was up but the crew were merry as mudlarks.'*

*From top left in a clockwise direction: SMS Seydlitz, SMS Moltke, SMS Blucher, SMS Von der Tann*

*HMS* Halcyon

Another man present at the action was Signalman Golding of HMS *Halcyon* who wrote to his sister:

'*I think it is an act of God that any of our ship's company are alive to tell the tale. It happened like this. We had anchored in Yarmouth Roads for the night and at six next morning we got up anchor and proceeded in a [censor line] direction.*

*About seven o'clock we spotted eight German ships and challenged them with our search-lights. They did not answer, so we challenged them three more and then they replied with three shots. They just missed us, so we turned round and they started firing broadsides at us.*

*It was a marvel we were not sunk in about a couple of minutes. Shells were falling all around us, and they shot our yardarm away and damaged the wireless. They shot a couple of holes on the bridge, one of them cutting the compass clean in halves and seriously wounding the man at the helm* [Able Seaman Harry Scotney]...*It cut a hole through the funnel. We fired seven shots from our 4.7 guns just to show them that they hadn't killed us, but they went miles short, as their guns hopelessly outranged ours.'*

The *Stralsund* had laid a line of 100 mines at 5.30am on her way to Smith's Knoll Passage and dropped her last 28 behind her squadron when they began to retire. HM Submarines *D3, D5* and *E10* had been sent out of Yarmouth with the orders to intercept the enemy off Terschelling. While proceeding on the surface to the interception point, *D5* struck a drifting mine and was sunk. The submarine had been running on the surface and only the five officers and men that were on the bridge survived the sinking out of a crew of 26.

The events on land on the morning of Tuesday 3 November 1914 were evocatively recorded in the *Yarmouth Mercury* where local residents were:

'...*ruthlessly disturbed by the rattling of windows and sound like the distant roll of thunder and the near slamming of big, noisy doors. Yet it was a calm morning with no wind. The banging and booming continued with alarming and ferocious frequency and a new noise, a screaming squeal in the air, made us all jump out of bed with a speed quite foreign to the leisurely movements of these autumn mornings. 'It's guns!' 'There's a fight!'*
 *The effect was the same as if anyone called 'Fire!' and the engine has been heard to tear past in a furious hurry. People issued from their houses, some properly dressed – the early risers – others variously garbed and even doing up their things as they ran with one accord along the roads to the Drive. And some women weren't excessively particular either. But no-one troubled to look at such trifles with great guns making the air start and quiver. It was just a pell-mell rush towards the sea afoot or on bicycles.'*

An eyewitness account recalls:
'Hundreds of inhabitants gazed out from along the front in awe over the sea touched with brightness by the rays of the rising sun, at the wonderful spectacle of shot and shell striking the surface of the sea almost on the horizon. By 7.15am when many local people had gathered at the end of Salisbury Road, the banging and the booming of the guns had become furious. No naval ships could be seen beyond the sands but there were fountains of water thrown up. As many as three of these cascades were in view at one time. They were not always in the same place, for whilst as seen from the north of Salisbury Road, some towered up over 60 or 70 feet, others appeared just like a piece of live coal dropping from the air and though judging distance on the water is the most deceptive thing in the world, it may have only been a mile or a mile and a half from the shore. The note of personal peril was quite absent, although it must be admitted that no one crossed the beach to the water's edge, they were content to remain in the openings and take in the fascinating spectacle from a safer distance.

'To many of those who were on the sands off Marine Parade it appeared the vessels were closing in on the town, for the firing certainly grew nearer and nearer; and there were apprehensions that some shot would come into the town. It was weird to see the flames of the explosion, and to see even the arc cut in the sky by the swift shell to feel the air shaken by detonations like thunder and yet different and all the time not to be able to see whence it was all coming. Many people considered it quite close enough and desired no nearer acquaintance with big guns. On the Denes a number of Scotch fisher girls were at work and the boom of the guns occasioned the greatest excitement among them. Some were seen to be crying and all the consoling efforts of the men folk proved of no avail. On the Fish Wharf the male workers jumped in all available carts and drove to the South Parade to see what was going on. The soldiers at the barracks were served instantly with ball cartridge and turned out on the sea front.'

Mr. J. H. B. Gedge, who lived at Caister facing the sea, was interviewed by the *Yarmouth Mercury* and as far as he could make out six vessels were firing and some of the shells landed between the Barber Sand and a passing steamer. Many women were sadly upset by the sound of the firing and ran out into the streets, only partially dressed, in great alarm. An eye-witness who was on the beach near the Wellington Pier immediately after the first shot stated he heard the shrill whistling of a shell and saw it burst into the sea within a few hundred yards of the Scenic Railway. The general estimate of spectators at Yarmouth that one hundred shots had been fired was later confirmed by the skipper of an Inverness drifter who witnessed the action at sea.

The troops billeted in Yarmouth were also mustered and preparations were made for defending the town, holding the main roads and going North and South to repel any possible landing. There was a naval ship of some kind at anchor in the Roads with wireless but she made no sign, though it was said by one observer there was semaphoring from her. Strangely enough, merchant vessels were steaming through the Roads all the time the firing was proceeding, together with drifters returning from the fishing ground and, to those viewing the events from the sea front 'none of them appeared to take the slightest notice of the awesome sight and sounds.'

Another rather surreal occurrence during the fateful quarter-hour was the passing of a train from Caister to the Beach Station which ran through during the thickest period of the firing oblivious to the action off the coast. The last quarter of an hour of the firing was heavy and momentarily the air was shaken by gunfire. It then began to slacken and ceased altogether before 8.00a.m. The firing was reported as being heard as far away as Stalham and Mundesley.

Many locals were left wondering what on earth had happened, some timid folk even went to the length of getting away from the town and all sorts of ingenious speculations were soon circulating. One gentleman said he saw a shell fall on the Barber Sands off Caister while others suggested they first heard the boom of a gun at 6.45. It was later revealed that a rumour had become currency in Norwich that Yarmouth had been left was in ruins after the bombardment!

## The Battle As Seen From Gorleston

'The first sound was heard just before 7.00am and came from the northward. Through a powerful glass from a point of advantage could be dimly discerned a number of warships making north. Suddenly, flash! flash! flash! Then after a perceptible interval the sound arrived in our ears. Then again flash! flash! flash! Meantime the scene of action was rapidly moving south. Lying in the Roads were two trawlers and it would seem as if they were a target, for within what appeared a very short distance of them the sea was ploughed with shot or shrapnel. Finding their position none too comfortable the trawler made tracks of their own – to the harbour.

While these events were happening the destroyers and submarine lying in the river proceeded to the scene of action and one saw visions of an extensive fight but before they had proceeded far, with three or four heavy crashes of big guns the whole thing ended. Nothing could be seen but a beautiful sunlit sea, a number of warships on the horizon, one of which was heliographing to the Naval Station and a cluster of fishing craft.

Throughout the morning the Pier Head was thronged by men and women and the vessels that entered the harbour were keenly observed with the object of discovering whether any of them had suffered as a result of the battle or whether there were any wounded on board. One of the first to return to Gorleston Harbour after the action was the steam drifter *Hastings Castle* whose skipper, George Wright, reported that many of the shells fired by the battleships passed over her and the deck hands laid flat on the deck to avoid being hit. Other skippers complained of similar experiences, a number of them cut their nets and fled the area with all speed. One Scotch boat had a mine explode in her nets, the shock causing considerable damage on board but the crew escaped injury, though they were thrown down in all directions and the vessel succeeded in making Yarmouth harbour safely.

Two hours after the return of *Hastings Castle* the Berwick Steam Drifter *Faithful* came in and moored at the Quay. On board were four members of the crew of the submarine D5 which had sunk when she struck a mine. One of the men was in such a serious condition that his removal to the Crossley Hospital on the South Denes was carried out as soon as possible using a steam pinnace. No further vessels, except Admiralty craft, were allowed to leave the harbour until Wednesday, when a fresh order was issued permitting fishing boats to go to sea again but they were limited to a prescribed zone.'

## Halcyon at Lowestoft

'The keenest excitement was aroused at Lowestoft, first by the sound of the guns and later by the arrival of the damaged gunboat *Halcyon* bearing external evidence of the danger through which she passed. At the north end of the town many residents noticed the rattling of their windows and not a few jumped to the conclusion that the cause was the firing at sea. By 7.30am numbers had made their way to the North Parade, where the flashes of the guns far out to sea were distinctly visible, while closer in the shells could be seen striking the sea sending up great columns of water. The shells fell in groups, as if broadsides were being fired and great columns of water sprang into the air.

The news spread quickly and when the *Halcyon* came into the Harbour the quaysides were thickly lined with excited people, who pointed out the wireless aerial hanging down, the cross-tree on the fore-mast had been partially shot away, there were shot holes in her after funnel and her bridge work has evidently suffered. The ship's company were heartily cheered by the naval staff on the North and South Piers as the vessel entered the Harbour. As soon as she reached the quayside a wounded man was landed and conveyed to the hospital in the horse ambulance. Before her wireless had been damaged the *Halcyon* was able to send a message announcing the presence of the enemy flotilla. The gunboat's captain, Commander Ballard, had received a cut to the back of his head, caused by a splinter of glass when the wheelhouse was struck by a shell; other members of the crew had also sustained minor injuries from flying splinters and glass.

The arrival of the enemy flotilla was as startling experience for the men of the Lowestoft fishing fleet as it had been for the Yarmouth boys. Shells had screamed high over some of the boats, while some of the drifters were so close to the enemy that on one boat the concussion smashed the wheel house windows. The steam drifter *Sam Richards* was close by the *Halcyon* and a destroyer when they were attacked and one of her crew stated shots fell all around them. Some fell so close to the drifter they feared she would be struck and they prepared their small boat for launching.

Robert Green, skipper of the Lowestoft steam drifter *Boy Daniel* said he saw the enemy steaming in from the eastward. He initially believed them to be British naval vessels but his engineer, who had been in the Navy, said they were German and so they proved to be. 'It was hazy, and we could not see what they were firing at.   The battleships came right along and fired broadsides as they steamed, the nearest German ship was only about a warship's length from us and the concussion of the first shot shattered my wheel-house window. The firing lasted about ten minutes. When they ceased firing the Germans steamed off in the direction from which they had come.'

Another Lowestoft skipper told what he saw in a letter to his sister:

*'We were coming in with £72 worth of herrings on Tuesday morning and about 7 o'clock we were about 4 miles off Lowestoft and about a mile below Corton float when we saw the gunboat Halcyon put up her flags. The next second I saw a shell burst alongside her and looking out to sea I saw eight German ships. For about a quarter of an hour the lot of them were just like lightening leaving their sides. How the Halcyon lived through it I don't know. Shells were exploding all around her in the air and others fell in the sea and sent up water like a fountain... some of our boats had narrow escapes from mines. One had just steamed over a mine when it blew up and blew the log-line off the boat's stern, but didn't hurt the boat.'*

Another mine exploded alongside *the John and Norah*. Pieces of the mine flew aboard, as well as a splendid codfish – fish and fragment were put on display at Mr. E. F. Thain's fish shop in Lowestoft the following day and attracted much interest.

The skipper of the Lowestoft drifter *Pilot Me* had seen 'a British submarine' [Submarine D 5] a short distance away, when suddenly her stern heaved up and then settled down in the water. Her stern then suddenly shot up into the air and she slipped beneath the waves. A Hull steamer, two other drifters and another British submarine were seen to circle round the spot for some considerable time, looking for survivors. One of them, the Steam Drifter *Homeland* was successful in this search and brought the last survivor of the D 5 (Able Seaman Albert D. Suttill) back to Lowestoft.

News also reached Lowestoft of the loss of steam drifter *Fraternal* (W. & S.A. Thacker of Kessingland) had been blown up by a mine. The drifter *Launch Out* brought in six survivors. Later in the afternoon the Lowestoft drifter *Primrose* brought in one of the crew of the Yarmouth steam drifter *Copious*. She was a fine vessel, built the previous March for Mr Harry Eastick of Gorleston and was returning to Yarmouth with a catch of herrings when she had struck a mine a short distance from the South Cross Sand Buoy. The victims of the disaster were :

George Symonds (Skipper)

John Richard Hill (Mate)

Robert Futter (Engineer)

William Waters (Hawseman)

William Symonds (Whaleman)

Frederick Veale Bonney (Net Ropeman)

Reginald Cecil Boast (Fireman)

Stanley James Baldry (Younker)

Joseph Fleming (Cook)

The sole survivor was Mr Frederick George Read (Younker) of Napoleon Place, Great Yarmouth who told his story to a reporter from the *Yarmouth Mercury*:

*'We crew were engaged in cleaning the nets when a sudden explosion was heard, which threw everyone down. When I got to my feet the bows of the boat were up in the air and the aft of the boat was sinking. I jumped overboard and found some broken wood to which I clung. I then saw the Copious going down but could not see anything of the rest of the crew.'*

After being in the water for about twenty minutes he was picked up from the top of the wheelhouse, to which he found he had been clinging. All the crew were Yarmouth residents with the exception of Waters whose home was at Burgh S. Margaret. Three years previously George Symonds was the skipper of the steam drifter *Piscatorial* who rescued the crew of the drifter *Montrose* in a heavy gale and was presented with a gold watch at the Town Hall for his gallant deed. Symonds left a widow and nine children; his brother, William Symonds, who was also a member of the crew, went down with the *Copious*.

Rumours soon spread that other vessels had also been blown up by mines. This proved only too true when news reached the town of the loss of the Lowestoft steam drifter *Will and Maggie* (owned by Mr. G. Westgate). The drifter *Qui Saint* rescued four of the crew. The other six were drowned. The fishing community were deeply affected by these losses and many refused to go to sea. It was to be long remembered as a black day for the fishermen of the East Coast.

## Postscript

### The *Lynn News* Diary – 3 November 1914

*Further Rumours and Scares*

*There was no definite news in the morning papers but presently very startling reports indeed began to come over the telephone from Yarmouth. The first story was regarded as a hoax but soon it became established as a fact that a German Squadron had fired shots very near the beach which is so familiar to all of us, that the Halcyon had been hit by shells and that a British submarine had been mined.*

*Needless to add, the actual facts – serious and thrilling enough in themselves became much distorted as the day wore on and during the evening I was told with the utmost earnestness that the Germans had landed an army, that their transports had been sunk by our fleet and that 60,000 of the enemy were in Norwich! Yarmouth and Lowestoft had, of course, been pretty well wiped out by gunfire and the Teutonic host was sweeping on to Lynn. What I wanted to know was this – why should Lynn be the main objective of the enemy's advance? It was at this stage my informant began to hesitate and to take refuge in the lame remark 'Well, of course, it's only what I've heard.' We have to draw the blinds of the trains when we go home at night now and the courting couples regard the precautionary measure without resentment.*

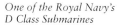

*One of the Royal Navy's D Class Submarines*

A total of five members of the crew of the submarine D5 were rescued, namely:

Lieut.- Commander Godfrey Herbert

Sub-Lieutenant Ian A. P. Macintyre

Chief Petty Officer Hebert A. Spiers

Able Seaman Charles H. Sexton

Able Seaman Albert D. Suttill

For their gallant rescue of the surviving crew members of HM Submarine *D 5* Mr. J. Collin, Skipper of Steam Drifter *Faithful* and Mr. A. Jenner, Skipper of Steam Drifter *Homeland* were each awarded The Board of Trade Sea Gallantry Medal.

Sadly, Able Seaman Harry Scotney (23) succumbed to the wounds he suffered to his head and abdomen during the attack on the *Halcyon* and died at Lowestoft Hospital about 12 hours after his arrival there. He was given full naval honours at his funeral on 5 November 1914; his coffin was draped with a Union Jack which was on a gun carriage to Lowestoft Cemetery followed by many members of the ship's company led by Commander Ballard and Captain Allison, Commander of the Lowestoft Naval base. The occasion was watched by a large gathering of townsfolk along the route.

*The Commonwealth War Graves headstone of Able Seaman Harry Scotney who died of the wounds he received aboard HMS* Halcyon *during the bombardment of Great Yarmouth.*

### Directions to the Public in the event of Bombardment or Invasion.

In case of BOMBARDMENT do NOT go into the STREET, but **keep in your cellar** or **on the ground floor of your home.**

In case of a hostile landing and the necessity arising of leaving the town, VEHICLES from **YARMOUTH** must travel by CAISTER ROAD.

FOOT PASSENGERS from Yarmouth must proceed past VAUXHALL STATION on to the ACLE NEW ROAD.

**Both Vehicles and Foot Passengers** from **SOUTHTOWN AND GORLESTON** must use the road to ST. OLAVES via BRADWELL AND ASHBY.

It must be borne in mind that in case of any of the roads being required for the movement of Troops, civilians must be prepared to move off the roads temporarily into adjacent fields if necessary in order that they may not hinder the movement of the Troops.

Persons leaving the Town should provide themselves with **food** and **warm clothing.**

If you wish for **advice** ask one of the SPECIAL CONSTABLES who will be on duty in case of danger, and be prepared to obey the directions given to you.

If any alarm comes during school hours, the **children attending the elementary schools** will be sent home at once.

**DAVID McCOWAN,**
*Mayor.*

TOWN HALL,
GREAT YARMOUTH.
6th February, 1915.

*Evacuation routes from Great Yarmouth in the event of bombardment or invasion, issued as a leaflet to local householders in February 1915.*

In the aftermath of the bombardment notices were produced and circulated and published in local newspapers by War Emergency Committees along the coast to reassure the public and advise them of the emergency procedures in the event of another

The following example comes from the coastal town of Sheringham where The Sheringham, Upper Sheringham, Beeston Regis and Weybourne Emergency Committee had been appointed under the authority of the Lord Lieutenant of the County, it consisted of Police Superintendent Collyer, Mr F. Edens, Mr R. W. Fetherstone, Rev. H. C. Finch, Mr H. R. Johnson, Mr W. B. Monement, Mr W. Shepherd, Mr H.M. Upcher, Mr B. A. Watts and Mr W. H. F. Wortley.

In an apparent attempt to allay fears the committee commented 'there is no reason to suppose that this part of the coast is likely to be bombarded, as in addition to the fact that it is an 'open' and undefended place and according to the laws of warfare should therefore be immune from such attack, it is difficult to imagine what the enemy could hope to gain thereby. Moreover past demonstrations have all been made against ports, which Sheringham is not.' Even so the committee considered it well to offer the following advice to the public in the event of bombardment:

*'The committee are advised the safest place in a house is the cellar, where a house is provided with one. Where there is no cellar, it should not be a difficult matter in a great many cases to dig a hole in the garden, and roof it over with something like railway sleepers, covered thickly with turf and soil. If it is intended to do this, the advice of the Council's surveyor, Mr. F. Hall Smith, should be asked, and would be readily given. Occupiers of houses with cellars or 'dug outs' should notify the fact in writing to the committee at the Council Offices, so that in the unlikely event of bombardment they could afterwards be inspected to confirm the safety of the occupants.*

*Failing this, the next safe place in a house is probably the ground floor room furthest away from the sea.*

*For those who prefer to leave their houses the best places are on the land side of the railway embankments, the south side of the Skeldon Hills and Beeston Hills and in holes and pits such as at the top of Sweetbriar Lane on the Golf Links and the old Lime Kilns near Beeston Hills.*

*The worst place would appear to be the streets and open spaces near buildings.*

*In the event of invasion the whole district would at once come under military law and any instructions given by the military must be implicitly obeyed. The main roads leading into the place would be required exclusively for military purposes, as would also the railways.*

*It is considered advisable for the inhabitants to leave the district, necessary directions as to roads would be given by special constables. As far as can be seen at present, the best roads to use out of Sheringham and Beeston would be:*

1. *The path through waterworks road*

2. *The road across Beeston Common, past the gamekeeper's cottage.*

3. *Briton's Lane*

4. *The road through Mrs. Cremer's yard at Beeston*

*Out of Upper Sheringham the best road would be past Heath Farm and across the heath to the mill. After reaching the top Cromer Road the public would have to use the bye-roads towards West Beckham and Gresham.*

*H. R. Johnson*
*Chairman, Emergency Committee*
*Sheringham, 24 December 1914.*

The next attack aimed at Great Yarmouth and Lowestoft came on 24 April 1916. 1st Scouting Group of the Imperial German Navy commanded by Rear Admiral Friedrich Bödicker, with the support of four light cruisers of the 2nd Scouting Group, two torpedo boat flotillas and their two light cruiser command vessels sailed across the North Sea bombard Lowestoft and Yarmouth. Four battlecruisers opened fire on Lowestoft at 04.10 am for 10 minutes damaging around 200 houses and destroying 40 destroyed and two gun batteries Lowestoft leaving over 20 people killed or wounded. As the cruisers carried on to Great Yarmouth fog hampered their vision but they did continue to bombard the town.

Three large shells also fell on Caister, one in a garden spattering the houses in mud for a 100 yard radius. Newtown also had a providential escape, shells falling on the Denes creating large craters just yards away from houses, doing no injury and blowing a few windows in. A huge crater was left by a shell at the Corporation Nursery adjoining the destructor on hurling enough soil onto the nearby Caister Road to block the tram lines and carriage way. While other shells exploded in the air showing fragments over Bradwell, Southtown and the North End where a number of 12-inch shells buried themselves in soft waste ground and caused no real damage. The only instance of significant damage was to a block of fishing premises belonging to Smith's Dock Trust Company Ltd which was struck and caught fire. The Fire Brigade were soon on the scene but despite their best efforts the building was destroyed. There were numerous stories of narrow escapes but fortunately there were no casualties. Local people especially youngsters sought out shell fragments which sold easily to souvenir hunters from one to ten shillings per piece according to size. The largest portion of shell fragment recovered in the immediate aftermath of the bombardment weighed forty pounds.

The final bombardment came surprisingly late in the war. At 10.55pm on Monday 14 January 1918, Great Yarmouth was again shelled by German warships. This time some shells did hit their mark, houses and buildings were damaged, windows were blown in, there were many lucky escapes but eight people were injured and four killed. Able Seaman Thomas Prigent (42) and ship's fireman John Simpson (17) were asleep on board their vessel in the harbour when the shell struck the forecastle deck. Both were recovered and rushed to hospital but later died of their wounds. Mr Alfred Sparks (53) and his wife Mary Ann (53) were also asleep when a shell struck their bedroom. Mrs Sparks had been killed instantly but Alfred was dug out of the rubble and removed to the hospital where he died from his wounds shortly after 10am the following morning.

## The U-Boat War

The censor was strict about publishing naval losses, hardly surprising as the losses off our coast on a single day were shocking at times. Often all that could be gleaned came from very short weekly announcements in local newspapers, for example on one week of heavy losses off the Norfolk coast, there was no reportage, just two lines under 'The Pirate's Record' published in the *Eastern Daily Press*:

> *'Two British vessels were sunk or captured during the week ending August 11th and 17 British fishing vessels were accounted for.'*

An attack from a U-Boat against a fishing vessel would often be preceded by the U-Boat surfacing, the Commander would appear in the conning tower and hail the crew of the fishing vessel with a megaphone and give a ten minute warning to surrender or be fired upon. The vessel would then be captured and boarded and the crew would be given a limited time to abandon their vessel then the U-Boat would fire upon it and scuttle it. Occasionally the fishermen would simply be left in the water, other times they would be taken aboard the U-Boat to become prisoners of war. Most of the vessels off Norfolk were lost in offensive actions by the U-Boats of the Flandern Flotilla, a formidable U-Boat force during the war which was responsible for the destruction of no less than 2554 merchant vessels (or about 4.5 million tons) plus damage and destruction of numerous fighting vessels of the Royal Navy.

## Losses to U-Boats off the Norfolk Coast during the First World War

### *'Bloody August' 1915*

### *Otto Steinbrinck, UB10*

**OFF PALLING**
*Fulgens*, Merchant steamer carrying a cargo of coal, 2,512 grt, **1 August 1915** sunk by torpedo from UB 10 under Kapitänleutnant Otto Steinbrinck 1 mile off Palling.

**OFF BLAKENEY**
*Rosalie*, Steamer (Cardiff), 4,243 grt (New Ruperra Steam Shipping Co. Ltd), **10 August 1915, 3 miles off Blakeney Buoy, torpedoed** by submarine UB10, under the command of Kapitänleutnant Otto Steinbrinck. No casualties.

**OFF CROMER**
*Esperance* (LT 1108), fishing smack, 46grt, (Arthur Evans, Lowestoft), **10 August 1915**, 17 miles NE by E from Cromer, captured by submarine UB10, under the command of Kapitänleutnant Otto Steinbrinck. Scuttled by gunfire. No casualties.

*Seamen captured from minesweepers and fishing trawlers photographed while prisoners of war in Germany c.1916.*

*Young Admiral* (LT 349), fishing smack, 60grt, (Samuel Ling, Lowestoft) **11 August 1915**, 17 miles E by N from Cromer, captured by submarine UB10, under the command of Kapitänleutnant Otto Steinbrinck. Scuttled by bomb. No casualties.

*Trevear* (LT 280), fishing smack, 47grt, **11 August 1915**, 17 miles E by N from Cromer, captured by submarine UB10, under the command of Kapitänleutnant Otto Steinbrinck. Scuttled by bomb. No casualties.

*Welcome* (LT 713), fishing smack, 56grt (Robert W. Linder, Lowestoft), **11 August 1915**, 17 miles E by N from Cromer, captured by submarine UB10, under the command of Kapitänleutnant Otto Steinbrinck. Scuttled by bomb. No casualties.

*Palm* (LT 190), fishing smack, 47grt (Henry R. Broadley, Lowestoft) **11 August 1915**, 17 miles E by N from Cromer, captured by submarine UB10, under the command of Kapitänleutnant Otto Steinbrinck. Scuttled by bomb. No casualties.

*Illustrious* (LT 546), fishing smack, 59grt (John Lang, Lowestoft), **11 August 1915**, 17 miles E by N from Cromer, captured by submarine UB10, under the command of Kapitänleutnant Otto Steinbrinck. Scuttled by bomb. No casualties.

*George Crabbe* (LT 1029), fishing smack, 42grt (John Chambers, Lowestoft), **11 August 1915**, 16 miles E by N from Cromer, captured by submarine UB10, under the command of Kapitänleutnant Otto Steinbrinck. Scuttled by bomb. No casualties.

*George Borrow* (LT 956), fishing smack, 62grt Charles G. Chambers, Lowestoft), **11 August 1915**, 15 miles ENE from Cromer, captured by submarine UB10, under the command of Kapitänleutnant Otto Steinbrinck. Scuttled by bomb. No casualties.

*Ocean's Gift* (LT 1009), fishing smack, 60grt (John C. Shepherd, Lowestoft), **11 August 1915**, 36 miles E. from Cromer, captured by submarine UB10, under the command of Kapitänleutnant Otto Steinbrinck. Scuttled by bomb. No casualties.

*Humphrey*, fishing smack, 41grt (W. H. Podd, Lowestoft), **11 August 1915**, 48 miles E ¾ S from Cromer, captured by submarine UB10, under the command of Kapitänleutnant Otto Steinbrinck. Scuttled by bomb. No casualties.

### *Oberleutnant zur See Wilhelm Smiths, UB 5*

*E. M. W.* (LT 314), fishing smack, 47grt, **13 August 1915**, 29 miles NE by N from Cromer, captured by submarine UB 5, under the command of Oberleutnant zur See Wilhelm Smits. Scuttled by bomb. No casualties.

*J.W. F. T.* (LT 597), fishing smack, 60grt, **13 August 1915**, 29 miles NE by N from Cromer, captured by submarine UB 5, under the command of Oberleutnant zur See Wilhelm Smits. Scuttled by bomb. No casualties.

*White City* (LT 268), fishing smack, 45grt, **14 August 1915**, At Cromer Knoll, captured by submarine UB 5, under the command of Oberleutnant zur See Wilhelm Smits. Scuttled by bomb. No casualties.

*Integrity* (LT 930), fishing smack, 52grt, **23 August 1915**, 24 miles ESE from Cromer, captured by submarine UB 12, under the command of Oberleutnant zur See Wilhelm Smiths. Scuttled by bomb. No casualties.

## OFF YARMOUTH

*Miura,* Navy Hired Trawler, 256 grt **23 August 1915** torpedoed by UB 2 under the command of Oberleutnant zur See Werner Fürbinger off Great Yarmouth Casualties 11.

*Sir William Stephenson*, Passenger Steamer, 1540 grt, **29 August 1915** mined by UC 6 under the command of Matthias Graf von Schmettow, off Cockle Light Vessel, sank in Yarmouth Roads (2 casualties).

## September 1915 – April 1918

### OFF CROMER

*Boy Ernie* (LT 282) fishing smack, 47grt, **10 September 1915**, 58 miles East of Cromer sunk by UB 2 under the command of Oberleutnant zur See Werner Fürbinger. No casualties.

*Research* (LT 1028) fishing smack, 44grt, **17 May 1916**, 35 miles East of Cromer. Stopped and scuttled by gunfire from UB 18 under the command of Kapitänleutnant Otto Steinbrinck. No casualties

*Dragoon* (LT 242) fishing smack, 30grt, **20 August 1916**, 36 miles NE by E for Cromer, captured by submarine UC10, under the command of Oberleutnant zur See Werner Albrecht. Scuttled by bomb. No casualties. On 21 Aug 1916 UC 10 was torpedoed in the North Sea and by HM Sub E54 off Schouwen Bank 5202N 0354E. 18 dead (all hands lost).

*Lanterna*, Merchant Vessel, 1685grt, **6 October 1916** sunk by a mined and sunk by UC 1, under the command of Oberleutnant zur See Heinrich Küstner, 2 ½ miles NE ½ E from Cromer. No casualties.

*Giralda* (LT 1100) fishing smack, 46grt, **3 June 1917** mined and sunk by UC 4, under the command of George Reimarus, 22 miles NE ½E from Cromer. No casualties.

### OFF YARMOUTH

*Cantatrice* RN hired trawler 302grt sunk by mine near Great Yarmouth on **5 November 1916**

*Doon* RN hired trawler 275 grt sunk by mine near Newarp Light Vessel, near Great Yarmouth **24 November 1916**.

### OFF SMITH'S KNOLL

*Superb* fishing smack 50grt sunk by gunfire from submarine 5 miles NE by E from Smith's Knoll **13 November 1916**

*Our Boys* fishing smack 50 grt sunk by gunfire from submarine 10 miles NE by N from Smith's Knoll **13 November 1916**

*Gold Seeker* fishing smack sunk by gunfire from submarine 4 miles from Smith's Knoll **13 November 1916**

## May – July 1918
## Götterdamerung

By 1918 the war against Germany had become one of attrition and the last real gambit of the U-Boat offensive occurred between May and July of that year. The main culprit for the losses off Norfolk was Oberleutnant zur See Hans Joachim Emsmann, commander of UB 40.

### OFF SMITH'S KNOLL

*Eclipse* (LT 684) fishing smack 47grt captured and sunk by gunfire from UB 40 under the command

*AB Samuel Johnson R.N.R. of Repps who was lost when the R.N. hired trawler* Cantatrice *was sunk by mine near Great Yarmouth on 5 November 1916.*

of Oberleutnant zur See Hans Joachim Emsmann 10 miles NE by N from Smith's Knoll Spar Buoy on **26 May 1918**. No Casualties

*Fortuna* (LT 547) fishing smack 61grt captured and sunk by a bomb by UB 40 under the command of Oberleutnant zur See Hans Joachim Emsmann 10 miles NE by N from Smith's Knoll Spar Buoy **26 May 1918**

*Dayspring* (LT 665) fishing smack 57grt sunk by gunfire from UB 40 under the command of Oberleutnant zur See Hans Joachim Emsmann 10 miles NE by N from Smith's Knoll Spar Buoy **26 May 1918**

*Dianthus* (LT 204) fishing smack 51grt captured and scuttled by bombs by UB 40 under the command of Oberleutnant zur See Hans Joachim Emsmann 5 miles N by ½E from Smith's Knoll Spar Buoy **6 June 1918**

*Active* (LT 513) fishing smack 57grt sunk by gunfire from UB 40 under the command of Oberleutnant zur See Hans Joachim Emsmann 10 miles NE by N from Smith's Knoll Spar Buoy **6 June 1918**.

*Beryl* (LT 275) fishing smack 57grt captured and sunk by gunfire from UB 40 under the command of Oberleutnant zur See Hans Joachim Emsmann 5 miles NE by N from Smith's Knoll Spar Buoy **6 June 1918**

### OFF HAPPISBURGH

*Fear Not* (LT 688) fishing smack 59grt captured and scuttled by a bomb from UB 40 under the command of Oberleutnant zur See Hans Joachim Emsmann 14 miles NNE from Haisbro' Light Vessel **27 July 1918**

*Passion Flower* (LT 95) fishing smack 46grt captured and scuttled by a bomb from UB 40 under the command of Oberleutnant zur See Hans Joachim Emsmann 14 miles NNE from Haisbro' Light Vessel **27 July 1918**

*I'll Try* (LT 320) fishing smack 51grt scuttled by a bomb from UB 40 under the command of Oberleutnant zur See Hans Joachim Emsmann 14 miles NNE from Haisbro' Light Vessel **27 July 1918**

*Valour* (LT 73) fishing smack 39grt captured and scuttled by a bomb from UB 40 under the command of Oberleutnant zur See Hans Joachim Emsmann 14 miles NNE from Haisbro' Light Vessel **27 July 1918**

*Paragon* (LT 362) fishing smack 56grt captured and scuttled by bomb from UB 40 under the command of Oberleutnant zur See Hans Joachim Emsmann 8 miles NE by N Haisbro' Light Vessel 27 July 1918

*Le Bijou* (LT 595) fishing smack 46grt captured and scuttled by bomb from UB 40 under the command of Oberleutnant zur See Hans Joachim Emsmann 9 miles NE from Haisbro' Light Vessel **27 July 1918**

*Two British 'H' class submarine lie alongside their war trophy, a captured German coastal type submarine at Hall Quay, Great Yarmouth 1919.*

*Success* (LT 1007) fishing smack 54grt captured and scuttled by gunfire from UB 40 under the command of Oberleutnant zur See Hans Joachim Emsmann 7 miles NE by E from Haisbro' Light Vessel **27 July 1918**

*Councellor* (LT 267) fishing smack 56grt captured and sunk with bomb by UB 40 under the command of Oberleutnant zur See Hans Joachim Emsmann 2½ miles N from Haisbro' Light Vessel **27 July 1918**

*Francis Robert* fishing smack 44grt captured and sunk by gunfire from UB 40 under the command of Oberleutnant zur See Hans Joachim Emsmann 8 miles NE from Haisbro' Light Vessel **27 July 1918**.

# 6 Air Raids

## The First Zeppelin Air Raid – 19 January 1915

While Britain's Navy still ruled the waves our Coastal Type airships or 'blimps' (nick-named Pulham Pigs in these parts after the airship station near the village) were fearfully inadequate in comparison to the Germans and their advanced classes of Zeppelins which were, in effect, the long-range heavy bombers of their day. Zeppelins could cross the North Sea from their bases in the Fatherland flying far beyond the range of battleship shells or field artillery they could literally take the fight to the enemy. General von Falkenhayen, Chief of the German Army General Staff was keen to commence combined operations against Britain but his plans and airships failed to impress the Imperial German Navy chiefs, they had their own plans.

Admiral Hugo von Pohl, Chief of Naval staff sought an audience with the Kaiser to obtain sanction to conduct air raids on Britain. The Kaiser was initially against any such action but after conference a compromise of only allowing bombs to be dropped on specifically targeted military installations and docks was agreed.

*Multi-view postcard of the Zeppelin bomb damage wrought on Great Yarmouth during the raid of 19 January 1915.*

During December and early January German airship reconnaissance pushed close up to the English coast and fears grew of aerial bombing attacks being carried out by Zeppelins. These fears lead to what may arguably be the first civilian casualty caused by Zeppelins (or at least the fear of their attacks). On Friday 15 January 1915 Mrs Alice Mary Cubitt (50), the wife of local bank manager, Henry Cubitt, was helping her neighbour Dr David Walter in the construction of a 'dug out' place of safety against air raids and bombardment in his garden at 2 Park Road, Gorleston Cliffs when the structure suddenly collapsed (probably due to the sodden soil caused by continued rainfall) burying the pair under a large quantity of struts, boards and earth. Dr. Walter managed to extricate himself, as he did so he called to his servants to summon the assistance of some of the military sappers at work on the cliffs who came running with spades to release Mrs Cubitt but she was found to be dead. Medical examination revealed she had a weak heart and the shock of the collapse had killed her.

Four days later, on the morning of 19 January 1915 Zeppelins L.3 under the command of Kapitanleutnant Johann Fritz and L.4 under Kapitanleutnant Magnus Count von Platen Hallermund, set out from their base at Fuhlsbuttel with orders to bomb key installations along the river Humber. Both Zeppelins were carrying crews of 16 men, eight 110lb explosive bombs, ten or eleven 25lb incendiary bombs and enough fuel for 30 hours flying.

*Admiral Hugo von Pohl, Chief of Imperial German Navy Staff c.1915*

These two Zeppelins were to be led across the North Sea by the L.6 that flew out of Nordholz carrying no lesser figure than Peter Strasser, Chief of the German Naval Airship Division. The L.6 had been given the 'prize' target of the Thames Estuary. The mission of the L.6 was, however, cut short when the crankshaft of the port engine broke while she was north-east of the Dutch island of Terschelling. It was still 90 miles to the English coast and fearing that the weight of the ice that might collect on the envelope of the Zeppelin would prove too much for her to carry with only two engines Strasser recorded he 'decided in agreement with the commander of L.6, but with a heavy heart, to turn back.'

When reading what follows next it is worthwhile keeping in mind the words of Horst von Buttlar Brandenfels, commander of the ill-fated L.6 and Zeppelin commander on numerous later raids who recorded the problems of navigation during these early operations in *Zeppelins over England*:

*'In those days we always flew as far as possible in sight of land in order to be able to determine our ship's position the more accurately and, above all, to have some means of checking the speed at which we were going. Our wind measurements, which we received before ascending, were extremely inadequate, and did not give us anything like a true idea of the conditions, more particularly as all observations regarding the west – and these were the most important and*

*Fregattenkapitän Peter Strasser, Chief of the German Naval Airship Division.*

*most valuable from our point of view – were altogether lacking. Whether the wind was increasing or abating could be determined only by ascertaining the position of the ship at various intervals, and these positions, as I have already pointed out, were fixed by keeping observation on the land. Later on, all this was entirely changed and we navigated our ships in accordance with wireless information.*

*Flying in sight of the Dutch coast had, of course, this disadvantage, that the ships were reported to England the moment they steered a westward course but, for the reasons above, we had to put up with this drawback. Moreover, in any case it was probable that English submarines, which were constantly busy in the North Sea laying mine barrages, reported the approach of the airships by wireless. Whether… we should succeed in reaching England or not was entirely dependent on whether our engines would be able to hold out.'*

The L.3 and L.4 Zeppelins approached the Norfolk coast in company, passed over the Happisburgh Lightship and were first spotted from land at 7.40pm, flying low, each 'carried a light' and were described by an observer at Ingham, a mile and a half from the sea, as 'like two bright stars moving, apparently 30 yards apart.' Before coming over land at 7.55pm, they separated, L.3, making landfall over Happisburgh, turned south-east and L.4 made for Bacton.

LZ 24. „L3."        1914.

*Zeppelin L.3, flown under the command of Kapitanleutnant Johann Fritz dropped the first bombs during a Zeppelin air raid on Great Britain on 19 January 1915.*

## L.3

A patrol of 6th (Cyclist) Battalion, The Norfolk Regiment T.F. spotted the Zeppelin L.3 as it passed over Eccles Gap. It then steered over Lessingham, Ingham (8.05pm) and Martham (8.15pm) where Kapitanleutnant Fritz attempted to find out where he was by dropping a flare. Mr Frank Gray, the landlord of the Royal Oak happened to be looking out and saw the flare which he described as looking like 'a big star' and was astonished at how the phenomenon 'stood out of the starless inkiness of the rest of the sky.' The casing from this flare was picked up in a lane near the hall at Martham and was described in the *Yarmouth Mercury* as being 'about two feet long and 3 ½ inches in diameter. At one end, which was solid except for a sort of turnscrew in the centre, where the figures 6, 12, 15, 18 at even distances round the edge and there were various German words on the tube itself.'

Shortly after 8.15pm the L.3 dropped its first bomb, an incendiary, on farmer George Humphrey's waterlogged paddocks near St Michael's Church at Little Ormesby leaving only a small crater about a foot and a half wide. Turning seaward to skirt the coastline it was spotted south of Caister (8.22) out to sea, turning almost immediately towards Great Yarmouth. Spotting the town, L.3 dropped a parachute flare to illuminate its target. The people below believed they were being swept by a searchlight and another small detachment of soldiers from the 1/6th Battalion, The Norfolk Regiment

(Cyclists) who were on coastal defence duty opened up with rifle fire. Crossing the town from North to South the L.3 dropped its second bomb, another incendiary, at 8.25pm, which landed on the back lawn of Mr Norwood Suffling's house at 6 Albemarle Road, overlooking the Wellesley Recreation Ground. This bomb 'burst with a loud report' but did little damage apart from gouging a two foot crater and splashing mud up the house. The third bomb, the first of the explosive bombs to be dropped, described in the *Yarmouth Mercury* as a 'diabolical thing', fell at the back of 78 Crown

Road, narrowly missing one of its elderly occupants Mrs Osborne who, at the moment of impact, was crossing the small back yard to the back door; still shaking as she spoke to the reporter she said of the sound 'It was like a big gun... If I had gone just a step or two further I must have been killed by it.' On the morning after the raid this bomb was dug out of the small crater it had made in the pavement by Norfolk National Reservists and taken to the York Road Drill Hall where the detonation mechanism (including a small air propeller operating on a fuse) was removed and the defused bomb became the object of much interest and curiosity to the large number of people who came to see it through the day. The fourth bomb, an incendiary, fell a few yards further west, failing to detonate it buried itself harmlessly against the gate post of Mr W. F. Miller's livery stables behind Crown Road.

*Norfolk Regiment Reservists recover the unexploded high explosive bomb dropped at the back of 78, Crown Road, Great Yarmouth.*

The people of the St Peter's Plain and Drake's Buildings area of the town were not to be so lucky. Here landed the fifth bomb, a devastating high explosive. Some of the windows of St Peter's Church and parsonage were blasted in and the front of St Peter's Villas, the home of fishworker Mr E. Ellis was brought down by the explosion. Luckily he was in the kitchen, the back door was blown off its hinges and fell on top of him, as did the kitchen window and sundry other wreckage but he only suffered cuts from flying glass and debris, and he was thankful, only minutes before he had been in the room that took the blast. He did suffer wounds severe enough to receive hospital treatment, a gash to his knee caused by the falling glass penetrated deep and caused him a lot of pain. He appears on several photographs, standing indignantly in front of his house with his head bandaged. Luckily his wife and family were away in Cornwall, where Mr Ellis was soon to join them for the mackerel fishing.

Opposite the Villas were the premises of J. E. Pestell, builder and undertaker, that received the full force of the explosion and suffered such extensive damage they had to be demolished. He lived on the premises with his young family and by some miracle they were all unhurt but the first casualties from the first Zeppelin air raid were incurred close by. Seventy-two-year-old spinster Martha Taylor, who lived at 2 Drakes Buildings with her twin sister Jane Eliza, was returning from a trip to the grocer's shop on Victoria Road when the bomb landed on St Peter's Plain. Her body was discovered by Pte Alexander Brown of the National Reserve who was on his way back from the Hippodrome when, turning the corner of St Peter's Plain, he stumbled over a 'bundle' outside Mr Pestell's corner office window. On closer examination he discovered it was the body of Miss Taylor whose clothes had been blown to rags. Running to the Drill Hall, he informed Cpl. Henry Hickling and they took a stretcher to where she lay. It was only when she was moved that was it revealed she had been badly injured in the lower part of her body and part of her arm that had been blown clean off and lay nearby.

Dr. R. H. Shaw examined Miss Taylor's body at the hospital and explained the extent of the injuries she had suffered at her inquest: 'The left side of the body was torn open from the hip to the shoulder and the organs dislodged. The right shoulder joint and bone and the right knee joint were broken. The ankle was also injured and the greater part of the left arm missing. Death was instantaneous.'

Left: *Injured but undaunted Mr E. Ellis stands in front of the wrecked frontage of his home, St Peter's Villa, Great Yarmouth.*

*Miss Martha Taylor*

*The bomb damage to St Peter's Plain viewed from Lancaster Road, Great Yarmouth. Miss Martha Taylor was killed by Pestell's corner office window, near where the soldiers are standing to the right of the photograph.*

Right: *The bomb-blasted premises of J. E. Pestell, viewed from within St Peter's Plain. Samuel Smith was killed at the end of the passage by the double gate entrance.*

A second body, that of shoemaker Samuel Alfred Smith (53) was next reported. He had evidently been standing at the end of the passage in which the door of his shop was situated to watch the passing raider. The passage, located opposite St Peter's Villas, had a large double gate at the end, one half open and the other half closed; the bomb fell 30ft away from Mr Smith. Several fragments of the bomb blast had been hurled in his direction, the gate was badly peppered and tragically Mr Smith was caught by some of the shrapnel, part of his head was torn away and left thigh badly lacerated. Found lying in a pool of blood it was clear he had stood no chance either. Other people close by were knocked off

*Mr Samuel Smith*

their feet by the blast, among them Mr W. J. Sayers and his eleven-year-old son Louis. They were just yards away from St Peter's Villa when the bomb went off, Mr Sayers got a 'rather nasty shaking' but his little boy received a flying fragment of glass in the shoulder. Mr Sayers said 'We went down like a pair of shot rabbits... I feel I must thank God that we are still alive. Less than thirty seconds before the bomb fell we had hurried over the very pavement it pulverised. There would not have been even enough of us for an inquest had we been slower.' William Storey and his family had recently occupied and furnished No. 17 St Peter's Plain and had been in the kitchen with his wife their two babies, one aged two the other nine months along with his sister and a female family friend. None of them heard anything until the explosion. Mr Storey explained 'The gas went out, glass and doors flew in every direction. The women screamed but when we got a light I was relieved to find no one was hurt but we were all unrecognisable because of soot and dust.' They had a narrow escape; a large bomb fragment had 'carried the front window away' tore a hole through the stairway door and penetrated nearly two feet into the solid bricks beyond.

The Rev. J. McCarthy, Minister of St. Peter's Church had just finished an intercession service and was talking with a parishioner when suddenly there was a crash and the windows of the north side of the church fell into the aisle and the vestry door was blown open, bending a heavy lock back at right angles. He fled with his family to take refuge in the cellar. When they emerged after the raid they discovered every window had been broken in the parsonage.

Mr. Frank Burton, Clerk to the Guardians had a very narrow escape from injury. He had been returning home from a meeting of the Guardians and was passing May's butcher's shop on the corner of Victoria Road when the bomb burst on St Peter's Plain. He was protected by the New Royal Standard which received the force of the blast and lost its windows and received several flying fragments that damaged the walls – any one of which could have proved fatal if they had hit someone in their path.

One notable incident was the case of Pte Poulter, a Territorial Army soldier from The Essex Regiment who was leaving the lavatory near St Peter's Church when the bomb went off and was wounded by shrapnel in the chest. It was Dr Leonard Ley who had the distinction of being the first doctor to operate on an air-raid victim. After successfully removing the piece of shrapnel he kept it and had it mounted as a tiepin, which he wore with great pride for years afterwards.

Harry Tunbridge, the manager of Britannia Pier, was a Section Leader in the 1st Yarmouth Voluntary Aid Detachment, British Red Cross Society and was drilling with the other members of the detachment in the basement of Messrs Boot's Stores on King Street when the caretaker rushed down and said 'Bombs are being dropped in the town!' The detachment divided themselves into three sections, one going down The Drive, another direct to the hospital and they scoured the area making enquiries as to anyone who had been injured. Mr Richards the detachment's pharmacist accompanied Mr Tunbridge; they obtained a lamp and rapidly received a report of a man being injured on St Peter's Plain. Rushing to the spot they found the body of Samuel Smith lying dead in the opening next to his workshop. Pharmacist T. Richards saw Smith was past any treatment and, when a group of soldiers with a stretcher arrived with Inspector Crisp soon after, they removed the body to the mortuary. Members of the Detachment then accompanied the police in their search for any wounded or unconscious people and then remained on duty through the night at Lady Crossley's Hospital where Messrs. Arnolds large covered motor car was in readiness for emergencies, The Detachment was finally dismissed at 6.00am on Wednesday.

The sixth and seventh bombs fell almost simultaneously, the first crashing through the roof of a stable abutting Garden Lane, near South Quay, owned by butcher William Mays. Failing to detonate, the bomb was found resting on a truss of hay beside a pony the following morning – bomb and pony both intact! This bomb was also recovered by National Reservists and was removed out to sea, sunk in 12 fathoms of water and exploded by a time fuse. This caused a great disturbance in the water and killed one fish – a 20lb cod – which showed its white belly on the surface and was brought ashore for a meal.

The seventh bomb fell with a 'huge, fiery flame', and landed opposite Messrs Woodger's shop, near the First and Last tavern on Southgate Road, near the Fish Wharf. There were no more casualties here but a number had narrow escapes. The damage was confined to a number of broken windows, lots of spattering of 'some grey substance on the walls of the houses' probably the accel-

*The Zeppelin bomb that crashed through the roof of butcher William May's stable which abutted Garden Lane, near South Quay, Great Yarmouth. Failing to detonate, the bomb was found resting on the hay beside the pony the following morning.*

erant from the incendiary, and a granite paving stone was fractured by the impact. Fragments from this bomb were soon on display in the pub. The Zeppelin then appears to have passed along the edge of the river dropping its ninth bomb which fell between two vessels, the drifter *Mishe Nahma* that was undergoing repairs and the pilot boat *Patrol*. Striking the river side of the dock gates of Beeching's South Dock it smashed through two planks causing it to flood on the tide.

The ninth bomb that fell failed to detonate and bounced off the stone quay of Trinity Wharf, narrowly missing a sentry from the National Reserve and the base of a crane turntable before falling harmlessly into the river.

The tenth bomb fell into the 'swill' ground at the back of the Fish Wharf and blasted the water tower and made a large hole in the ground, fractured a water main and blew a nearby electric light standard to smithereens. Almost the entire glass roof of the wharf was smashed and the fish sales offices badly damaged (it was estimated £500-£600 of damage was caused to the Fish Wharf). Several enormous chunks of the building's foundation had simply been blasted away and the refreshment rooms opposite had every window smashed – both front and back. Most of the family and staff were out and it was miraculous Miss Steel, who was in the building playing the piano, escaped injury but was severely shaken. Two small children also had a narrow escape; they were in bed and uninjured after the blast but their covers were smothered in broken glass fragments. Miraculously, the only casualty here was Captain Smith, the Fish Wharf Master, who suffered a cut to his hand from flying glass.

The eleventh bomb was another high explosive that fell by the river blasting a hole in the stern quarter, 'started' the timbers and blowing the rigging wire 'out like cotton' of Mr Harry Eastick's steam drifter, *Piscatorial*. It was to be his second casualty of war as he had recently lost his drifter *Copious* that sank taking nine lives with it when striking a mine shortly after the bombardment in November 1914. Debris and bomb casing from the blast also damaged the grain store of Messrs Combe and Co. Maltsters on Malthouse Lane where a chunk of ragged steel casing was recovered measuring 7½ inches by 1½ inches and a number of windows were smashed on the Southtown side.

The last bomb, the twelfth to fall during the ten minute attack, landed at the back of the racecourse grandstand on South Denes a short distance from the Auxiliary War Hospital. Leaving the largest crater of the attack, it blew down the paddock palisading, destroyed a number of fish baskets and killed a dog.

L.3 left its trail of bombs behind it and droned off, following the coast to Runton where she turned seaward and headed back to base at 10.00pm.

# L.4

*The first bomb dropped by Zeppelin L.4 fell upon the home of Robert Smith and his family at Whitehall Yard off Windham Street, Sheringham; fortunately it did not explode.*

L.4 followed the coast from Bacton to Cromer from the east shortly before 8.30pm. The lights of the town had been shaded for a number of weeks but when the Zeppelin arrived over the town the local military had received warning of 'hostile aircraft' over Great Yarmouth and warned all shopkeepers to turn out all their lights and the town was in darkness. Local people, not considering the danger, ran into the streets and looked up at the raider. Most folks who saw it over Cromer agreed it was so low it almost caught on the pinnacles of the church tower. As the Zeppelin passed over the G.E.R. station it appeared to lose its bearings, missed the main street and struck right across to the electric light station where it appeared to encircle the tall chimney and then left in the direction of Sheringham and was spotted circling round to the S.E., between Weybourne and Sheringham at 8.35pm.

Travelling in an easterly direction over Sheringham, von Platen brought the L.4 down to 800ft and dropped a flare. Mr Stanley Simons who lived on Augusta Street was watching the Zeppelin and saw it drop the flare which he described as 'a small object which burst with a slight noise and a bright glare'

L.4 then dropped an incendiary bomb that fell on Whitehall Yard, Wyndham Street, where it entered the roof of one of the houses and passed through a bedroom down to the ground floor, dropping near the fireplace. The house was occupied by local bricklayer Robert Smith, his wife and daughter May (14), who was fortunate to escape with only a few scratches. *The Cromer and North Norfolk Post* reported:

> *'The chair in which she was sitting was slightly damaged. The family were naturally terrified. Our representative who visited this house found the bedroom in great disorder. Hardly a pane of glass was left in the windows, a large hole was made in the roof and the boards were torn up. Considerable damage was also done downstairs to the floor and furniture. The scene was one of utter disorder. The landlord, Mr. Jordan, is not insured.*
>
> *Another little girl, a companion of May Smith who was sitting in the same room received an injury to her wrist and her hair was singed. 'I never had such a fright in my life. I shall never forget it to my dying day' remarked Mrs. Smith, 'I never want to go through it again.' The bomb was about 4½ inches in diameter. The shell itself must have weighed about twelve pounds. If it had exploded probably the whole square of houses would have been wrecked and lives lost. Mr. Smith the occupier of the house said 'It all came so suddenly. The bomb fell near the fireplace and it is a wonder how we escaped serious injury. My impression is that it was a fire-ball and that the object of the raiders was to burn the houses.'*

Many Sheringham residents ran out into the streets to see what was going on. A missionary meeting being held in the Church Room was stopped and abandoned as several members of the audience rushed into the street to watch the murderous machine make off. Special and emergency constables went on duty at once and proceeded to give instructions as to lights and generally assist the police in dealing with the situation. The night although a little hazy, was 'decently fair' and there was no wind. Mr R. C. West, a coal merchant, who was on duty as a special constable with Mr Gooch at the Gas Works, near the Sheringham Hotel saw a huge body floating in the air an apparently coming in the direction of the lifeboat sheds.

L.4 then dropped a second incendiary on a building plot between the back of The Avenue (near Mr Lee's house) and Priory Road, leaving a small crater. A man who was walking along Beeston Road said the bomb nearly struck him. He had an anxious time, as for some yards he was endeavouring to get out of the way but was firmly of the belief the Zeppelin was so low down if he had had a gun he could have shot it. Inspector Carter was on duty on the Cromer Road and witnessed the dropping of the bomb upon The Avenue and rushed to the police station to telephone Norwich and other places. Newspaper reports stated the engine of the Zeppelin made 'a terrific noise' as it passed low over Sheringham, eye-witnesses believing that it nearly touched the Roman Catholic church in Cromer Road and it also went near St Peter's Church and the Grand Hotel.

The airship, which had a tremendously long body, was described by locals as looking 'like a gigantic sausage'. First two bombs gone, L.4 then flew over the golf links and was then lost sight of travelling in a north-west direction off the coast towards Blakeney and Wells.

*Unexploded explosive bomb dropped by L.4 on field near the high road leading from Old Hunstanton to New Hunstanton.*

L.4 followed the coast and came overland again at Thornham at 9.50pm dropping its third bomb on The Green, then eastward to Brancaster Staithe but returned to Brancaster village, where a fourth bomb, another incendiary, was dropped near the church, about 50 yards from Dormy House and approximately 150 yards from the local auxiliary war hospital. Then, after passing over Holme-next-the-Sea, the Zeppelin proceeded to Hunstanton where its fifth bomb landed at 10.15pm (but did not explode) near the centre of a field on the high road leading from Old Hunstanton to New Hunstanton. It was suggested in the press at the time that the Zeppelin may well have been drawn by the beam of the lighthouse, whereas in the *Report of the Intelligence Section GHQ GB on the Airship Raids from Jan to Jun 1915* states 'at 10.15 an HE bomb aimed at the wireless station dropped in a field about 300 yards away. After circling the town, which was in total darkness, it went out to sea twice, but returned each time and then made off along the coast to Heacham...'.

The L.4 droned over Heacham at about 10.40 and a number of residents came on to the roads or craned their heads out of bedroom windows to look at the Zeppelin as it passed overhead. Bombs six and seven were dropped here; one HE fell by Mrs Pattrick's cottage in Lord's Lane, after clipping the edge of a window sill and damaging some of the bricks in the wall, smashed part of the roof of the adjoining wash house and fell into a rainwater tub – promptly blowing it to pieces – a narrow miss indeed. The second bomb did not explode and was only discovered a couple of weeks later by a lad named Dix who had been walking across Mr Brasnett's field between the council school and the chalk pit.

*A sentry from the locally based 1/1ˢᵗ Lincolnshire Yeomanry, the local constable and villagers gather around the bomb removed to the lawn of 'Homemead' at Heacham.*

The 1/1ˢᵗ Lincolnshire Yeomanry were based in Heacham at the time dug the bomb from the ground and removed it to the lawn of 'Homemead' where the officers were staying. A sentry was posted and with the local policeman in attendance the local populace soon gathered to look at the bomb. On the Sunday an officer drove all the way up from Woolwich Arsenal to collect the bomb and remove it for further examination, but before leaving he did confirm it was a 100lb bomb and if it had gone off would have damaged anything within a 100 yard radius.

Zeppelin L.4 continued its flight south reaching Snettisham at about 10.45. The Reverend Ilsley W. Charlton, Vicar of Snettisham wrote his account of what happened next, published in the *News and County Press*: 'Supposing that the distant noise was the hum of an ordinary aeroplane, and that some lights would be visible, my wife and I and a lady friend were walking about in the garden, trying to penetrate the darkness and discover the aircraft. The drone of the engine was so much louder than usual that we were quite prepared to descry at length, exactly overhead, the outline of a Zeppelin hovering over the church and Vicarage at a great height, appearing at the distance, to be only about fifteen or twenty yards long.

'No sooner had we identified it as probably a German airship, than suddenly all doubt was dispelled by a long, loud hissing sound; a confused streak of light; and a tremendous crash. The next moment was made up of apprehension, relief and mutual enquiries, and then all was dark and still, as the sound of the retiring Zeppelin speedily died away.'

The Zeppelin had circled the village and was so low that the light shining through the opening of the trap door on the release of the bomb were clearly seen. L.4 then dropped its eighth bomb, an HE, which landed about four yards from the Sedgeford Road in Mr Coleridge's meadows causing an explosion that was felt across the village. The houses in the immediate vicinity suffered a number of broken windows, but the worst of the blast was suffered by the St Mary's church. Rev. Charlton concluded 'That there was no loss of life, and that the church (with the exception of 22 windows) escaped damage, we owe, humanely speaking to the fact that the bomb fell on a soft, rain soaked meadow, with a hedge and a wall between it and the church.' After the war the windows were repaired, and the east window replaced with stained glass 'as a thank offering for preservation and in memory of the men of this parish who fell in the Great War'.

The Zeppelin then passed over Ingoldisthorpe, Dersingham, Sandringham (Wolferton), Babingley, Castle Rising, South Wootton and Gaywood but dropped no bombs, however the *News and Country Press* were keen to point out the 'peculiar gusto' and 'special pleasure' of the reportage in the *Hamburger Nachricten* which claimed 'On the way to King's Lynn, Sandringham, the present residence of King

*One of the windows of St Mary's Church, Snettisham shattered by blast of the Zeppelin bomb that dropped nearby on Mr Coleridge's meadows.*

George was not over looked. Bombs fell in the neighbourhood of Sandringham and a loud crash notified the King of England that the Germans were not far off... Our Zeppelins have shown that they could find the hidden Royal residence. In any case, they did not intend to hit it, and only gave audible notification of their presence in the immediate neighbourhood.'

As he approached King's Lynn von Platen saw many lights and was convinced he was not over the Humber but north of it when he spotted what he thought to be 'a big city' and claiming he had been fired upon by both 'heavy artillery and infantry fire' he proceeded to bomb Lynn. He steered the L.4 towards the town from the Gaywood district and appearing to take the railway lines as its guide.

Charles Hunt, the King's Lynn Chief Constable, had received an unofficial report of a Zeppelin raider dropping bombs on Yarmouth and Sheringham. In his report of 5 February 1915 he stated upon hearing the explosion: 'I immediately communicated with the Electrical Engineer of this Borough and asked him to put the street lights out as soon as possible. He stated that his men had started putting them out and he would put further men on and get them out as soon as he could... I at once communicated with Major Astley who is in charge of the National Guard in this town, also the Officer Commanding the Worcestershire Yeomanry who are billeted here... About 10.45pm when I was trying to get through to Dersingham the Superintendent there rang me up and stated that a Zeppelin had passed over Dersingham and had dropped bombs in that neighbourhood. Before a message was complete I heard bombs being dropped close to this Borough. Immediately on hearing these explosions the Electrical Engineer put out all lights by switching off at the main, not only putting out lights in the streets but also in private residences as well. The aircraft was soon over our building and several bomb explosions were heard almost immediately.' On the commencement of the bombardment the members of the fire brigade assembled at the station to be ready if needed. Mr G. E. Kendrick and the engineer were the first to arrive and they made the appliances ready. The Intelligence Report commented, however, 'Lynn seems to have had a considerable amount of light showing and probably presented a very clear target.' The airship picked up the railway at Gaywood and came over the station at Lynn. In all, eight bombs (seven H.E. and one incendiary) were dropped on the town

A letter published in the *Lynn News* from Inspector R. Woodbine at Lynn Station recorded his experiences:

*King's Lynn Chief Constable Charles Hunt examining an unexploded Zeppelin bomb.*

'*I had arrived in our junction signal box just before the first bomb fell. The signalman had told me he noticed a distant report which had shaken his windows and looking out of his box windows I heard a noise resembling an aeroplane. I remarked, as the noise grew in volume, that is no Britisher and told him to put his lights down as the visitor was evidently coming for us. He also told Exton's Road signalman to do the same. The noise seemed in a direct line with the signal box coming from the direction of the Ship Inn on Gaywood Road. I could distinctly see the movement of the propeller but not the body of the machine owing to it being straight in front of me. I called the signalman to have a look but before he reached the window the first crash came. You may imagine, if you can, our feelings. I cannot describe them and never wish to experience such another fright. I remained in the signal box until three bombs had fallen; they appeared to fall all over the station and I thought from the sound that the royal carriage shed and the station were struck by the second and third bombs. I was anxious to get back to the station to see what was done but found no damage to either building of course.*'

The first bomb had landed on a field adjoining the railway at the junction of the Hunstanton and Norwich lines near Tennyson Avenue; a number of houses in the area had their windows smashed by the blast. This was followed close after by a second bomb which exploded 'with a grey-blue flash' on allotments that ran along the Walks side of the railway at the Tennyson Road end, making a crater some sixteen feet across and seven feet deep and blowing in the windows of the carriages standing near the nearby railway sheds.

*Troops of the Worcestershire Yeomanry in and round the crater of the bomb that exploded on allotments at the Walks side of the railway at the Tennyson Road end at King's Lynn.*

After droning its way menacingly over St John's church and St James's Park the carnage began when the third bomb was dropped on Bentinck Street – a typical Victorian street, lined with poor quality terraced housing, built for working folk. It was also one of the most densely populated parts of the town and nothing short of a miracle that the casualties were as few as there were. The home of fitter's mate John Goate and his family at 12 Bentinck Street received a direct hit, fourteen year-old Percy was killed outright, father and mother had been crushed and wounded and his four-year old sister Ethel was stunned. Mrs Goate's testimony at the inquest revealed what happened on that fateful night: 'We were all upstairs in bed, me and my husband, and the baby and Percy, when I heard a buzzing noise. My husband put out the lamp and I saw a bomb drop through the

Below: *A Kings Lynn policeman talks to Mr Fayers and troops from the Worcestershire Yeomanry guarding the wreckage of the homes of the Goate and Fayers families on Bentick Street where Percy Goate and Maude Gazley died.*

skylight and strike the pillow where Percy was lying. I tried to wake him, but he was dead. Then the house fell in. I don't remember any more.' PC John Fisher also gave evidence that just after the bombardment a message was received at the police station stating that an ambulance was required at Bentinck Street. He and other constables rushed there with two ambulances. On arrival they were informed that young Percy Goate had been got out of the ruins but he was dead and his body had been taken to a house in Clough Lane. When one of the ambulances returned after their first run to the hospital, the boy's body was removed to the mortuary.

The other Lynn fatality was Mrs Alice Maud Gazley a widow at just 26; her husband, Percy had been a porter at South Lynn Station but as a Reservist had been called up and sent to France with the B.E.F. and had been killed in action on 27 October 1914 while serving with the 3rd Battalion, The Rifle Brigade. Mrs Gazley lived at Rose Cottage on Bentinck Street but she had gone the Fayers family, about four doors away for supper. Giving her account of the events on that fateful night at the inquest, Mrs. Fayers recalled they had just finished their meal together when Mrs. Gazley remarked 'There's a dreadful noise!' Shortly after there was 'a terrible bang', which frightened both of them Mrs Gazley said 'Oh, good God, what is it?' and made to rush out into the street. Tragically, the Fayers were neighbours of the Goates and their house collapsed moments after the direct hit upon their neighbours' house. The Fayers all sustained minor injuries. Shortly after the raid Mr Henry Rowe (Mrs Alice Gazley's father), went to check on his daughter at Rose Cottage. He found the windows were shattered but there was so sign of her. He spent the rest of the night searching for her. At about 6.30 Mr Rowe went to the police office to let them know he had not found his daughter and stated 'I think she is under the ruins of Mr. Fayers house.' Police Sergeant Beaumont asked Rowe to wait until daylight then between the hours of seven and eight the following morning, Sgt Beaumont, Mr Rowe and others began to search the wreckage of Mr Fayers house and it was there they found the body of Mrs Gazley, which was then recovered from the wreckage and removed to the mortuary by police ambulance.

*Mrs Alice Maude Gazley*

Incredibly, a stable close to the two wrecked houses on Bentinck Street contained a horse belonging to Mr. Cork, the baker of Blackfriars Street. Despite the stable being badly damaged the horse was got out safely and unscathed the day after the raid.

At the inquest, Dr G. R. Chadwick stated he had examined both victims of the air raid at the mortuary. He found Percy Goate had suffered wounds on his face and one on his chest. Mrs Gazley suffered bruising to her face and abrasions on the front of the right thigh. Dr Chadwick was very much of the opinion that the injuries suffered by both victims had not been insufficient to be life threatening and that both had died as a result of shock. Their death certificates both recorded their cause of deaths, as suggested by Dr H. C. Allinson, the Deputy Borough Coroner, as 'From the effects of the acts of the King's Enemies', although the foreman of the inquest jury was compelled to state some of the jury felt it should be recorded as murder.

The fourth bomb exploded at the junction of Albert Avenue and East Street, at the back of the property owned by vet and blacksmith Mr T. H. Walden causing extensive damage to the terraced houses in the area. Several people were trapped and required assistance to get out of the rubble of their former homes.

The fifth bomb, an incendiary, fell on No. 63 Cresswell Street, the home of Mr J. C. Savage and his family. They all had a lucky escape; the bomb fell through the roof, crashed through the floor in the back bedroom, through a tin box and into a basket of linen in the kitchen. It had caused a fire to the bedroom on the way through and the fire brigade were summoned but by the time they arrived it had been extinguished by neighbours.

*Zeppelin bomb damage on East Street, King's Lynn*

The sixth bomb fell on a Mr Wyatt's allotment, at the end of Great Lewis Street near Cresswell Street causing a crater 15ft across. It wrecked fences, trees and shattered windows but luckily no-one was hurt and caused no real damage. The seventh device buried itself in a garden at the back of a house in the occupation of Mr Kerner Greenwood near the docks also causing minimal damage.

The eighth hit the power station of the King's Lynn Docks & Railway Co., causing extensive damage to the engine house, destroying its two boilers and the hydraulic gear that operated the Alexandra Dock gates and caused considerable damage to surrounding buildings. Just as in Yarmouth, the Zeppelin had been over Lynn for about ten minutes before it steered off into the darkness again. Many were treated for shock as a result of the raid on Lynn, a total of 13 people received treatment in the West Norfolk and Lynn Hospital and many others suffered minor injuries caused by the flying debris and were treated at home. A list of those who required hospital treatment was published in the *Lynn Advertiser* viz;

Mr Goate – cut face and swollen ankle

Mrs Goate – Leg damaged

Ethel Goate, aged 4 years – stunned

Mr Fayers – cut on head

Mrs Fayers – cut on face

G. Hanson – back of hand cut by glass

D. Skipper – face and head cut

Mrs Skipper – injured leg

G. Parlett – forehead cut and head wound

R. Wykes – cut head

R. Howard – face cut in two places

G. W. Clarke – cut lips

W. Anderson – wrist lacerated

L.4 droned over the Grimston Road station at 11.15pm, then turned south-east over Gayton and Westacre then east again, passing north of East Dereham at 11.35pm, flying over Mousehold Heath near Norwich at 11.50, then over Acle at about midnight and finally passed out to sea north of Great Yarmouth before 12.30pm.

## Aftermath

Francis Perrott, a journalist on the *Manchester Guardian* until his death in 1926, was regarded as one of the finest reporters of his day. He visited Great Yarmouth the day after the air raid occurred and recorded his impressions of what he saw in the town:

*Yarmouth has taken the visitation with remarkable calm and cheerfulness. I found people even pleasantly excited by what has happened and willing to make the most of it as a winter's tale. When first the threatening hum of the propellers was heard in the starless sky, people seem to have obeyed the powerful human instinct of curiosity and ran out into the street to see what was going on but in a short time they remembered the official instructions and made for cover. The authorities turned off all the lights and Yarmouth spent the rest of the evening in dead darkness. Towards midnight the throbbing of engines was heard again over the town but if this really was the noise of Zeppelins returning home no one saw them* [this was the L.4 taking its circuitous route across the county after bombing King's Lynn].

*I could find no one in Yarmouth who actually saw the aircraft, although there are vague stories of 'long black shapes' and things in the sky 'like a big black cigar.' The best evidence on the point of whether they were airships or aeroplanes is the size of the bombs dropped. Two unexploded bombs were on view in the Drill Hall this afternoon, where an interested crowd inspected them. They are bulky pear-shaped things two feet long, forty inches round the base and weigh about sixty pounds. Yarmouth is convinced that only a Zeppelin could throw bombs of that size about wholesale.*

*The first sign of interest seen in the streets was a group of sightseers round a shop window where bits of bomb were shown as relics. Down on the South Quay the publican of the 'First and Last' tavern showed me a handful of fragments picked up in his bar just after a bomb had burst outside his doorstep. 'There was some nasty, sticky, yellow stuff inside it' he said. I came nearest the reality of the raid in the little open space behind St. Peter's Church where people were collected staring hard at a mess of ravaged houses, broken windows and littered roadway. Here the bomb fell which killed old Miss Taylor and Samuel Smith the cobbler. It dropped on the pavement across from the St. Peter's church and outside a modest villa. It stripped half the wall of the villa and made mincemeat of the content. The man inside escaped with a cut head. I found him hovering about the hole in the road as if he could not leave it twenty hours later... The dwellers in the houses round the church that had been torn open to daylight, like doll's houses with the front opened, were standing about looking as if they felt the importance conferred by the calamity. They gladly took you over what was left of their homes and related marvellous escapes. A queer sight was the furniture of the villa piled in the street, with a forlorn doll holding out its arms in horror at the ruin wrought by the bomb.*

*From St. Peter's church the raiders steered along the quay. Following in the track, I found the deep bruise in the roadway, where the Germans tried to destroy the tavern, only to give the innkeeper a grievance because the War Office had claimed his cherished bits of shell, and also the ruin caused on the Fish Quay. Here the bomb fell in a heap of empty basket nets close to the salt water tank. It burrowed a hole in which you could stand up to your knees, knocked a warehouse about and damaged an eating house. On the wall of a wrecked office the only thing left untouched was the barometer at 'set fair'.*

*The last call of the Germans before quitting Yarmouth was the race course, where the grand stand was splintered. In some parts of the town men were filling carts with tons of broken glass. The fishermen on the quay were chiefly interested in a steam drifter which was riddled with shell fragments. 'Looks as if she'd been taking on the German Navy all by herself' said one.*

The relics of the air raid also drew considerable interest in King's Lynn as the *Lynn News* reported:

*The bomb shell in the possession of the Lynn police, with portions of other bombs discovered in the borough, was placed in the Stone Hall on Tuesday afternoon for public inspection. Sixpence per head was charged for admission and the proceeds, nearly £3, were in aid of those who have suffered damage. Mr William Fayers, one of those injured by the falling house in Bentinck Street was present and two members of the National Guard, through the kindness of Major Astley, were on duty.*

An interesting perspective on how the news was viewed at the time was recorded in the diary kept by a senior member of the staff published in the *Lynn News*:

*January 21: Needless to say, the London papers are crowded to-day with photographs of Lynn wreckage – many of the prints are excellent – and with full narratives, which are not so excellent. The editorial comments are scathing in the extreme, as was but to be expected* [many of the reports criticised the King's Lynn engineer for opting to turn out the street lights individually rather than throwing the switches to turn off all the lights in the town be they on the streets or in people's homes].

*Though the tragedy of the whole horrible occurrence weighs upon one's imagination, stories of a host of humorous incidents have reached me. Many of these tales would make excellent reading if they could be published but discretion is the better part of a diarist's valour.*

*Talking of valour, one of two episodes brought to my knowledge confirm the theory that moral courage is a very different thing from physical pluck. As to the fact that the loudest talkers and the bullies are seldom brave when real danger of death threatens, that goes without saying, of course. On Tuesday night several individuals who in normal times are of a domineering disposition were in a pitiable state of fear. I have even heard of men who left their wives and children in order selfishly to seek a fancied security for themselves!*

*It is more pleasing to dwell on the stories of the quiet bravery of men who, in ordinary conditions, make no pretence of being endued with strength and, above all, the tales of the women's silent endurance thrill one. I have heard of several women who, showing hardly a sign of emotion while the bombs were raining from the skies, have since suffered a physical collapse – a fact that proves the enormous mental suffering they rigidly endured on Tuesday night.*

In the bombed towns anger at their dearth of defences and the need for protection in the event of another raid saw a Lynn editorial suggest 'Lynn Corporation, despairing of protection by the War Office and Admiralty, should itself purchase high angle guns and an aeroplane.' On a more prosaic level, Mr R. O. Ridley, the Mayor of King's Lynn wrote to Prime Minister Herbert Asquith on 22 January 1915:

*Sir,*

*In reference to the raid of this town by the enemy's aircraft on Tuesday evening last, the 19th inst. I am directed to inform you that considerable damage was done to property of the very poorest classes. As a result various persons are homeless and others are suffering greatly in consequence of the loss and damage to their furniture.*

*I shall be glad of an early intimation of the Government to compensate the people injuriously affected. In the meantime, may I ask that some steps may be taken to relieve cases of immediate necessity?*

*I am to further call your attention to the fact that no protection of any kind is afforded to the town against raids of the above description and I beg to strongly urge that in view of the great probability of further occurrences of a like nature, some steps be devised to deal with them. I believe I am fully alive to the difficulties of the situation and I know that great efforts are being made by His Majesty's Government in connection with the conduct of the war. I do suggest, however, that the matter referred to is of great importance and calls for some action to be taken.*

The reply from 10, Downing Street was swift, dated 25 January 1915:

*Dear Sir,*

*I am desired by the Prime Minister to acknowledge the receipt of your letter of January 22ⁿᵈ and to inform you in reply that it is the intention of the Government to take measures to deal with the damage suffered by reason of the recent air raid on King's Lynn similar to those adopted in the case of the recent bombardment of Hartlepool, Scarborough and other places.*

*The other matters referred to in your letter are receiving careful consideration.*

In the immediate aftermath of the raids the German papers were plastered with accounts of successful attacks on fortified places between the Tyne and Humber or the 'fortified place at Yarmouth' as well as warnings to the King. Only after the German authorities gained sight of the copies of British and international newspapers did the Zeppelin crews discover the places they had actually attacked.

With their reportage of the raid the local newspapers were quick to publish a set of 'Safety Rules' in the event of further air raids, such as this example from the *Cromer Post* published on 22 January 1915:

*'It is essential in the common interest that the public should become conversant with these regulations, which are designed to prevent confusion, to assist the military and civil author-ities, as well as to protect the civil population. The following summary of the official advices gives a clear idea of the best course to follow:*

*To those who happen to be in the street – Take cover immediately*

*There is danger from bombs from aircraft and also from fragments of shell and from bullets from the guns and against the raiders.*

*The assembly of large crowds might prove fatal.*

*The nearest basement would be the safest place.*

*Any fragment of shells should be handed to the police, in order that the War Officer may ascertain the size and nature of the missile.*

*To School Teachers –*

*Continue the lessons as far as possible in the normal way.*

*Remove children from the neighbourhood of windows.*

*Children should not be brought from upper floors to crowd ground floor class-rooms or basement. In the event of damage to the building the children should be marched as in a fire drill.*

*To those in Private Houses – Stay there! Preferably in the basement.*

The national press reflected the outrage of the British people with articles headlined 'The Coming of the Aerial Baby Killers' and reports such as in the *Daily Mirror* 'Germany overjoyed by news of "gallant" air huns murder raid' that included 'Berlin's War Whoop: Copenhagen, Jan. 20 – I have just received a private telegram from Berlin which describes the people's joy at the success of the Zeppelin attack as being widely enthusiastic. I have an intuitive feeling that the joy could not have been greater even if Dr Barnardo's Homes had been destroyed.' The international press is typified by the *New York Tribune*, 'A Disgrace to Civilization' that spoke of a 'wanton disregard of Hague rules and humane principles. The raid belongs in the worst acts of German militarism in the present war... It is savagery which civilised opinion of the world has already condemned, which must stand condemned for all time.'

The New York *World* echoed:

> *They accomplish no military purpose and the wanton slaughter of women arouses a world-wide resentment against Germany... Germany will not begin to realise what these raids cost her until she comes to make peace. Her military authorities seem to forget that the war is not going to last forever and that when it is over Germany will have to live in the world with all the other nations. How does she propose to deal with the vast body of hatred that she is building up for herself? How many years will it take for her to live down the record she is making?*

The reports of the air raid in the international press stirred disquiet in the corridors of power in Germany and Chancellor Theobald von Bethmann-Hollweg did not mince his words in a letter to Admiral von Pohl:

> *According to information received, for Zeppelins to drop bombs on apparently undefended places makes a very unfavourable impression on foreign neutrals, particularly in America. Also doubt exists in reasonable circles there, as military importance and success is not readily apparent. Prompt explanation to this effect seems urgently necessary.*

German propaganda card produced after the Zeppelin raid showing Great Yarmouth Town Hall under attack – not exactly what happened!

The Kaiser publicly praised the conduct of the raid and the crews of the L.3 and L.4 were all decorated with Iron Crosses for their part in the action but was quick to reiterate to his ministers that only the docks of London, military establishments of the lower Thames and the British coast could be taken as bombing targets, but royal palaces – including Sandringham – were not to be bombed. The bombing campaign would continue but the crews of the L.3 and L.4 would have their wars abruptly ended when less than a month later both Zeppelins were lost during a scouting mission along the Norwegian coast. The L.3 had one engine down when she encountered a severe snow storm and strong head winds, fearing he would not make the return journey Fritz put L.3 down on the beach of the North Sea island of Fanø off the south western coast of Denmark. Despite a hard landing the crew escaped uninjured. Fritz then burned the ships' papers and then set the whole Zeppelin on fire with a signal gun. The crew were detained in Odense for the rest of the war.

L.4 was caught in that same storm of 17 February 1915, suffered the loss of electric power, the radios went down and with the engines failing Hallermund forced an emergency landing at the shore near Blaavands Huk, Denmark. The Zeppelin was wrecked beyond repair, four crew members lost their lives and the remaining members of the crew were interned. Hallermund escaped at the end of 1917. He subsequently served in Finland, fighting the Bolsheviks alongside White forces.

In the aftermath of the air raids it is also intriguing to read in the *Daily Telegraph* the account from the correspondent they had despatched to Lynn: 'That the hostile aircraft that attacked Lynn was guided by a pilot who was familiar with the countryside over which he flew there can be little doubt. The military and police authorities here are satisfied this is so.' Moreover, among all the reportage after the raid one question was raised again and again – were spies at work? In Great Yarmouth the *Mercury* was quick to dismiss the stories: 'It seems a great pity that the authors of such rumours who have a disturbing effect upon the community cannot be discovered and brought to book. Many of these fairy tales concern the capture of alleged spies, and the absurd stories range from the arrest of a small crowd of Germans in an empty Howard Street shop to the detention of a young girl, a German of course, in empty business premises in the Market Place in the very act of flashing signals out to sea.' The *Mercury* took particular exception to a report in another local paper that stated: 'A signal is said to have been given from Yarmouth on Tuesday evening to direct the German airship as to the best place to place bombs', and concluded, with some vitriol over this matter: 'We, however, feel compelled to enter a protest when the local press give publicity to such tarradiddles.'

*Lighting restriction proclamations issued in the wake of the first Zeppelin raid.*

## DEFENCE OF THE REALM REGULATIONS, 1914.

### NOTICE.

After this date and until further notice no Street Lights are to be lit and all House Lights as well as Lights in Business Premises are to be screened and blinds drawn down within an area of Ten Miles from the Coast, from King's Lynn to Lowestoft inclusive.

BY ORDER
**ALFRED A. ELLISON,**
Captain-in-Charge.

24th January, 1915.      Lowestoft and Yarmouth.

JARROLD & SONS, Ltd. Printers, King Street, Great Yarmouth.

## CITY OF NORWICH.

### IMPORTANT MILITARY ORDER.

The Military Authorities Order that all Lights other than those not visible from outside of any House, Premises or Buildings, whatsoever, must be Extinguished in Norwich, between the hours of 5 p.m. and 7.30 a.m. to-day, and until further notice.

Signed **E. F. WINCH,**
Chief Constable.

Norwich, January 26th.

In the west of the county questions over the presence of spies and stories such as a light being shone on to the Greyfriars Tower at Lynn or a similar account at Snettisham where 'the church spire was being constantly flashed upon' on the night of the raid were taken more seriously; above all there were accounts of a motor car that was said to have guided the Zeppelin raiders to their targets with 'brilliant headlights' or 'that flashed upwards to the sky.'

Mr Holcombe Ingleby, MP for King's Lynn expressed his concerns in a letter to *The Times* published on 22 January 1915: 'I have myself tested the evidence of some of the most trustworthy of the inhabitants and the evidence seems to be worth recording. The Zeppelin is said to have been accompanied by two motor cars, one on the road to the right, the other on the road to the left. These cars occasionally sent upwards doubles flashes, and on one occasion these flashes from the car on the right lit up the church, on which the Zeppelin attempted to drop a bomb. Fortunately the missile fell on the grass meadow... After this attempt at wanton mischief the Zeppelin made for King's Lynn, and here again there is further evidence that it was accompanied by a car with powerful lights which were at one time directed on the Grammar School. The car was stopped in the town and attention was called to the lights as a breach of the regulations. Having put them out the driver turned the car quickly round and made off at a rapid pace for the open country. Seven bombs were dropped in King's Lynn, two of them right in the heart of the crowded streets. Possibly they were intended for more important buildings, which, without the aid of the car, it was difficult to distinguish...'.

*Mr Holcombe Ingleby, MP for King's Lynn.*

The official response to the concerns voiced by Ingleby was to dismiss the existence of the car but after Ingleby's letter and official response were also published in the local press a number of west Norfolk residents wrote to him with testimony about the mysterious signalling car. Having drawn together so many earnest accounts he brought the entire matter to the notice of the Home Secretary and published the now rare and collectable booklet *The Zeppelin Raid in West Norfolk* in 1915.

Spies or spy scares aside, Britain had been bombed and its air defences needed to be vigorously re-addressed. As Ingleby put it in the latter part of his letter to *The Times* 'A couple of biplanes at King's Lynn and a couple at Hunstanton might make such a raid as to which we have been subjected impossible of success. If they could not destroy a Zeppelin they might at least drive it off.' Although plans and construction work for a limited number of airfields in Norfolk, mostly for experimental aircraft, had been made in the years immediately before the First World War it took the first Zeppelin raid to persuade the authorities to take serious action on service airfield development in the county.

### Subsequent Air Raids

Enemy Zeppelins would frequently traverse Norfolk on their way to their targets, often using the Happisburgh lights as guides, although foul weather and efficient blackouts regularly stymied their navigations. Reporting restrictions were tight and little or nothing appeared in the newspapers of these later raids. Admittedly, most of the bombs that were dropped on Norfolk fell on open fields and only caused minor damage but the fact that Zeppelins did regularly drone over our county during the First World War is not widely known and is worth recording, especially the many places where bombs fell and the fact that a further three fatalities did occur as a result of those air raids. By including the following accounts I hope it will evoke some idea of the climate of fear that existed at that time – created by those dark shadows that brought death in the night.

What follows are accounts of the most significant air raids and aerial actions over the county between 1915 and 1918 drawn predominantly from the information recorded in the once-classified 'Secret' reports on air raids compiled during the First World War by Intelligence Section, General Headquarters, Great Britain .

## 15/16 April 1915

### L.7
Under Oblt-z-S Werner Peterson, carrying Zeppelin Chief Peter Strasser, spent an hour skirting the coast from Hunstanton to Yarmouth in high winds and frustrated by the blacked out county below them headed back to Germany without dropping a single bomb.

## 6/7 June 1915

### L.9
Kptlt. Heinrich Mathy, in command of Zeppelin L.9, decided soon after departure from his base that conditions made it more prudent to attack Hull rather than London. Using the sea and landmarks of Norfolk to fly over the county until he crossed The Wash he then flew over Mablethorpe in Lincolnshire to Bridlington and eventually Hull in Yorkshire where he dropped ten HE and 50 incendiary bombs resulting in 20 fatalities and 40 injured – the heaviest air raid casualties of the war to date.

## 8/9 September 1915

Zeppelins L.13 under Kptlt. Heinrich Mathy and L.14 under Kptlt. Alois Böcker were on a mission to attack London and made landfall over the Norfolk Coast.

### L.13
Zeppelin L.13 was first heard at sea off the coast north of Holkham at 7.35pm where some armed trawlers opened fire upon her and she went out to sea again, seen coming over land again at Brancaster at 8.05pm. Mathy was feeling his way to mouth of The Wash, which he did not reach until 8.25pm. He then turned, followed the coast and passed over Hunstanton at 8.30, near Sedgeford at 8.35, went out to sea and was seen by a fishing boat. At 8.45 L.13 was over the Mouth of the Lynn Cut, where the Zeppelin was observed by the S.S. *Annandale* going slowly up the river. For a full four minutes she stopped at an elevation of about 1,500 to 2,000 feet to observe her position. At 8.49pm she started

---

### Precautions in the event of Zeppelin Air Raids – 1915

Further air raids during the war saw new and renewed precautions announced to the public in the press, on posters and on hand bills. Lighting restrictions, employed to reduced the danger of bombardment from the sea, had been in place at the request of the Admiralty since September 1914 and had been tightened up and publicity renewed along the coast in the immediate aftermath of the Zeppelin raid of 19 January 1915.

A month after the first raid the dangers of moving around streets in darkness and in reduced lighting saw Norwich City Engineer Mr A. E. Collins whiten the edges of street kerbs at street corners with lime wash, along with the carriageway crossings of footpaths. The work was carried out by a steam wagon installed with a pneumatic painting machine.

In May 1915 Dr H. J. Starling, Chairman of the Norwich Division of the R.M.A. circulated printed notices of the medical arrangements for casualties occurring in the City of Norwich caused by enemy aircraft. The climate of fear of air attacks during 1915 was such that to avoid any panic the doctor was quick to point out first in his announcement 'It cannot be strongly emphasized that the existence of such a scheme in no way adds to the probability of such air raids taking place and is drawn up for the sole purpose of reassuring the public and to avoid congestion at the Norfolk and Norwich Hospital.'

The public were thus requested to direct all casualties in the first instance to the nearest dressing station. Seven schools were set up as dressing stations for the City of Norwich, namely, Bull Close, Avenue Road, Crook's Place, Wensum View, Heigham Street, Surrey Road, Thorpe Road. Each school was provided with 'all appliances for first aid, dressings, splints, stimulants etc.' At least three doctors were appointed to each school and would give first aid to all casualties brought there. The Red Cross would also provide two sections, each with its own doctor and stretcher bearers to attend each school to work in the streets of the neighbourhood to search for and recover the injured then to direct, aid or remove them by stretcher to the nearest dressing station. The Chief Constable would also direct appointed members of the Norwich War Emergency Corps to assist those whose houses had been damaged by incendiary or explosive bombs.

*The full RNAS Honours funeral cortège of Flt. Sub-Lieut. G. W. Hilliard passing along St. Peter's Road, Great Yarmouth.*

again, passing between Lynn and Terrington St Clement and picked up the course of the Ouse near Wiggenhall St Germans, Mathy then set his course following the river and railway to Downham Market (9.00pm), then he followed the Bedford Level and headed for London where he dropped fifteen high explosive bombs across Golder's Green, Middlesex and the City and County of London killing a total of 22 men, women and children and injured 87. Mathy then crossed Norfolk again, leaving the destruction on London behind him, flying over Wymondham (1.20am), passing over Norwich (1.30am), Martham (1.45am), and heading out to sea between Caister and Great Yarmouth at 2.00am.

Three planes from RNAS Great Yarmouth were sent to hunt down L.14 but tragically each drew a negative, two had lucky escapes, but the third pilot was not so fortunate:

Squadron Commander C.W. P. Ireland was first in the air at 19.45 but he was back less than ten minutes later when his patrol was cut short after four of his engine cylinders cracked. Flt J. M. R. Cripps was in the air at 19.50 and he too had a remarkable escape when his engine spluttered to a stop half way through his patrol. He could see no landing area so allowed his B.E.2c to glide down and he threw himself clear just before it landed. He was unhurt and his aircraft came down with only minor damage – both man and plane had landed on the Caister Marshes.

After a two-hour sortie patrolling between Cromer and Lowestoft, Flt. Sub-Lieut. G. W. Hilliard was attempting to land at the night landing ground at Bacton. Despite the flares being lit on the runway Hilliard misjudged his approach and touched down heavily in an adjoining field. His B.E.2c's undercarriage collapsed, his bombs exploded in their frames and he was killed instantly. This brave 30 year old pilot was buried with full RNAS honours in Great Yarmouth (Caister) cemetery.

## L.14

Zeppelin L.14 under the command of Kptlt. Alois Böcker was first heard off Haisbro' Lightship, was spotted just off Overstrand at 7.20pm and was close to Cromer at 7.50pm. L.14 skirted the coast westward as far as Blakeney where at 8.10pm she came over the land developing engine trouble soon after turning inland near Cromer, going south-west. Passing near Walsingham (8.20pm), Foulsham (8.35pm) she was at Bawdeswell at 8.40pm. Five minutes later she dropped her first bomb at Bylaugh Park, where there was a Yeomanry Camp in which lights were showing. Böcker brought L.14 down lower, circled the camp and dropped one H.E. bomb that fell 150 yards from the camp and a further 14 incendiary bombs. They did no damage and caused no casualties beyond a cow. They also dropped a German officer's cap (or it was knocked/blown off) and a parachute was found in a meadow at Scarning; the latter contained German newspapers and a leave pass dated Nordholz, 7 September 1915, signed by Oberleutnant z. See Frankenberg, L.14. Frankenberg was second in command of the airship.

At 8.55 Böcker was over East Dereham. He was aware he had flown to the centre of the county and, believing he was over Norwich, he unloaded his bombs causing the most severe air raid casualties inflicted upon the county during the war.

L.14 swept over the town from the direction of Scarning. The first four bombs dropped on Church Farm meadows causing little more damage other than blasting a gate by a barley stack and blowing

*The view down Church Street, East Dereham, the morning after the raid of 8 September 1915. The severely damaged White Lion pub is on the right.*

the leaves off a hedge, but it did cause the patients in the War Hospital to run out in their night attire and investigate what was going on. The next three bombs landed on marshy meadows blowing stinking black mud over a large area. The next bombs caused increasingly serious damage; one landed on the roadway near the Guildhall leaving a crater 6ft across and 4ft deep, bringing down part of the Guildhall outbuildings, badly damaging the roof of the infant school on the opposite side of the road and smashing some of the glass in the church windows.

The worst damage was caused by the bombs dropped on Church Street. The premises of H. H. Aldiss's shop on the High Street corner was almost completely wrecked, the windows of the King's Arms and Cave's photographers were blasted in, the White Lion pub was so badly damaged it never opened again and two patrons, Mr Harry and Mrs Sylvia Johnson were badly injured. In this upper area of the street the body of L/Cpl Alfred Pomeroy was found, his left leg, abdomen and pelvis horribly mangled from the blast, parts of his body were found on the roof of a building next to the Corn Hall. Mr James Taylor was passing along the top of Church Street to post a letter when the bomb landed. His body was found lying in the road near the National Provincial Bank 'shot in the abdomen by a piece of shell case'. The frontage of Hamerton's grocery shop was blown out and cottages in White Lion Yard were badly damaged, one of them collapsing on top of its occupants, Mr and Mrs Taylor. On the opposite side of the road many houses were scarred by the flying shrapnel and the orderly rooms of 5th Battalion, The Norfolk Regiment (T.F.) had its windows shattered and roof smashed. The body of Harry Patterson was found in the entrance of the headquarters building of the battalion, a piece of steel shell casing having penetrated his chest.

The Corn Hall had its glass roof smashed and a bomb fell on a nearby house demolishing it. The occupant, Mr. Catton had heard the commotion outside and ran out to investigate as a soldier ran inside to take shelter; he was extracted alive from the collapsed building but died later from his injuries. The bank and other buildings had their windows smashed along with the Alexander family memorial

windows in the Cowper Memorial Church. The Zeppelin then swept away towards Bayfield Hall, leaving a trail of bombs along the way, most of which fell on farm and estate land. But then, ominously, the Zeppelin turned again and made another pass over Dereham. On this second run an incendiary was dropped on Bradley's ironmongers in the Market Place, setting fire to the oil store and adjacent cartridge store with ammunition exploding in the intense heat. Terry Davy in *Dereham in the Great War* recorded what happened next: 'The fire brigade is summoned by the firing of maroons, and immediately the fire broke out at Bradley's, Mr Herbert Leech, who had a men's outfitting business at the other end of the Market Place, ran to the King's Arms Hotel where the maroons are kept. He found all the occupants down the cellar and, as bombs were falling rapidly, nobody answered his request for the maroons to be fired. Eventually he was given the key to the outbuilding where the maroons were kept. Mr Leech enlisted the assistance of a passing soldier and they got the maroons out. He knew nothing about firing them and actually held the match in his hand whilst lighting the fuse! When the first maroon was fired the soldier rolled over amongst the cabbages in the garden and bolted! Mr Leech fired the second maroon as the Zeppelin was hanging directly over head and it immediately fled. The Zeppelin's departure was attributed by many to Mr Leech's courage and for this he has been complimented by military officers and prominent people of the town.'

The casualties were listed as:

**Killed**

James Taylor (61) an Earthenware, China and General dealer, 27 High Street, Dereham
Harry Patterson (44), watchmaker and jeweller, High Street, Dereham
Lance Corporal Alfred Edward Pomeroy 2/1st City of London Yeomanry (Rough Riders)

**Died of Wounds**

Pte Leslie Frank McDonald 2/1st City of London Yeomanry (Rough Riders)
Pte H G Parkinson 2/1st City of London Yeomanry (Rough Riders)

**Injured**

Mr and Mrs Johnson, Baxter's Row, Dereham – Wounded by shrapnel
Mr and Mrs Taylor, White Lion Yard, Dereham – Injured by house collapsing on them
Miss Dawson, Scarning Fen – Injury to ankle
Pte A W Quinton London Mounted Brigade Field Ambulance RAMC – Wounded in leg.

*The view across Dereham Market Place to the Corn Hall and nearby houses that received a direct hit which killed a soldier sheltering inside.*

At about 9.00pm the raiding Zeppelin went off in a north-easterly direction towards Fakenham, was at North Elmham at 9.10, passed Ryburgh and Pensthorpe and at 9.30 was near Walsingham again whence she seems to have turned off eastward towards Holt, and going back across the sea.

Kptlt. Alois Böcker, formerly an officer in the Mercantile Marine had flown a number of missions and raids before the attack on East Dereham and would fly more until he was captured after he was forced to land the damaged L.33 at Little Wigborough, Essex early in the morning of 24 September 1916. Early in 1918 he was returned to Germany in an exchange of prisoners, with the usual stipulation that he should not fly in combat again. He did end the war in the air though, in his old Zeppelin L.14 as Director of Airship Training at Nordholz.

### 13/14 October 1915
On the morning of 13 October 1915 five Zeppelins left their sheds with orders to bomb London. L.13, 14, 15 and 16 all came in over the Bacton area almost at the same time while the L.11 came in too far south and had to retrace her course to find Happisburgh and Bacton.

### L.13
After hovering between Haisbro' Lightship and the coast for nearly an hour the L.13 under Kptlt. Heinrich Mathy was first to make landfall when she came in over Happisburgh at 6.15pm. Turning south -west the Zeppelin picked up the Midland & Great Northern Railway line at Lenwade and followed a train going to Norwich, till the driver, who had sighted the Zeppelin, stopped at Drayton. After hovering for some time L.13 went westwards to East Dereham and passed over the town at 7.15pm. She then turned south-west and pursued a direct course, passing Griston and Watton (7.25pm) and on to bomb Hatfield (Hertfordshire), Shalford (Surrey) and Woolwich.

### L.15
Under the command of Kptlt. Joachim Breithaupt, the L.15 came in at Bacton at 6.25pm closely followed by L.14 and 16 all of whom were fired on by the Maxims section of the Mobile Section of the Royal Naval Air Service Anti-Aircraft Brigade. L.15 then went inland on a south-westerly course, passing Aylsham (6.35pm), Honingham (6.55) and threw a flare west of Thetford, over Elvedon, at 7.25pm. Changing course southward L.15 passed over Bury St Edmunds in Suffolk and went on to bomb Rushmere (Suffolk), Broxbourne (Hertfordshire) and London.

### L.14
L.14 under the command of Kptlt. Alois Böcker came in at Bacton at 6.30pm, passed North Walsham

### Women's Fire Brigade

Owing to the large numbers of male workers at Chamberlin's, a Norfolk manufacturers of khaki clothing supplying the War Office, who joined the army the firm began a ladies fire brigade in September 1915, the first of its kind in the Eastern Counties. The main objective was to establish an efficient body of fire fighters who could deal with an outbreak of fire following a Zeppelin raid. The Captain and sub-Captain were men but all the other members of the Brigade were female members of staff from the firm.

at 6.35pm and was fired on for a second time, in this instance by the machine guns of the 6th Battalion, The Norfolk Regiment (Cyclists) T.F. posted there but after this fiery reception L.14 traversed the rest of the county via Felthorpe and Thetford unmolested and proceeded to bomb Otterpool Camp, Westenhanger and Tunbridge Wells (Kent), Frant (Sussex), and Croydon (Surrey).

## L.16

L.16 under Oblt z. S. Werner Peterson made landfall at Bacton at 6.40pm then travelled west-south-west and dropped a bomb at Banningham at around 6.50pm. No damage was done. Peterson then altered course to a southerly course passing over Costessey (7.20pm), then north-west to Attlebridge and then south-west to Attleborough where she dropped a petrol tank at 7.50pm and another a few minutes later at Eccles. Passing East Harling (8.00pm) and to the west of Thetford 10 minutes later and went on to bomb Hertford.

## L.11

L.11, under Oblt z. S. Horst von Buttlar eventually came in over Bacton at 8.25pm and made her way inland until 8.45pm when she circled over the parishes of Horstead, Coltishall and Great Hautbois dropping bombs. Four H.E. and three incendiary bombs fell in Horstead parish in open fields breaking a few panes of glass in the cottages nearby. In Coltishall and Great Hautbois the L.11 dropped nine H.E. bombs, two of which did not explode. All these dropped in fields not far from the Great Eastern Railway Station at Coltishall. The only damage done was a shed partly blown down and a few more panes of glass broken. Seven incendiary bombs were also dropped around three cottages. These bombs were quickly put out by pails of water. There were no casualties. The Zeppelin then went eastward to Wroxham (8.50pm) and south-west to Thorpe, near Norwich (9.00pm) where just north of this latter location the L.11 was fired upon by the 1/1st Leicestershire Royal Horse Artillery (T.F.) on Mousehold Heath. From Thorpe she headed towards Acle (9.10pm) and out to sea at Great Yarmouth at 9.15pm.

Buttlar described this short and futile trip over Norfolk as a significant attack in West Ham and Woolwich, but did claim he 'had great difficulty in fixing his position owing to being fired at.'

### 1916

The German Naval Air Service developed plans to bomb the whole of England and had divided the country into three areas for the purpose of issuing simple attack orders:

England North – Edinburgh and secondarily the Tyne

England Middle – Liverpool and secondarily the Humber

England South – London and secondarily Great Yarmouth and Eastern Counties

### 31 January/1 February 1916

This raid had been planned as an attack against Midland towns. Nine airships crossed the North Sea but were hampered in their navigation by the mist and fog that were prevalent along the Norfolk coast where seven of them made landfall on that night: L.21 North of Mundesley, L.13 North of Mundesley, L.15. North of Mundesley, L.16 Near Hunstanton, L.14 North of Holkham, L.19 Near Sheringham and L.17 West of Sheringham

Many of the Zeppelins traversed Norfolk and travelled north to bomb locations in the Midlands, but they were often widely inaccurate in identifying exactly where they had bombed in their reports.

Two of the Zeppelins involved in this raid were significant to Norfolk.

## L.16

It had not been a good crossing for Oblt-z-S. Werner Peterson and his crew because L.16 had developed engine problems, was left with just two reliable motors and was heavily loaded with snow and ice. Giving up on his attack on Liverpool as a target too far, he decided to bomb Great Yarmouth. Believing he was over the coastal town Peterson reported that he had dropped his two tons of bombs from 7,000 feet on 'such factories as could be made out'. He had, in fact, been flying over Norfolk and had dropped two H.E. bombs (one of which did not explode) near Swaffham, causing no damage. L.16 then seems to have wandered for nearly two hours in southern Norfolk and was next found at 8.30pm near Pulham where she appeared to have followed the course of the River Waveney towards Bungay and went out to sea at Lowestoft. No further bombs were located.

## L.17

Kptlt. Herbert Ehrlich reported he was having problems determining his location due to dense cloud when suddenly a searchlight broke through the overcast to starboard. He claimed he saw the glow of 'blast furnaces' nearby and that he came under small arms fire as he steered to attack. Ehrlich made two runs over the 'industrial area' during which he claimed to have silenced the battery attacking him

**Zeppelin Commander Horst von Buttlar recoded his personal account of one of the early missions he flew in for his book *Zeppelins Over England* (1931)**

*We started off at 10.00am, made the North Sea coast an hour later, and then, shaping a westerly course, kept the German and Dutch coast in sight. At twilight our position was just north of Terschelling, and at an altitude of about 2500 feet we veered west and continued our journey. According to my calculations we ought to have made the English coast between 11 and 11.15pm. The ship was darkened; that is to say, all lights were put out in the car and even the use of pocket electric torches was forbidden, our object being to approach the coast as secretly as possible and without being observed by any craft searching out at sea.*

*It was 11.30pm and still there was no sign that we were approaching land, although the shipping below certainly seemed to be growing more plentiful. Here and there through the pitch-black night we had been able to observe the side-lights of the small steamers and now and again also the lights of fishing smacks. It now occurred to me that the ship was making less headway, for the lights below us took longer to move away. The west wind, which during the day had been only a gentle breeze, had now apparently grown somewhat stronger and was making our progress more difficult; the consequence was that it was taking us longer to reach the English coast than we had reckoned it would. I looked at the clock and was horrified. It was midnight! And still there was no land in sight.*

*Half past twelve and still no land! Since we had last ascertained our position near Terschelling a good four hours had elapsed. I had our fuel gauged; it was terribly reduced. Should we turn back? We had only enough petrol for another seven hours and still there was no sign of England!*

*After coming all that distance, however, and on the very point of reaching the English coast, I was determined to push on at all costs. On our return journey we should be able to find some way out of the difficulty. For if the wind from the west really had increased in force, it would be a great help for us on our way back and we should reach home all the quicker. I therefore decided to continue on our westward course until 1.00am at the very latest and if by that time I had not made the English coast I should turn back for otherwise I would most certainly never be able to reach the most westerly airship base at Hage, near Norden, in East Friesland.*

*At that time a flight of this kind was much more of a strain than it is today (1931). For instance the cars were open on all sides and this made it extremely cold up in the air, particularly as it was mid-winter. The only car that possessed a small windscreen was the forward one, but it was just sufficient to protect the steersman and the maps on his chart-table, from the icy blast during the flight. It was 1.00am and still no land was in sight! Should I turn back after all? Suddenly a thin shaft of light came into view. The misty arm of a searchlight darted across the sky. It was probably looking for us. We were over England! Then we saw a number of faint lights beneath us, myriads of them. We must be over some town. Let fly therefore!*

*Schiller hurried aft to drop the hundredweight bombs. I was just able hurriedly to discuss my plan of action with him and told him that I proposed to sweep over the town, which we could just faintly discern, by coming up from the south, turning west and then going off east and arranged with him that when a bell rang he was to begin dropping the bombs.*

*Steering a south-westerly course, we kept over our objective and climbed to a height of about 3500 feet. It was impossible to take the ship up any higher and I did not wish to make her too heavy, for if an engine broke down or one of our gasbags got hit, I should not have any reserve buoyancy left with which to control her. By this time Schiller must be at his post – now! Then the lights could be seen below. Whitish-green beams came up through the mist again and began searching the sky. They crossed each other. Drew nearer, their light grew brighter and suddenly covered the ship's envelope in a blinding glare. They've got us! Little red spots of fire appear below. They were the anti-aircraft batteries. I gave Schiller the sign. Then I climbed slowly in a spiral to a height of 4500 feet above our objective.*

*The chief engineer artificer helped the Wachoffizier in the bomb-cabin to drop the bombs, for the incendiary bombs had to be thrown out by hand. A pin had to be taken out to make the 'live,' after which they were flung in a gentle curve overboard, to crash and burn below a moment later and burn merrily. Meanwhile the Wachoffizier dropped the three one-hundredweight bombs. By this time the space between us and the ground had become a perfect inferno of gunfire and bursting shells – shrapnel meant for us.*

*When all the bombs had been thrown, I leant well out of the car and saw a fiery '6' burning gaily below. Now we must get back. At a height of 4500 feet we were soon out of reach of the English anti-aircraft batteries and steered a course south-east by south back toward the North Sea.*

and extinguished the light. In reality he had drifted in over Sheringham and had been caught in the searchlight of the Naval Air Station at Bayfield near Holt and had jettisoned the majority of his bomb load on to it. Ten H.E. bombs fell about 200 yards from the station, five in a field to the south-east and five more to the south, some 400 yards away causing no greater damage than a few craters in open ground. Five more bombs and an incendiary fell on Bayfield Lodge nearby. One of these wrecked a barn and a greenhouse, blasting out tiles and glass but, fortunately, injuring no one. The L.17 then turned south to Letheringsett, dropping 14 incendiary bombs in a field and in a wood near Bayfield Hall on the way. A further H.E. bomb was dropped in Letheringsett, the *History of 25th County of London Cyclists* records:

> In late January 1916 a Zeppelin raided Holt and every telephone line west of it was broken. No lives were lost, but a draft of recruits just arrived from the Depot had a shake-up in their quarters at Letheringsett, which was close to a searchlight station the Zeppelin was apparently anxious to locate and destroy.

L.17 remained in the Holt area for some time then headed south-west by way of Reepham and north of Norwich, where she was spotted at 8.10pm and was finally spotted out to sea south of Great Yarmouth at 8.30pm.

## 24/25 April 1916

The raid of 24/25 April 1916 was closely bound up with the bombardment of Lowestoft and Yarmouth by a German cruiser squadron early on 25 April. British intelligence suggested: 'In view of the climatic conditions prevailing on that day the raiding airships would not in all probability have attempted to raid if the naval operations had not demanded an accompanying aerial demonstration. The naval attack was in turn connected with the political crisis in Ireland. The raid is unlike earlier attacks in that it had no definite objective on land.' Intelligence was correct only in parts. The German government had sought to support the Easter Rising in Ireland and had taken the Irish nationalist leader, Roger Casement from his exile in Germany by submarine to Banna Strand in Tralee Bay. The bombardment of Lowestoft had been planned by Admiral Scheer as a diversion and the Zeppelin raid was independent to the naval operation. Eight Zeppelins had set out to 'attack England south, London if possible.' Their mission, however, was badly hampered by the wind over the central North Sea (40-50 miles per hour at 1,500 feet) and the mist and cloud that hung over much of the coastline. Four of the Zeppelins on this mission are of particular significance to Norfolk.

### L.16
Commanded by Oblt-z-S. Werner Peterson crossed the Norfolk coast at Trimingham at 10.15pm and pursued a winding course in a south-westerly direction, by way of Hanworth, Colby, Aylsham, Cawston, Ringland and Kimberley where a small parachute was dropped with a bundle of German newspapers attached to it. Then on it droned to Hardingham, Attleborough and west of East Harling to the neighbourhood of Thetford, which it reached about 11.30pm and circled north of the town for about 20 minutes then on over Suffolk where he dropped bombs on Newmarket and Snailwell. Passing back into Norfolk West of Thetford at 12.55am, dropped five incendiary bombs at Honingham about 1.15am that fell in fields of wheat near the hall and caused no real damage but the fifth fell within yards of a large oat straw stack, the flames were fanned by a good breeze and the stack soon caught fire and damaged farm sheds known as 'Read's Sheds' owned by farmer Walter Bartram. It was reported that the occupants of a cottage adjoining these buildings were unaware of anything untoward happening until they were roused by the police. The only other damage done in this neighbourhood was the destruction of an old straw stack ladder that also caught fire and a hen turkey that was roasted alive on her nest. L.16 then made for the coast to the coast via Ringland and North Walsham (where she was spotted at 1.30am) and then back out across sea near Mundesley at 1.35am.

### L.23
Under the command of Kptlt. Otto von Schubert, came in at Caister at 11.50pm and immediately dropped three incendiary bombs, of which only one exploded. Next seen over Filby at midnight, L.23 seemed to follow the line of the Broads, north-west, at low speed to Stalham, which she passed at 12.10pm. Arriving over Ridlington at 12.30 the Zeppelin dropped nine H.E. bombs breaking windows and killing a bullock at Church Farm and partially wrecked a cottage but fortunately there were no casualties. Windows were smashed and damage was also caused to the parish church of St. Peter. The Zeppelin then dropped a further six H.E. bombs near the R.N.A.S. station at Bacton, damaging glass and woodwork of the windows in two houses known as 'Beech Bough' and 'The Croft' the blast also displacing the searchlight. The L.21 then turned seaward and departed.

## L.21

L.21, under the command of Kptlt. Max Dietrich made landfall at Kessingland, south of Lowestoft at 11.10pm dropping nine H.E. bombs on two farms at Old Newton (near Stowmarket) before crossing into Norfolk. Passing over Diss (12.25am), Banham (12.35am), New Buckenham (12.40am), Wymondham (12.25am), Horsford (1.15am), Coltishall (1.20am) and Worstead (1.25am), five minutes later the L.21 dropped a H.E. bomb that landed on Witton Park causing no damage. The Zeppelin then made for the coast and went out to sea near Bacton at 1.35am.

## L.11

Under Kvtkpt V. Schütze made landfall near Bacton shortly after 12.30am and went over Honing Hall and shortly after emptied what was probably her entire cargo of bombs – 19 H.E. and 26 incendiaries over Honing and Dilham. Only one of the H.E. did not explode and the blasts from the others stripped many tiles from farm premises at Dairy House Farm and four nearby cottages while another four cottages had numerous panes of glass broken. Seventy-nine year old widow, Mrs Fanny Gaze was living with her son at the farmhouse of Hall Farm near where the bombs fell died of shock. The L.11 then turned east, passed Stalham at 1.05am and was sighted at Palling heading out to sea at 1.18am where she turned north-west and skirted the coat as far as Bacton, where at 1.25am she was fired on by the section of 3-pdr. guns of the Royal Navy Anti-Aircraft Corps. L.11 then turned out across the sea and flew back to base.

### Aftermath

The inquest into the death of Mrs. Fanny Gaze was held on Wednesday 26 April 1915 before the Norwich District Coroner Mr. H. Culley. Her son, William Bowyer Gaze, with whom she was living, confirmed she had previously enjoyed fairly good health; she had suffered with rheumatism 'but was able to get about.' She had retired to bed about 10.00pm. William Gaze stated had been awakened between one and two on Tuesday morning by '...terrific explosions. Four within the period of a minute'. He went outside and saw a Zeppelin. Not more than five minutes elapsed between the time he first heard the explosions and his seeing the aircraft. The bombs had dropped in a field about a quarter to half a mile from the house. On returning indoors he went to check on his mother and found her in a state of collapse and unconscious. He called up their servants to help him but Mrs Gaze did not revive. He then ran to get help, seeing Robert Earle the gamekeeper, he sent him to summon the District Nurse but by the time she arrived Mrs Gaze was already dead. The findings of the inquest were recorded on her death certificate - 'Heart Failure from shock endured by the terrifying effect of explosions produced by bombs unlawfully dropped from a Zeppelin aircraft.'

A personal memoir of this Zeppelin raid was written by Edith Everitt Owen (1873–1946) who, at the time, was living with her sister Alice and their widowed father, the Revd Canon John Smith Owen, at Witton Vicarage.

*April 24th 1916 Easter Bank Holiday*

*The night was dark but starlit with a strongish westerly breeze which had been more evident during the day. Father retired as usual about 10 o'clock and Alice soon after but returned to tell me that the aerodrome was illuminated and the search lights were being used. On going into the garden I heard one of our biplanes but though I could trace his course by the whine of the engine I could not see the machine. I came indoors about 11.00pm and went upstairs soon after. When I heard a shell explosion which I put down (rightly as we afterwards heard) to our airman letting off his red flare to show he was descending. The subsequent intermittent purring of his engine told me he was landing. I would have dropped off to sleep but was awakened at 11.45 by a deafening report, quickly followed by several others, all sounding very near.*

*The household was active by this time, the maids in the kitchen and Alden, Alice and myself in hastily dressed clothes in father's room. Bombs fell at greater intervals and apparently at a greater distance and finally ceased altogether the last one sounding a long way off. Of us all Father took it all in, I think, with the greatest composure but the noise of the explosion of the bombs was ear splitting and the whole place shook and the windows rattled so that we expected every moment to hear the crack of shattered glass. Going out into the garden I saw the beam of the search light still lighting the sky but the raider had apparently made off and presently the search light went out and we agreed to go to bed again though some determined to keep some of their clothes on. Personally I undressed and consequently had the trouble of searching for raiment in the dark again when a second Zeppelin began dropping bombs about a quarter of an hour afterwards. Three fell in quick succession, the flashes of the explosions lighting up the entrance of the hall through the skylight and roar of the exploding bombs telling of their proximity. This time father, somewhat reluctantly, consented to get up and dress and we all retired to the cellars where we drank hot coffee and sat on uncomfortable chairs. All the time bombs were dropping at frequent intervals but seemingly further away. After a lull we decided that the dining room was preferably to the cellars and we accordingly adjourned thither and the maids going into the kitchen. Someone remarked that the wind was rising and we listened, I going to the front door. It was no rising of the wind but a third Zeppelin for as I stepped out there was a flash and a fearful bang. I turned to go indoors and as I did so flash after flash lit the garden tree tops and several bombs (five in reality) dropped a distance of 200 to 300 yards away their reports succeeding one another so rapidly as to merge into one stupefying roar. The mighty 'swish' that the five made, falling in such rapid succession, was distinctly audible, we sat up in the dining room until 2.45 when everything being quiet we all turned in, the sun having risen by that time.*

*I must have slept for over an hour when the shaking of the windows awoke me again. It was daylight, the sun was rising - a glorious morning. I lay and listened. A distant deep throated growl followed at an interval of a few seconds, by a rattling crash that made the house quiver awakened father's inquiry, from the next room, as to whether the Zeppelin had returned, but eventually suggested a naval bombardment, probably Yarmouth. For about 20 minutes we lay listening to the reports of the guns and the crash of the exploding shells as they fell (as we afterwards learnt) Yarmouth and Lowestoft.*

*The sun was nearly above the horizon and between the distant muttering of the guns and the succeeding explosions I more than once (and father also) heard the cry of an imperturbable cuckoo for the first time this year. The firing gradually lessened, grew more distant, faded to mutterings and ceased. We went to sleep.*

*To describe one's feelings during the actual bomb dropping is almost impossible. Fear was there without a doubt but no unreasoning panic. Anger at our utter helplessness coupled with the desire to keep a 'stiff upper lip' as a help to each other predominated I think. It was perhaps curious but easily to be understood that we gave little thought to anyone outside our immediate neighbourhood where we afterwards found that people living some little distance from us outside the range of the bombs were almost, if not quite, as disturbed as we were and told us that they thought the bombs dropped were surely meant for them. But some of them have heard them really close. Let's hope they weren't.*

*The damage done was mercifully small. One bomb dropped in Mrs Cozen's garden, breaking the palings and glass in her house and the adjoining one (Mrs. Baine's). The five bombs above referred to dropped in Brady's field between us and Bacton making holes 10-12 feet across and 5-6ft deep. Mrs Randall Cubitt's house had all windows broken and doors wrenched off. She, bare footed as she was, carried her baby to Ridlington vicarage. The bomb that wrecked her house dropped within 20 yards of her door, close by the wall of a barn, carrying away a large piece of the wall but injuring none of the 6 horses in it. The South windows of Ridlington Church were all broken and the lock at the south door freed. One old lady in Honing died of shock. Mrs. Cubitt of the Grange, Bacton, aged 93, slept soundly though it all. Forty three bombs dropped within a radius of 4 miles from us some of them fell on the shore but failed to explode.*

### 28/29 July 1916

On 28 July 1916 the weather conditions were most favourable for Zeppelin navigation on the European side of the North Sea and ten naval airships set off to bomb England, the problem for them was when they arrived they encountered unexpected sea fog on the East Coast. Four Zeppelins turned back before making landfall. L.24, L.17, L.13 made landfall over the Humber and Lincolnshire then conducted their missions over the Midlands. L.31 came in at Corton, circled over Suffolk and left without dropping a bomb while L.16 and L.11 droned over Norfolk.

### L.16

The L.16, under the command of Kptlt. Erich Sommerfeldt was first spotted over Brancaster Bay at 12.50am, passed inland over Thornham (12.55am), dropped a 'water-indicating bomb' at Ringstead and went over Hunstanton (1.05am) to Heacham (1.15am). She then circled first south-east, then south-west, dropped two incendiary bombs at Snettisham, went out over the Wash, returned to Heacham (1.40am) and went out to sea over Thornham at 1.45am.

### L.11

The L.11, under the command of Lt-z-S. Otto Mieth, first appeared off the Norfolk coast at Sheringham at 2.35am where she dropped a H.E. bomb in the sea. The Zeppelin then came inland at Weybourne (2.40am), dropping an H.E. bomb on the cliff edge which killed a cow and damaged some tiles on a farm building. Then manoeuvring south-west L.11 dropped an illuminating flare at Holt and while passing Sharrington, where at 2.45am a third H.E. bomb was dropped, a few minutes later a fourth was dropped on Gunthorpe, neither caused any damage. From Gunthorpe she pursued her way south, to the neighbourhood of Melton Constable, where about 2.50am she suddenly turned and flew at high speed eastwards, passing over Hanworth (3.00am), North Walsham (3.10am) and Paston (3.20am) where a H.E. bomb was dropped, The Zeppelin then went out to sea at Mundesley, flying very high, about 3.25am, dropping as she went one H.E. and one incendiary bomb. L.11 was last seen off Happisburgh by the Danish steamer *Rai*, evidently heading out to sea, and was finally heard from the Haisboro' and Wold Lightships going North-East.

### 30/31 July 1916 Mirage?

On the night of 30/31 July 1916 reports were received from units of the North Army, Home Defence, that two Zeppelins were seen North-East of Wells-next-the-Sea between 7.50 and 8.20pm. British Intelligence indicated at least one Zeppelin was far out in the North Sea on the afternoon of 30 July and she may have reached our coast in company with another on a reconnoitring cruise about the time given. But at the same time there was much mist at sea and it was suggested that two of the funnel-less motor patrol boats showing beyond the mist in a sort of mirage may have accounted for the report.

The observers, eleven in number, were, however, very confident about the accuracy of their reports and it is worth of note that Flight Sub-Lieutenant J. C. Northrop flying a Blackburn BE.26 (No.8612) engaged a Zeppelin 30 miles east of Covehithe at 5.15am on 31 July. The problem was as Northrop was firing his Lewis gun vertically upwards the magazine came away and hit him in the face, stunning him. When he recovered control the airship had disappeared.

### 31 July/1 August 1916

On the afternoon of 31 July 1915, ten Naval Zeppelins left their sheds on the North German coast and flew over the North Sea with orders to attack London and England South. Five of them are significant to Norfolk.

### *L.11*

About midnight the L.11, under the command of Kvtkpt Viktor Schütze, was heard in the neighbourhood of the Haisbro' Lightship from Cromer, on the one side and from the Newarp Light Vessel on the other. From other indications she is known to have been immediately North of Cromer at 1.18am. She came in West of Cley at 2.04am, dropping an incendiary bomb on the sands at Warham Hole and proceeded South to Binham, where she dropped an incendiary bomb. Changing course South-East, L.11 steadily pursued this direction, showing a flare at Field Dalling, dropped and incendiary bomb at Galthorpe, a H.E. bomb at Briningham, a fourth incendiary bomb at Briston, a fifth incendiary and another H.E. at Thurning (which did some damage and injured two bullocks), a sixth incendiary bomb at Wood Dalling and a seventh at Cawston. Here, at 2.30am, her course was slightly altered to the eastward; an incendiary bomb was dropped at Wroxham at 2.45am, another at Hoveton St. John and another at Neatishead. The Zeppelin went out to sea between Horsey and Winterton at 3.00am.

### *L.13*

The L.13, under the command of Kptlt. Eduard Prölss, came in over the Wash and was first signalled near Sutton Bridge at 11.55pm. At midnight she dropped her first bomb (an incendiary) at Walpole St Peter. At 12.05am she was spotted north-east of Wisbech, where she seems to have turned abruptly north-east and passing King's Lynn, reached West Newton near Sandringham where she dropped another incendiary bomb and changed course due east. On the way she dropped a third incendiary at West Rudham at 12.25am and then on over Guist where L.13 dropped its first H.E. bomb of the raid. At 12.40am she was near Cawston when she dropped one incendiary and two H.E. bombs. Moving northward, she passed over Blickling (12.50am), Roughton (12.57am) then back over the coast at Cromer (1.00am) where she turned south-west approaching the coast again at Sheringham and finally out to sea in a north-easterly direction at 1.05am.

### *L.16*

L.16, under the command of Kptlt. Erich Sommerfeldt, came in over Lincolnshire where she dropped six incendiary bombs, flying south over the Wash and coming overland again at Sutton Bridge at 12.10am on 1 August, the Zeppelin then lipped into Cambridgeshire and dropped two H.E. and two incendiaries at March, then flew north of Littleport. Crossing over the border into Norfolk, L.16 dropped an incendiary bomb at Hockwold shortly after 1.00am, passed over Mundford and Lynford Hall and dropped seven H.E. and one incendiary bomb on Croxton Heath. At 1.40am, the Zeppelin passed north of Thetford, East Harling (1.40am), Bunwell (1.45am) dropping two incendiary bombs, then on over Long Stratton (1.50am). About 2.00am L.16 dropped an incendiary bomb half a mile east of Buckenham railway station, then changed course south-east, passing Reedham, where four H.E. bombs were dropped at 2.05 am. Finally, she went out to sea south of Great Yarmouth (2.15am), passing over the Cross Sand Light Vessel at 2.25am, heading east-north-east.

## L.17

L.17, under the command of Kptlt. Herbert Erlich, passed over the Cross Sand Light Vessel at 11.25pm, made landfall at Ormesby, north of Great Yarmouth (11.45pm) and followed the river Yare to Loddon (12.15am) where she turned north-west at moderate speed in the direction of Norwich, dropping and incendiary bomb at Bixley, passed south of the city over Stoke Holy Cross and headed towards Tuddenham at 12.30am. Apparently drawn to the aeroplane searchlight at Honingham and the flares of Tuddenham aerodrome. The searchlight may have induced the belief that a battery was close at hand and unloaded the majority of its H.E. Bombs. Ten dropping on Tuddenham, the raider then turned east, dropping seven more H.E. and five incendiary bombs between Tuddenham and Honingham. The Zeppelin passed over Costessey at 1.00am then Wroxham (1.15am) and finally, out to sea between Mundesley and Bacton at 1.40am.

## L.22

L.22, under the command of Kptlt. Martin Dietrich, crossed the coast near Lowestoft at 10.30pm and passing over Suffolk she dropped her first bomb (an incendiary) on Clare, four H.E. on the aerodrome at West Wickham, dropped six incendiary bombs near Haverhill, five at Withersfield and an H.E. at Great Wratting and three more at Snarehall near Thetford (1.25am). While crossing over the border into Norfolk via Croxton Heath L.22 showed a flare that started a small fire on the heath, which also attracted L.16, who probably thought some target had been found, and also dropped an incendiary. She then made off at very high speed north-east, passed near Attleborough (1.30am) then over Honingham to Hevingham where about 2.00am six H.E. and four incendiary bombs were dropped, with the result that one horse was slightly injured. Further on at Burgh-Next-Aylsham, an incendiary bomb was dropped. The Zeppelin then passed by North Walsham and out to sea between Mundesley and Happisburgh about 2.10am.

### 2/3 August 1916

On the afternoon of 2 August six Zeppelins left their shed and flew westwards over the North Sea, by 7.30pm British Intelligence had located all of them.

L.11 and L.16 raided Suffolk and Essex, L. 31 south-east Kent while L.21, L.13, and L.17 raided Norfolk and Suffolk.

## L.21

Before coming inland L.21, under the command of Hptmn. August Stelling, cruised out to sea north of the coast of Norfolk, between Cromer and Wells-next-the-Sea. She was heard at 9.30pm from Wells and between 10.40 and 10.55pm from the Cromer Lighthouse, flying from east to west. She reappeared and made landfall at Wells-next-the-Sea at 11.55pm flying south-west. She momentarily changed her course at 11.59pm to the north-west but very soon turned south again. At 12.0am she passed over Little Walsingham, flying fast in a southerly direction. Passing Fakenham at 12.09 am she seemed to reduce speed and carried on in a southerly direction. She was next seen from Wendling to the north going south-west(12.20am) and arrived over Swaffham at about 12.26 am. She hung over this place for about three minutes and then went due south, making for Thetford. Heard at Ickburgh and Mundford (12.37am), L.21 was attracted by the flares of Thetford Aerodrome and dropped five H.E. bombs. She then altered course to the eastward, flew between Attleborough and East Harling and passed New Buckenham at 1.00am. Twenty-five minutes later she was over Suffolk, passed across the county and out to sea over Covehithe dropping two incendiary bombs as he did so, eight more H.E. bombs fell into the sea close by.

## L.13

L.13, under the command of Kptlt. Eduard Prölss was heard over the Haisbro' lightship going south-west at 11.37pm and made landfall over Bacton at 11.45pm. Fire was at once opened by the mobile anti-aircraft guns at Bacton Coast Guard station and at 11.47pm the airship was driven off along the coast in the direction of Happisburgh where L.13 changed course at 11.52pm to the south-west and passed over Stalham (11.44pm), changed course and passed over Horning at midnight, Wroxham (12.05am), turned due south, dropped and incendiary bomb at Panxworth and went over Blofield (12.10pm) passing over Mundham at about 12.25am the Zeppelin dropped three incendiary bombs that damaged five panes of glass at Grange Farm. Progressing towards the Norfolk/Suffolk border

L.13 dropped five H.E. and three incendiary bombs on Ditchingham, damaging some 70 panes of glass at Ditchingham Hall, fortunately there were no casualties. Flying over Suffolk, the Zeppelin dropped four incendiary bombs on Earsham soon after. Manoeuvrering west and slightly north she dropped thee H.E. over Shelton that broke a few windows, then turned north-west, arriving over Tacolnestone at 12.55am where it dropped one incendiary and six H.E. bombs. Still bearing north-west, she passed Silfield at 1.10am where she dropped three H.E. that damaged two farm houses and two cottages and smashed twenty windows.

L.13 then passed to Wymondham, where she dropped one incendiary bomb. North of Wymondham she turned north and then sharply to the east at 1.12 am. Between 1.15 and 1.25 she circled round Stoke Holy Cross, Shotesham All Saints, Saxlingham, Thorpe, Shotesham St Mary and back to Stoke Holy Cross. It was thought by military observers that L.13 was looking for Norwich. At about 1.25am, when the Zeppelin arrived over Stoke Holy Cross for a second time, she seems to have abandoned the attempt, as she turned north-west and arrived at Costessey at 1.35am and steered off in the direction of the coast, passing over Horsford (1.45am), hovered over North Walsham at 1.55am, she then flew in the direction of Mundesley turning south-east towards Bacton as she approached and was observed flying out to sea between these villages by the Mundesley coastguard at 2.15am.

## L.16

L.16, under the command of Kptlt. Erich Sommerfeldt was cruising off the Norfolk coast between 9.35pm – 10.15pm between the Haisbro' Lightship and Mundesley. She was again sighted over the Cockle Lightship at 12.15am flying south-west and was believed to have made landfall over Hemsby at 12.25am. She then flew south-west and after passing Ormesby St Margaret turned towards Acle (12.40am). Going due south she passed over Cantley (12.45am), then west to Rockland St Mary, south over Brooke (12.55am), then south-west to Hempnall (1.00am). Setting a westerly course L.16 was over Long Stratton at 1.10am where she dropped three incendiary bombs. The Zeppelin was next spotted at Bunwell at 1.20am but her course taken after that was lost until she reached Ashby St Mary where she dropped four H.E. and three incendiary bombs, breaking all the windows in Ashby Lodge and two nearby cottages. On leaving Ashby the Zeppelin seems to have reduced its speed and was next seen over Limpenhoe (before 1.55am) and Acle (2.00am). L.16 was last seen flying out to sea over Yarmouth.

## L.17

L. 17, under the command of Kptlt. Herbert Ehrlich, passed over the Cockle Lightship at midnight and made landfall between Caister and Great Yarmouth at 12.20am. At 12.30 she was seen in the neighbourhood of Ormesby St Margaret in company with the L.16. She was next seen over Halver-gate (12.30am), turned South and passed over Reedham (12.35am), Loddon (12.45am) manoeuvred south-west to Pulham where the Zeppelin dropped three H.E. bombs and then followed the valley of the river Waveney to Eye in Suffolk. Turning due west she dropped an incendiary bomb on the Great Eastern Railway line at Mellis at 1.03am. Returning to Eye (1.10am) she went down the Waveney passed over Thorpe Abbots (1.15am) then, while over Billingford, she dropped three H.E. bombs killing six horses, then a further three H.E. and three incendiary bombs that damaged a farmhouse at Brockdish between 1.15am and 1.20am. Turning north she arrived at Hardwick (1.30am) where she dropped five H.E. bombs doing no damage. At Long Stratton she dropped 2 H.E. (1.37am), then a single incendiary bomb on Fornsett St Mary (1.40am) which landed near an up-starting signal on the Great Eastern Railway, doing no damage to the permanent way. She then turned south-east again to the valley of the Waveney, dropping two H.E. bombs at Starston before 1.45am, which killed three horses and injured one. From Starston she next went to Redenhall where she dropped one H.E. bomb doing no damage at about 1.45am, then to Denton, at about 1.50am, where she dropped six incendiary bombs. The Zeppelin then turned north-east to Broome, where she dropped three incendiary bombs between 1.50 and 1.55am. She was then thought to have headed direct for Southwold, no further bombs were dropped and was last seen over Southwold Lighthouse going out to sea at 2.15am.

## Aftermath

Scaremongering during the Zeppelin offensive was taken very seriously and some of those who repeated rumours even ended up in being brought before the magistrates, such as this case reported in the *Norfolk Chronicle*:

> *At Wymondham Petty Sessions, John Quantrill of Silfield, Wymondham was charged with unlawfully spreading a false report, viz that twenty-two Zeppelins were crossing the channel. Florence Ellen Chilvers, a single woman said that on 3 August she saw Quantrill at work in his garden. He said there were twenty-two Zeppelins crossing the channel. This was at 8.00pm, she was with two other women at the time. She then went to Bunwell and told some people there*

*and the consequence was the report soon spread all over the parish. Quantrill claimed his boy had been to Wymondham and when he came back he said he had been told of the report and that the news had come from Norwich and had been sent on to Wymondham to let the people in the town and surrounding villages know. The Chairman (Mr. W. B. Fryer) said it was the first case of this kind to come before the Bench at Wymondham and they would deal leniently with the defendant but added it was, however, quite time that the public should know reports of this nature must not be spread around without taking steps to ascertain if they were true. The defendant had rendered himself liable to a fine of £100 and they would deal severely with any future case of this kind. Quantrill was fined five shillings.*

### 8/9 August 1916

Nine Zeppelins raided parts of the Midlands, North and Scotland; only one Zeppelin raider came over Norfolk.

## L.16

The L.16, under the command of Kptlt. Erich Sommerfeldt, was observed by the Master of the Inner Dowsing Lightship observed an airship coming from the south-east, flying so high it could only be seen with binoculars, although the night was clear and starlit. Turning west, then north of the Inner Dowsing, the Zeppelin then came in over the Wash, making landfall at Brancaster about 12.30am. Flying S.S.W. to Fring the L.16 arrived over Dersingham at 12.40am and dropped ten H.E. and 10 incendiary bombs causing blast damage to a number of private houses. Five minutes later eight H.E. and seven incendiary bombs were dropped at Wolferton, but these cause no damage. Having disposed of her bombs, the Zeppelin went north along the coast and out to sea at Hunstanton at 1.09am.

### 2/3 September 1916

This raid included both army and naval Zeppelins and was intended by Strasser to be his last 'big push' to bomb Britain to surrender. Sixteen Zeppelins set out to attack London but their attack was badly hampered by adverse winds with belts of heavy rain and ensuing ice which forced two of them to turn back before they made landfall over Britain. Nine of the remaining Zeppelins dropped bombs on Norfolk.

It was also during this raid that first the airship SL.11 , (to be precise it was actually a wooden framed Schütte-Lanz rather than a duralumin framed Zeppelin) became the first to be shot down on British soil, landing at Cuffley, Hertfordshire. The 'kill' was achieved by Lieutenant William Leefe Robinson R.F.C. using the new explosive and incendiary ammunition. Robinson was awarded the Victoria Cross and became a national hero.

## L.16

L.16, under the command of Kptlt. Erich Sommerfeldt, crossed the Norfolk coast at 10.40pm at Salthouse, passed Hindolvestone (11.00pm), Billingford (11.08pm), Mattishall (11.15pm) and dropped its first bomb (an incendiary), at Kimberley at 11.28pm. At 11.35pm she was over Attleborough in company with L.21 and pursued a parallel course with that of the latter for some time. L.16 crossed into Suffolk and went on to bomb London and some of its surrounding area. Returning via Essex and Suffolk, when passing over Raveningham at 4.10am, a blue naval cap was dropped. At 4.15am she passed over Reedham and went out to sea near Yarmouth at about 4.20am.

## L.32

L.32, under the command of Oblt-z-S. Werner Peterson was first heard north-west of Cromer at 9.30pm, going south-west, but did not make landfall until 10.00pm when she came in over Sheringham, passing Edgfield (10.15pm), east to Erpingham (10.35pm), south to Aylsham (10.40pm). At 11.00pm the Zeppelin passed over Honingham and turned west-south-west, dropping a flare at Whinburgh and her first three bombs at Ovington, followed by a further three on Saham Toney at about 11.10pm. Turning south when east of Mundford she dropped a further two incendiary bombs at Two Mile Bottom, near Thetford. Sweeping over Suffolk L.32 was heading across Hertfordshire and dropping bombs believing she was over 'Kensington and the City'. On their return the crew witnessed the destruction of S.L.11 over the port bow of the Zeppelin. L.32 dropped the remainder of the bomb load over Hertfordshire and headed for the sea, passing over Corton, Suffolk at about 4.15am.

## L.21

L.21, under Oblt-z-S. Kurt Frankenberg made landfall at Mundesley at 10.20pm, invisible in the clouds, so she was not fired at although she sounded to be just 5,000-6,000 feet up. She steered a south-westerly course, passing Knapton (10.25pm), between North Walsham and Aylsham (10.40pm),

Buxton Lamas (11.00pm) and Drayton, near Norwich at 11.15pm. At 11.35pm she was at Attleborough, in company with L.16. The two, however, soon parted company, but for some time kept on the same parallel course at a distance of about 6 miles from each other. L.21 then proceeded across Suffolk, Bedfordshire, Hertfordshire and then back into Norfolk via Cambridgeshire. Crossing the border, the Zeppelin dropped one H.E. and one incendiary bomb at Tilney St. Lawrence about 3.35am, then two H.E. to the west and two incendiaries to the north of Lynn at 3.40am. As L.21 passed over Wolferton (3.40am) it dropped a single incendiary then seven H.E. bombs. As the Zeppelin travelled away from Wolferton in the direction of Dersingham at 3.45am it was estimated to be some 6,000 feet up and was engaged by a 75mm gun of the Royal Naval Mobile Brigade at Sandringham, which fired 12 rounds, the second of which was claimed to have been a hit. As it passed over Dersingham, L.21 dropped seven H.E. and two more incendiary bombs causing serious damage to six dwelling houses and minor damage to eight at Dodds Hill, injuring three people, one of whom, Violet Ellen Dungar (36), subsequently died of her injuries. At Snettisham four H.E. and three incendiaries were dropped (3.50am), six H.E. and four incendiaries at Sedgeford (4.00am) and one incendiary at Thornham before the Zeppelin finally passed out to sea.

The death of Violet Dungar, like so many details about the air raids, could not be reported in any newspapers but the Dersingham burial register bears mute testimony to the local tributes to her as the Reverend Arthur Rowland Grant, the Rector of Sandringham and Domestic Chaplain to the King, conducted the service. In addition to Grant's entry in the register the local Rector, Reverend Robert Lewis, annotated that she 'Died of wounds inflicted by a Zeppelin bomb.'

## L.14

L.14 under the command of Hptmn. Kuno Manger made landfall east of Wells about 9.50pm, dropped an incendiary bomb and passed inland east of Burnham Market at 9.55pm and at 10.00pm she was south of Thornham. Next heard of at Ringstead at 10.30pm, where she dropped a single H.E. bomb, causing no damage. She then passed out west over the Wash to Terrington Marsh, where about 10.55pm she dropped an incendiary bomb. She then circles south of Lynn, being near Wiggenhall (11.10pm) then northwards east of Lynn to Gayton, where she dropped two H.E. bombs about 11,30pm and turned south by Wormegay Fen dropping a H.E. bomb about 11.35pm, followed by three H.E. on the Warren, Shouldham. No damage was caused by these bombs. Manoeuvring southwestward she passed over Downham Market (11.45pm), Upwell (11.55pm) and on over Cambridgeshire, Essex and Suffolk where she dropped further bombs and fled back over to Norfolk, passing over Diss (3.10am), Long Stratton (3.15am), Shotesham (3.20am), Blofield (3.30am), Wroxham (3.45am) and back over the sea at Bacton at 4.05am, pursued by an aeroplane but she could not be picked up by the searchlights owing to the thick and low clouds.

## S.L. 8

S.L. 8, under the command of Kptlt. Guido Wolff, crossed the Norfolk coast making landfall north of Holkham at 11.05pm and dropped two incendiary bombs at Burnham Thorpe at 11.15pm but caused no damage. She then went west, afterwards turning south to the neighbourhood of Wendling (11.40pm) and Swaffham (12.20am) heading west. At 12.30am she passed Downham Market and turned south crossing the border into Cambridgeshire and Suffolk reappearing over Norfolk at East Winch (2.55am). The airship commander was thought to have followed the long, straight line of the Bedford Level, the twin canals of which extend in a direct line for a distance of 22 miles from Earith Bridge, immediately west of Haddenham in Cambridgeshire, to Downham Market. Further over Norfolk at she started dropping bombs again, with three H.E. and three incendiary bombs dropped on Congham at 3.00am breaking windows and damaging tiles in two cottages and one incendiary at Harpley Dams, Flitcham, two or three minutes later. She then turned north-east, to East Rudham, when at 3.05am three H.E. bombs fell at Syderstone and two at South Creake where a further four cottages suffered damage to windows and tiles. At 3.15am one H.E. bomb fell at Great Walsingham and two shortly afterwards at Wighton, causing no damage. About 3.20am the airship went out to sea at Cley, dropping one H.E. bomb on land and eight into the sea as she went.

## L.24

L. 24, under the command of Kptlt. Robert Koch, came inland near Trimingham at about 12.30am and dropped a flare soon after over Gunton. At 12.40am she was at Blickling and turned west, passing Saxthorpe (12.45am) and dropped two H.E. bombs at Briston at 12.50am, which caused no damage. Zeppelin then turned north, dropped an incendiary bomb at Plumstead near Holt and then turned east, appearing shortly after 1.00am over Bacton where she was fired upon but without result. The airship then turned north near the coast and was fired at by the Royal Naval Mobile Brigade 3 pdr gun as it passed Mundesley at 1.12am. Her height there was estimated at only 4,000 feet. On being fired at she circled north and dropped five H.E. bombs which fell on the beach just below high tide, at the base of the cliff on which the gun stands and within 60 to 100 yards of it. No damage was done. The airship then turned inland and dropped two incendiary bombs at Trunch about 1.25am, followed by 13 H.E. and 27 incendiary bombs at Ridlington at 1.30am. Remarkably, these caused no damage and nobody was injured. It was thought the Zeppelin had been drawn to drop its bobs at these last two locations by the flares that had been lit up for the landing strip at Bacton aerodrome. The airship then approached Bacton from the south-west and was fired on again by the two 75mm guns and the 3-pdr of the Royal Naval Mobile Brigade. Visibility was, however so bad owing to low clouds and mist that she was only momentarily picked up and was not hit. Her height was estimated from 6,000 to 8,000 feet, rising as she went out to sea at Bacton.

## L.30

L.30 under the command of Kptlt. Horst von Buttlar, came in at Southwold, Suffolk at 10.40pm, crossed over into Norfolk at about 11.00pm when she was picked up by the Pulham searchlight and immediately turning north-east, dropping nine H.E. and 12 incendiary bombs as she did so and causing damage to two farmhouses and injuring one man. Two minutes later she passed Mettingham and dropped eight H.E. bombs and one incendiary bomb of Bungay Common, killing two cows and injuring three others. At 11.15pm L.30 dropped six H.E. Bombs at Ditchingham, smashing glass and displacing tiles, followed three minutes later by four H.E. bombs at Broome, which smashed some windows. Zeppelin then went off north-east to the coast, was fired at by anti-aircraft guns at Fritton, then passed out to sea south of Great Yarmouth at about 11.25pm.

## L.11

L. 11, under to command of Kvtkpt. Viktor Schütze , approached Great Yarmouth from the north-east at 10.00pm and passed over the St Nicholas Lightship at 10.05pm. Five minutes later she dropped several bombs which landed in the sea, made landfall at 10.15pm, dropping one H.E. and one incendiary bomb about half a mile west of Southtown Railway Station. Both landed on marshy ground and did no damage. Anti-aircraft guns opened up on her and L.11 went swiftly back out to sea again, dropping more bombs as she went. She then passed south along the coast and at 11.30pm came in again north of Lowestoft and went on to raid Harwich Harbour.

## L.23

Under the command of Kptlt. Wilhelm Ganzel passed over the Lynn Well light vessel at 10.00pm, threw a flare and eventually  approached the Norfolk coast at Snettisham (10.15pm) dropping a number of incendiary bombs that fell in the sea. Of these, three were later recovered and brought ashore. L.23 then made across the Wash in a westerly direction and went on to bomb Boston and other locations in Lincolnshire then left that county over Donna Nook to cross the sea back to base.

### Aftermath

The statement for Berlin published in the German and European newspapers regarding this raid fell, as ever, rather short of the truth. After proclaiming 'another successful attack' on London it went on to claim:

> *'Other Zeppelins attacked factories and fortifications at Norwich, where strong explosions and fires were caused. Searchlight batteries and industrial works in Oxford, Harwich, Boston and on the Humber were bombed and numerous fires caused there. In Yarmouth the gas works and aerodrome were attacked and a battery silenced.'*

### 23/24 September 1916

Nine Zeppelins raided England between the Humber, London and the south coast of Kent.  Only one of them came directly towards the Norfolk coast in what the Intelligence Report could not disguise its contempt in describing as 'a very half-hearted attack upon the Norfolk coast.'

## L. 23

L.23, under the command of Kptlt. Wilhelm Ganzel,passed near Haisbro' Light Vessel at 8.35pm the L.23 was heard dropping bombs in the sea north of Cromer at 8.55pm. Then she seems to have approached the land and dropped bombs at Overstrand at 9.20pm but none of these bombs fell on the shore, let alone on land. L.23 was heard to drop ten bombs in all, presumed to be H.E. in the sea between 8.55pm and 10.05pm and then returned towards her base.

### 1/2 October 1916

Eleven Zeppelins left their shed to raid England, four of them however, failed to make the crossing and fly over Britain, those that did make landfall mostly did so between Cromer and Theddlethorpe

**Decorated Zeppelin Commander Horst Freiherr Treusch von Buttlar evokes the atmosphere of missions at the height of the campaign in *Zeppelins Over England* (1931)**

Our raids over England were much alike as the airships which carried them out, and which, as they hung in the sky along the German coast at sunset, could hardly be distinguished from one another.

Even the course our raids pursued was always the same. The scene at our departure, the scene when twilight began to fall, when the darkness of night spread over the sea and the first lights of the English coast began to gleam in the distance – all this was always the same, even to the great island suddenly plunging itself into the deepest gloom the moment the news of our raid had been reported to the authorities.

Then came the same gleaming white searchlights, exploring every corner of the heavens for airships, until one here and there suddenly shone out all milky-white; the same white clouds of shrapnel smoke, thinning out into diaphanous veils; the same red lights from the gun flashes below on the ground, the same fires kindled by our bombs, which poured out pools of burning red flame.

Sometimes five, sometimes nine, sometimes as many as seventeen ships received orders to carry out a simultaneous attack on England and drop bombs on some particular area of the country. Whether they went to the North, to the Midlands or to the South, with London as their main objective, depended entirely upon the weather conditions to be expected in the west.

The first ship went up at twelve noon. As soon as she was up, the ground staff hastened to deal with the next, and thus one ship after another left her shed and steered a westerly course.

It was always the same routine. We flew at a height of a few hundred feet over Heligoland Bight and exchanged signals with outpost aeroplanes. We could see our friends come from Tondern in the north, observed the airships ascending and setting out as we passed Wittmundhaven and Hage, and saw the Ahlhorn airships arriving from the south and steering north towards us.

We never flew in squadron formation or in line ahead or anything of that sort. Each of us flew independently, though there were always some ships which kept close to others. This was the case chiefly with the beginners, who always clung to the airship commanded by an experienced man. For the great problem was, in the first place, to determine the position of one's ship and next to discover a spot along the English coast which would enable one, as far as possible, to pass unobserved.

(Lincolnshire) between the hours of 9.20pm and 1.45am, the exception being the L.31 under the command of Kptlt. Heinrich Mathy made landfall off Lowestoft and was brought down over Potters Bar, Hertfordshire by Lieut. Wulstan Joseph Tempest R.F.C.

Some of the Zeppelins had come in close enough to attract the attention of the coastal guns, such as the L.22 that was spotted off the coast of Happisburgh about 9.30pm, it was fired at from Bacton, dropped four H.E. bombs in the water in reply then sheered off from the coast and back out to sea. Those that made landfall and dropped bombs on the county were:

### L.34

L. 34, under the command of Kptlt. Max Dietrich, was first heard travelling south-east of the Haisbro' Light Vessel at 9.36pm, L.34 made landfall at Overstrand (9.42pm), travelling W.S.W. passing Felbrigg (9.45pm) and Melton Constable (10.00pm), then south-west passing west of Foulsham (10.05pm) and dropped a flare over Kempston at 10.15pm. Maintaining the same course she passed over Swaffham (10.25pm) and Stoke Ferry (10.35pm). Altering course westward she passed West Dereham (10.45pm) and Downham Market at 10.50pm, crossing over into Cambridgeshire via Outwell at 10.55pm, dropping her bombs around Kirby Hall and the southern entrance to the Corby tunnel. L.34 then exited via Norfolk going out to sea between Palling and Horsey at 1.40am, being observed to drop three or more H. E. bombs in the sea as it departed.

### L. 21

L.21, under the command of Oblt-z-S. Kurt Krankenberg, made landfall at Weybourne (9.20pm) and skirted the coast going west, passing Warham (9.30pm), Burnham Overy Staithe (9.40pm) where she turned south-west, passing Docking (9.50pm) and when over Heacham (10.00pm) L.21 dropped two incendiary bombs, which did no damage. Turning south, she then followed the coastline of the Wash, past Wolferton (10.10pm) and up into Lincolnshire via Sutton Bridge (10.25pm). Dropping just one H.E. and an incendiary, she clearly could find a suitable target and went out to sea near Donna Nook at 1.10am and was heard dropping bombs in the sea from the Spurn Lighthouse shortly afterwards.

### L.17

L.17, under the command of Kptlt. Hermann Kraushaar, dropped at flare at 1.35am followed by three H.E. bombs off the Norfolk coast between 1.40am and 1.43am, then came in over Weybourne at 1.45am. Passed over Baconsthorpe (1.50am) and Hindolvestone (2.10am) where she altered course to the eastward to Guestwick (2.10am), then south-west near Reepham (2.20am), east of Dereham (2.30am) and Shipdam (2.35am) and remained in that area for some time. L.17 was next spotted over Binham where she turned north-east and dropped a single H.E. bomb when passing over Marlingford at 3.10am, quickly followed by another that landed at Easton, neither of which did any damage. Now flying eastward, she was north of Norwich passing near Blofield (3.16am), Salhouse (3.20am) and while over Martham (3.30am) she was seen to change course south-eastward and passed out to sea at Caister 5 minutes later. Passing over Cross Sand Light Vessel at 3.45am, she was heard to drop seven H.E. bombs into the sea five minutes later.

### Fighting Zeppelins: A Pilot's Perspective

This fascinating account was written by a pilot who had flown in action during in the great Zeppelin offensive of 1916. It is also worthy of note he placed more store in bombs than machine guns (or did not wish to give away the new secret to Zeppelin killing – the Brock-Pomeroy exploding phosphorous bullets). Sadly he remains anonymous for the account was published under the name of 'An Air Pilot' in 'B.P.' *The Works Magazine of Boulton & Paul Ltd, Norwich* December 1916.

Fourteen or fifteen airships participated in the attack on Great Britain last night; two of the raiders were brought down.' Hard official words these, that read in cold black and white of print, fail entirely to bring to the reader's mind a true idea of the romance, the danger and nerve wracking conditions under which this novel form of warfare is fought out.

Let us imagine, if we can, the difficulties the aeroplane pilot has to face. It is dark, pitch dark, sky and earth are alike indistinguishable. Flying at the best of times contains more than a comfortable element of danger and in the darkness is accentuated. The darkness deprives the air pilot of all senses of direction and of locality, greatly hampers him in the manoeuvring of his craft and renders unpleasantly possible a collision with another aeroplane on similar errand bent.

Starting out there are a hundred and one small details to be attended to, as the testing of the engine, the trying of elevators and ailerons and the examination of petrol and the oil tanks in order to ascertain if there is a sufficiency of both to last a two or three hour trip. All this to be performed in the pitch dark, with the engine screeching loud so that a man may not hear a word and the attendant mechanics indistinguishable in the gloom. Fortunately for the pilot a small dry-cell electric lighting set is installed in the body of every machine and by this means the pilot is able to distinguish his instruments – a most necessary adjunct to safe flying – as the altimeter which records the height, the revimeter which indicates the speed of the engine and the compass, more necessary than any other instrument for night flying.

Getting off from the ground is by no means a pleasant sensation. There are hangars, high roofs and chimney stacks all waiting to be collided with, patches of thin and rarified air, which will bump the machine down as much as 30ft at a time; the ever present danger of engine failure, necessitating a descent to the darkened earth beneath, always so full of death traps for the airman and his craft.

Clear of the earth at about 1000ft there are, here and there, faint patches of light and dark grey and the subdued reddish glow of the distant metropolis; the locomotive of a passenger train, bright as a searchlight for a brief moment, then passing away into the outer darkness. Higher and yet higher and the sensation! The mind of a Jules Verne of an H. G. Wells could not imagine a feeling more eerie, more strange than this. Noise and darkness, the incessant deafening purr of the engine, the pitch blackness on all sides, relieved by the one tiny light inside the fuselage as welcome and cheery to the airman as a distant lighthouse to a sailor in a storm.

Then the searchlights begin to blaze, creeping up across the sky in ribbons of shining brightness. One plays for a moment on the machine, the pilot is almost blinded, before it passes on, in its strange search across the heavens. For an encounter with the raiding airship is not at all probable at an altitude of below 6,000 ft and from that height up to 15,000; the only likely encounter is with the observation car of a Zepp. This car is usually suspended hundreds of feet beneath the mothercraft by means of a stout aluminium cable or cables; is about 7ft by 5ft, composed entirely of aluminium and contains sufficient space for one observer, who is in telephone communication with the commander.

At last the pilot of the aeroplane has a feeling; he cannot hear, because of the noise of his own engine and he cannot see because of the intensity of the darkness all around him that the Zeppelin is near at hand.

The combat between the aeroplane and the Zeppelin might be compared to that between a British destroyer and the German Dreadnought in the recent Jutland battle; for once above the Zeppelin, the aeroplane pilot can use his bombs, which are considerably more effective than a machine gun, and the broad back of the gas-bag offers a target which can hardly be missed.

With regard to the matter of manoeuvring, the aeroplane has the great advantage of being remarkably quick both in turning, climbing and coming down, whereas the Zeppelin is a slow and clumsy beast at the best of times. The Zeppelin is very susceptible to flame and explosion of any kind; the gas in the envelope, a mixture of hydrogen and air, forms an extremely explosive mixture. The aeroplane, owing to the fabric of which is composed and the petrol needed for propulsion is, to a certain degree, inflammable, but not nearly to the extent of the airship. Per contra the airship possesses a distinct advantage in that it is able to shut off its engines, and to hover, which is impossible for an aeroplane to do. Again in the matter of speed in a forward direction, and for that matter backwards also, for the Zepp engines are reversible – the aeroplane holds palm.

The combat finished the aeroplane pilot has yet to make a landing, surely the most dangerous and tricky manoeuvre of the whole flight. The difficulties and dangers thus encountered are too obvious to need explanation, further than to say that the landing has to be effected in the dark, with only an electric ground light for guidance.

## 27-28 November 1916

Ten airships left their sheds with orders to attack the Midlands and Tyneside, two of them failed to make landfall over England. One is of particular significance to Norfolk and Suffolk.

### L.21

L.21, under the command of Oblt-z-S. Kurt Frankenberg. the L.21 made its first landfall at Atwick, East Riding of Yorkshire at 9.20pm and immediately came under fire from the Barmston guns. Steering north-east and out to sea but soon returned and evaded more anti-aircraft fire as it droning up to the Potteries, where she dropped her bombs. The Zeppelin then crossed the Midlands from west to east where she was pursued by aeroplanes in Leicestershire, she escaped them and was spotted over King's Lynn at 3.50am. Here her commander slowed down and verified his position and probably recognised the proximity of the Wash and was intending to go out to sea by it. Proceeding slowly to Narborough (4.14am), he went north to Hillington (4.20am) perhaps wondering if his petrol supply would carry him across the North Sea he changed direction and appeared to be making for Belgium. The north-west wind carried the airship along at a slow rate in an E.S.E. direction past Swaffham (4.40am) and East Dereham (4.55am). About this time L.21 was almost caught up by an aeroplane piloted by Lieut. W. R. Gayner of R.F.C. Marham, who had been attracted to the Zeppelin by a light which she was showing. She was at a height of 7,500 feet but when almost within striking distance of her, the aviator's engine revolutions dropped and he was compelled to land at Tibenham. L.21 had had another lucky escape and made off north-eastward in the direction of Reepham, where she arrived at 5.05am. The Zeppelin then drifted slowly over Taverham (5.15am), it was then spotted north of Norwich (5.30am), Wroxham (5.40am), Acle (5.50am) to the coast, which she neared north of Great Yarmouth at 6.00am, drifting at a great height over the post at 6.05am when she was fired upon by the anti-aircraft guns at Bradwell and by a monitor in the Roads. At 6.18am she passed east of Lowestoft, still under fire, and hovered near the coastline for some minutes.

As day was breaking the Zeppelin was visible by ordinary observation without the aid of the search-lights she made out to sea at 6.30am. Meanwhile, both military and naval aeroplanes were on her track. Owing to the approach of day they could clearly follow the Zeppelin, which was steering E.S.E. from Lowestoft. At 6.35am, two naval aeroplanes, a pair of B.E. 2c's (machine No.8625) piloted by Flight Lieutenant Egbert Cadbury and (machine No. 8420) Flight Sub-Lieutenant G. W. R. Fane (machine No. 8420), had risen from R.N.A.S. Burgh Castle on the approach of the airship from the west, overtook her a few miles E.S.E. of Lowestoft.

The following description of the combat that ensued is taken from the reports of the aviators. Lieutenant Cadbury got under her at about 700 feet distance and fired his Lewis gun into her after part, being at the same time under heavy machine-gun fire from the airship. His first magazine not having the desired effect, he changed magazines and repeated his action, still without effect. He put four magazines through his Lewis until his ammunition was exhausted. The airship commander increased his speed to 55mph on being attacked. On perceiving that Cadbury had exhausted his ammunition, Flight Sub Lieutenant Fane then approached to within 100 feet of the starboard side of the airship and tried to open fire but his Lewis gun jammed owing to the cold and the oil having frozen. Flight Sub-Lieutenant Pulling, who had been on patrol in B.E. 2c (machine No. 8626) from R.N.A.S. Bacton witnessed the two previous attacks, then approached to with 60 feet of the airship. He opened fire under a continuous fusillade from those of the airship's machine guns that could bear on him. After he had fired 10 rounds the airship caught fire and in a few seconds was 'nothing but a fiery furnace.' Pulling immediately dived to starboard to avoid falling debris and even though they were ablaze the crew of the airship continued to fire at him for some appreciable time. The Zeppelin then fell stern foremost into the sea, where she sank at once, shortly after 6.40am, leaving no trace but a large area of oil-covered water about 8 miles east of Lowestoft. There were no survivors.

With the crash of L.21 into the sea came the final conclusion to a dogfight that had been watched by thousands of spectators who gathered along the sea fronts of Great Yarmouth and Lowestoft. The *Eastern Daily Press* well captured the atmosphere on the ground:

'...*there were no sign of the invaders in this district until about six o'clock in the morning when the people were disturbed by the booming of guns. Shortly afterwards the Zeppelin, a huge monster, could be seen with the naked eye blotting out the dazzling stars as she was speeding her way seawards...The hundreds of people who were gazing, particularly those who had the use of glasses, got a fine view of the airship as the stars disappeared and dawn approached. Now and again the guns would cease and there were mingled feelings among the onlookers. Some tried to shout because they thought she was hit, others groaned, for they feared she would escape.*'

On land the spectators were not sure if the gunners had scored a hit or the aircraft had achieved similar effect bur there came a moment when it appeared the Zeppelin had become disabled, nor was she at any great altitude or elevation; another correspondent who witnessed the scene noted:

'*There she hung, going a little one way and then another but never making any headway. Suddenly a bright flash came from her and the assembled crowds shouted 'She's hit.' They were right and in the second or so succeeding the flash flames burst all along the Zeppelin, which dropped into the sea in a cascade of red and gold, leaving a trail of smoke behind.'*

There had been a spell of the gravest anxiety and then the whole town rang out with one great spontaneous cheer and the ships sounded their sirens freely, for as the *Eastern Daily Press* reporter concluded: '*the air monster, which had given the gunners the hardest twenty minutes of their lives, burst into flames and fell into the sea. How far she was away did not matter; our seaplanes had fixed her and all that could be seen a few minutes later was a large cloud of black smoke which gradually gave way to the grey dawn.*'

### 23/24 May 1917

Six Zeppelins set off to attack England on the afternoon of 23 May 1917. L.42, under the command of Kptlt. Max Dietrich, came in over Walton-on-the-Naze at 12.20am, dropped bombs as it traversed Essex and Suffolk and crossed into Norfolk at 2.40am and dropped five H.E. bombs at Hockwold, causing slight damage to two farm buildings and two fields. At 2.42am two H.E. bombs were dropped on Weeting Heath, doing no damage, followed at 2.42am with two more (one of which did not explode), at Cranwich. Soon after another incendiary fell at Ickburgh followed by two more that landed in field at Hilborough. No further damage was done. The Zeppelin then bore off north-east, passing Swaffham (2.50am), East Dereham (2.55am) and Reepham (3.00am) and was seen heading south-east near Hindolvestone at 3.13am. L.42 then turned north, was spotted at Briningham, Stody and Brinton, it passed between Hot and Bodham at 3.20am and went out to sea between Weybourne and Sheringham five minutes later.

### L.45

L.45, under the command of Kptlt. Waldemar Kolle, made landfall at Hollesley Bay, Suffolk, traversed the county passing over Stradbroke and came over the Norfolk border, dropping an incendiary bomb at Banham on the way. L.45 was next reported over Swaffham and Litcham. The weather had taken a turn for the worse and there was heavy rain and thunder as the Zeppelin passed over Docking at 2.20am and dropped one H.E. and one incendiary bomb on the village. No damage was caused. The Zeppelin was last heard passing out to sea at Thornham.

On her way back across the sea L.45 was pursued and attacked by a seaplane (Large America No.8666) from R.N.A.S. Great Yarmouth piloted by Flight Lieutenant Galpin and Flight Sub-Lieutenant Leckie about 6.38am when she was ten miles north-east of Terschelling (where they had destroyed L.22 back on 14 May). They fired one magazine of ammunition at a range of 300 yards before the Zeppelin disappeared into the clouds and could not be found again. Galpin and Leckie were also unfortunate enough for their seaplane to run out of petrol on its homeward flight. Safely landed on the sea at Cromer Knoll men and machine were returned in tow.

### L.43

L.43, under the command of Kptlt. Hermann Kraushaar, made landfall at Hollesley Bay, Suffolk, traversed the county and crossed the Norfolk border via Redgrave at 2.55am, dropping a couple of petrol tanks at South and North Lopham soon after. Shortly after 3.00am L.43 passed East Harling, going north and dropped five incendiary bombs at Wrentham five minutes later. No damage was caused.

At 3.10am another incendiary bomb fell at Tottington, followed by a flare thrown out at Saham Toney. The Zeppelin now circled to the east and south, dropping another petrol tank at Carbrooke about 3.20am. Steering west towards Little Cressingham two incendiary bombs were dropped there at 3.25am. The Zeppelin then resumed her northerly route, dropping a H.E. bomb at Houghton-on-the-Hill at 3.30am and two more at North Pickenham causing damage to crops and to the windows and tiles of a farm house. At 3.35am six H.E. bombs fell at Little Dunham, breaking seven panes of glass in a cottage window. At 3.40am two incendiary bombs were dropped at West Lexham, both of which failed to ignite, another incendiary was dropped at Weasenham St. Peter at 3.45am causing no damage. Three H.E. bombs were then dropped at Wellingham, damaging a farmhouse, five cottages and a chapel. Farm labourer Frederick Pile (45) had just called his employer to warn him of the approach of aircraft but a moment after he left the house a bomb fell on the public road demolishing a stone wall. Mr. Pile's body was discovered on the road, a few yards from the crater.

About two minutes later three H.E. and two incendiary bombs were dropped while the Zeppelin was over East Raynham, breaking the glass in the windows of three houses and seven cottages, blowing tiles off roofs and smashing 250 panes of glass in greenhouses at Raynham Hall, damaging trees in the park, uprooting a large white hawthorn and depositing the main portion of the tree fifty yards away. One bomb in a small wood felled a tall oak tree at a considerable distance from the spot where it exploded Another bomb killed two fine cart horses (mares) in a meadow.

A further five H.E. and two incendiary bombs at South Raynham where one cottage was wrecked, several windows and doors of others were blown out and the windows of the church, the vicarage, a private house and 14 cottages were broken. In all these villages, the cottages affected by the blast from the bombs not only lost windows but it was also 'no uncommon thing' for their ceilings to fall in too. It was reported one unfortunate girl of fifteen was in bed when the ceiling fell and buried her under the debris. She was lucky to escape unhurt. A man in another cottage was blown out of bed and fell heavily on the floorboards. He was injured too, with a slight cut to his upper lip from a small piece of shell.

It was now daylight and L.43 made a dash for the sea, and despite being warned of the danger many people came out onto the street upon hearing its approach or in the hope of spotting it. The Zeppelin passed between East Rudham and Fakenham, South Creake and Walsingham and finally, out to sea between Wells and Burrow Gap about 4.05am under a heavy stream of fire from the Mobile Anti-Aircraft 3 pdr. Vickers Quick Firing gun at Holkham, where it eventually disappeared into the clouds out at sea.

Frederick Pile was laid to rest at Wellingham on 26 May 1917 in a service conducted by the local rector, the Reverend L. K. Digby, who annotated the entry he made in the Dersingham burial register 'Killed by a bomb dropped from German Zeppelin.'

The L.43 returned to its base safely but a few days later fell victim to a R.N.A.S. seaplane in the North Sea on 14 June 1917. There were no survivors.

## Norfolk Constabulary.
## PUBLIC NOTICE.
## DAYLIGHT
## HOSTILE AIR RAIDS

When hostile aircraft are within such a distance of

## NORTH WALSHAM

as to render an attack possible, the public will be warned thereof by the following signals:—

### Each Day of the week (including Sunday)
### "Danger" Signal.

Police and Special Constables will patrol the streets on cycles exhibiting cards bearing the words, "POLICE NOTICE, TAKE COVER."
The Constables will blow whistles frequently to attract attention.

### "All Clear" Signal.

Police and Special Constables will patrol the streets on cycles exhibiting cards bearing the words, "POLICE NOTICE, ALL CLEAR."
The Constables will blow whistles frequently to attract attention.

The signals will be given during the period of **half-an-hour before sunrise to half-an-hour after sunset.** Every effort will be made to give **timely** warning of the approach of hostile aircraft, but the public should remember that the "**Danger**" signal will be given when **Real Danger** is apprehended in which event they should **Seek Shelter** with all speed.

Persons still in the open should take what shelter is afforded by lying in ditches, hollows in the ground, &c.

It is recommended that, in the event of raids during school hours, children should be kept in the school until the "**All Clear**" signal is given. Likewise, workpeople at factories, etc., should remain on the premises in whatever shelter is afforded.

Horses and other animals should be stabled or secured in some manner and should not be abandoned in the streets.

### J. H. MANDER, Captain,
Chief Constable.

*County Police Station,*
*Castle Meadow, Norwich.*

## L.40

The L.40, under the command of Kptlt. Erich Sommerfeld was first heard off Lowestoft at 12.10am and came inland over Kessingland at 12.18am. Dense, low lying cloud prevented her being spotted or fired up as she flew overhead. Pursuing a course in the direction of Norwich, the Zeppelin passed over Loddon (12.35am) and Rockland St. Mary (12.40am), passing eastward of Norwich and dropped a 300kg bomb on Little Plumstead. The only damage consisted of glass broken in two cottages and a greenhouse, value estimated at £3 2s 6d. Travelling northwards, the Zeppelin dropped two petrol tanks, one at Horstead at 12.50am and the other at Worstead at 12.55am. Passing North Walsham about 1.00am, L.40 dropped a H.E. bomb at Knapton which demolished some telegraph wires for a distance of 50 yards but did no other damage. Passing out to sea at Mundesley at 1.05am; dropping the remainder of her bombs in the sea as she went. Fourteen explosions were heard from the Cockle and Newarp Light Vessels, growing gradually fainter as the airship proceeded north-east.

### 12/13 April 1918

Five naval airships left their bases to attack the Midlands. Only one of them came in over Norfolk.

## L.62

The L.62, under the command of Hptmn. Kuno Manger, crossed the Norfolk coast at Overstrand at 9.30pm pursued a steady W.S.W. course towards her target of Birmingham. Passing Bodham and Corpusty (9.45pm), Foulsham (9.50), Litcham (10.00) she was over Swaffham at 10.05. Turning west, the Zeppelin passed Downham Market (10.15pm) and then veered off to the north-west dropping her first bombs 200 yards west of Middle Drove Station at 10.20pm. The two 100-kg bombs both exploded breaking some windows in the properties near where they fell. The intelligence summary recorded that a searchlight located about a mile from where the bomb dropped 'was probably the objective.' L.62 then made its way to the West Midlands dropping bombs upon Northamptonshire and Warwickshire. Returning to Norfolk via Brandon (2.20am), she was spotted north of Thetford (2.25am), Attleborough (2.35) and Forncett (2.45). From 2.46am to 2.49am one of the Pulham 18-pdr Anti-Aircraft guns at 'The Beeches' was in action against her firing seventeen Anti-Zeppelin (A-Z) rounds. At 2.50 she passed Long Stratton, and five minutes later was west of Loddon. Here she appeared to stop her engines in order to ascertain her whereabouts and then went past Loddon at about 3.00am. There were several British planes in the neighbourhood. Owing to the heavy mist prevailing at that time 'she was generally invisible' and the sound of her engines appears to have been confused with that of the aircraft pursing her. Seen from Pakefield (Suffolk) at 3.10am, she descended to 11,000 feet to escape the headwind and approached Yarmouth from the west. Yarmouth was cloaked in fog so the 3-inch, 20 cwt. A.A. gun at Nelson's Monument could only open fire to her sound at 3.20. The firing was suspended soon afterwards on account of the presence of British aircraft in pursuit of the Zeppelin. The firing, however, had driven L.63 south-westward, it passed over Herringfleet (3.25am) then went over Gorleston (3.34am) going north-east out to sea.

### 5/6 August 1918

On the afternoon of 5 August 1918 five airships were despatched to carry out a raid on the Midlands, three of them the L 53(under the command of Kptlt, Eduard Prölss), L 65, (under the command of Kptlt. Walter Dose)and L 70, under the command of Kptlt. Johann von Lossnitzer which was also carrying Peter Strasser, Head of the German Naval Airship Division, approached the coast together. At 8.10pm these three Zeppelins were sighted by the Leman Trail Lightship bearing east about eight miles, steering W.N.W. and flying low. Messages were relayed across the sea until the East Coast defences were alerted and the daylight warning was sounded. The *Eastern Daily Press* reported: 'There was no sign of alarm; just the anxiety to get cover in the event of anything happening. The police and special constables took up their positions and all arrangements in case of emergency were made.'

At 9.25pm the leading pair, L.70 and L.65, were seen from the Haisboro' Lightship bearing E.N.E. about 12 miles at a very high altitude. Both were plainly visible in a clear patch of sky. They then passed behind the clouds and were not spotted again until half an hour later when the L.53, which had fallen behind, passed north of the Leman Trail Lightship at 9.25pm, went directly over the Haisbro' Lightship heading south-west. The three airships were thus disposed in a 'V' formation and the leading pair appeared due north of Cromer at 9.50pm, dropping flares. Ten minutes later they were north of Wells and the L.70 dropped three bombs that fell in the sea very close by the schooner *Amethyst*.

In the meantime, the telephone of the Great Yarmouth RNAS station had rung with the warning of the approach of the Zeppelins. Duty Officer, Captain Robert Leckie commander of 228 Squadron, the 'Boat Flight' acted immediately. Informing the station commander, Lt. Col. Nicholl, orderlies were sent post haste across the town to call in officers and men, including Temporary Major Egbert Cadbury, commander of 212 Squadron from Wellington Pier where he had been in the audience of a charity concert where his wife had been due to sing (they were newly married too, it had been a wartime romance - she was Mary, the eldest daughter of the Revd. Forbes Phillips, Rector of Gorleston.)

At the cinema, the film clattered to a stop and the glass lantern slide projected on the screen stating: 'All officers wanted at Air Station immediately.' Rushing back on foot, bicycle or bundling onto the station's Ford tender the aircrew and pilots knew the drill and soon thirteen aircraft; DH-4s, DH-9s and Sopwith Camels, were in the air from Great Yarmouth, Burgh Castle and Covehithe, with twenty more soon joining them in the air over the county from airfields farther inland. Leckie turned over the station to its permanent commander and jumped in the observer-gunner seat behind Cadbury, in a DH-4 as its 375-hp Rolls-Royce Eagle warmed up. Both Cadbury and Leckie were seasoned in Zeppelin combat, both had already shot down airships and had been recognised for their gallantry.

Once over the sea, in an attempt to increase his rate of climb Cadbury ditched the two 100-pound bombs used against surface craft that had been fitted to the DH-4's rack. This appeared to make little or no difference; Cadbury put it down to the barometric pressure. At 9pm Strasser sent a Morse code message to his command: 'To all airships, attack according to plan from Karl 727. Wind at 5,000 meters [16,250 feet] west-south-west three doms [13.5 mph]. Leader of Airships.'

At 9.25pm the three Zeppelins were sighted by the pursuing aircraft 'in line abreast with their noses pointing landward.' The other two airship L 56 and L 63, which were near Yarmouth at the time were, apparently, not observed.

At 9.45pm Cadbury emerged from cloud to see the shadowy shapes of the Zeppelins altering course north-westward at 17,000 feet, some 2,000 feet above the DH-4. The little aircrafts' climb was painfully slow, ten minutes later Cadbury was 400 feet below the Zeppelins when he pointed to the airship in the centre, indicating it to Leckie as their target. Once they were within range at approximately 10.10pm Cadbury concentrated on keeping the plane steady head-on, slightly to port as Leckie took aim with the twin Lewis guns and rattled a steady concentration of Pomeroy explosive bullets into of the bow of the L 70 blowing a great hole in the fabric and a fire was started which quickly ran along the whole length of the airship.

The burning Zeppelin was seen from the Leman Trail Lightship, about 40 miles away and was described as 'a large red flame' the glare of which was seen on land as far away as Reedham (25 miles away). West of Blakeney Bell Buoy and having been narrowly missed by the bombs it dropped, the *Amethyst* had another lucky escape when the Zeppelin was coming down several more bombs fell near the ship, followed soon after by the flaming superstructure of the L.70 that landed about 300 yards from the schooner!

On seeing the fate of their companion the other two airships immediately altered course east and made off at high speed. At about 10.25pm L. 53 dropped a large number of bombs in the sea. Major Cadbury's engine now failed temporarily but he managed to get it going again and closed with the L.65. He again attacked bow on, and Captain Leckie opened fire when within 500 feet of it. Fire immediately broke out in the midships gondola, owing probably to the ignition of a deposit of oil and grit accumulated from the exhaust of the forward engine on the underside of the gondola. There is little doubt that this Zeppelin would have also been destroyed had Captain Leckie's gun not jammed at the critical moment owing to a double feed which in the darkness and perishing cold conditions could not be cleared, a situation made that was not helped because in the rush to leave Yarmouth Leckie had forgotten his gauntlets.

The fire in the gondola was extinguished by the crew of the Zeppelin and though Major Cadbury maintained contact with L.65 for about five minutes the gun could not be got into working order again and the action had to be broken off. The machine gun fire from the Zeppelin during the attack had been heavy but fortunately also inaccurate.

Another aeroplane attempted to attack L.65 after Cadbury had broken off the fight, but it was too low, being 2,000 to 2,500 feet beneath the target. L.65 and L. 63 were fortunate enough to effect their escape into the now dark and rainy night and eventually returned to their sheds.

The remaining two airships, L56 (under Kptlt. Walter Zaeschmar) and L.63 (under Kptlt Michael von Freudenreich) had proceeded from Great Yarmouth up the coast, being seen from Caister (over which one of them passed), the Newarp Lightship and Winterton between 9.10pm and 9.36pm and off Happisburgh at 9.42pm. They appear to have dropped flares between Mundesley and Overstrand at 10.05pm. The catastrophe to L. 70 occurred at 10.25, Kptlt. Freudenreich, was to record:

> 'I was nearing the coast when we suddenly saw an outbreak of flame on the L 70, amidships or a little aft. Then the whole ship was on fire. One could see flames all over her. It looked like a huge sun. Then she stood up erect and went down like a burning shaft. The whole thing lasted thirty, maybe forty-five seconds.'

Fearing the same fate should befall him and his crew the L.63 made off N.N.E., making a considerable detour in order to ensure her safe return, while L.56 went south-east back along the coast and over an hour later, at 11.45pm, appeared off Great Yarmouth. The Intelligence Section notes state:

> Apparently her commander had no mind to return to Germany without having attempted to do some damage and the danger from aeroplanes which had attacked L.70 and L.65 having now presumably been evaded, he essayed an attack upon Lowestoft. Three bombs were dropped in the sea and then the airship seems to have crossed the coast at 11.56pm flew from north-west to south-east over Lowestoft (evidently without her commander knowing where he was, as she dropped no bombs) and out to sea again and between midnight and 12.15am dropped fourteen or fifteen bombs in the water. No damage was done to any craft.

Meanwhile Cadbury and Leckie were a long way from their base at Yarmouth but sighting the flares of Sedgeford made a safe landing at 11.05pm . It was only when he jumped down from the cockpit that Cadbury realized why the DH-4 had climbed so sluggishly. The two bombs that he thought he had released into the sea were still in place, *and primed*, but by some miracle still intact despite a rough landing. Just one more jolt and the DH-4 could well have been blown to pieces! Later, both Cadbury and Leckie were recognised for their action with the award of the Distinguished Flying Cross.

The German official communiqué was particularly imaginative in its account of the action:

> *'In the night 5th-6th August the so often successful leader of our airship attacked, Fregatten-Kapitän Strasser, with one of our airship squadrons, again damaged severely the east coast of Middle England with effectual bomb attacks, especially on Boston, Norwich and the fortifications at the mouth of the Humber. He probably met a hero's death in the raid with the brave crew of his flagship. All the other airships that took part in the attack returned without loss or damage in spite of strong opposition. Besides their experienced fallen leader the airship commanders Korvetten Kapitän J. R. Prölls, Kapt.-Leutnants Walther Zaeschmar, von Freudenreich and Dose took part with their brave crews in the success.'*

A search of the sea soon revealed neither Strasser nor any of his twenty-two crew had survived. The British military authorities did not wait for the sea to give up its dead. Within two days a trawler in naval service had located and buoyed the wreckage of L 70. Over the following three weeks much of the wreck was recovered by divers and wire drags. From this watery grave came code books and all manner of airship intelligence, even the barograph that recorded she had just reached 5,500 metres when she fell.

The body of Peter Strasser and a number of crew were also found, others were washed up on the nearby coastline. All were buried at sea and with them the future of the German military airship in modern warfare.

*Major Egbert Cadbury and Captain Robert Leckie photographed at RNAS Great Yarmouth a few hours after they shot down Zeppelin L.70.*

# 7 For King and Country
## Your Country Needs You

On the 5 August 1914, the day after the Liberal government of Herbert Asquith announced that Britain had declared war on Germany, Field Marshal Horatio Herbert Kitchener, 1st Earl of Khartoum and Aspall, was made Secretary of State for War. Kitchener, or 'K of K' (Kitchener of Khartoum) as he was often known, was a national hero who had come to prominence during the colonial wars of the second half of the nineteenth century, notably at the Battle of Omdurman in 1898, and later against the Boers in South Africa. The Field Marshal was an illustrator's dream, looking every inch the epitome of the senior British Army officer, and his apparently imperturbable and sternly martial features regularly appeared in newspapers and magazines and on all manner of patriotic souvenirs from Sunday school prize books and certificates to decorative plates and tea caddies. Kitchener was one of few senior British officers far-sighted enough to see that a major European the war was not going to be over by Christmas. To have sufficient numbers of trained soldiers to fight for Britain, a country in which conscription was not introduced until January 1916, he would have to step up recruitment. Kitchener had been opposed to the creation of what he termed the 'unwieldy' Territorial Force in 1908 and was not prepared to expand the Territorials to fill the manpower gap. Kitchener wanted a New Army, with soldiers who were proud to say that they were 'Kitchener's men'.

On 11 August 1914 Kitchener's famous call to arms, 'Your King and Country Need You', was published. This called for 100,000 men between the ages of 19 and 30 to enlist; former soldiers were accepted up to the age of 45. The appeal was met with an outburst of patriotic zeal. Recruiting drives were held in every town, and public meetings were led by local dignitaries, with the clergy and military officers delivering speeches voicing 'appeals to patriotism', and military bands filled marketplaces with music as flags and bunting flapped in the breeze. The pressure was on. The British Empire was a force to be reckoned with and worth fighting for, while the generation targeted by Kitchener had been educated to possess a sense of duty and obligation to both King and country. The iconic image of Kitchener, with his pointing finger and hypnotic eyes looking directly at a young chap, appeared everywhere. Alongside the Kitchener poster were many others calling for men to 'Join our Happy Throng' and defend Britain and all it stood for from 'the marauding Huns'. Some posters ignored the appeal to patriotism and instead questioned any man's motives for *not* joining up. One quoted the words of

another national hero, the late Lord 'Bobs' Roberts, asking men to 'make sure your reason for not joining is not a feeble excuse', while young women were asked to consider 'Why is *your* boy not in khaki?' Such appeals to patriotism saw groups of young girls arm themselves with white feathers, which could be presented to any coward not thought to be 'doing his bit'. The problem in Norfolk and other rural counties was that when war broke out there was still a harvest to be gathered in, the pay on offer was at least double that offered by the army and, despite criticism, recruiting in Norfolk only really took off 'when all was safely gathered in.'

The upsurge in recruiting in Norwich was reported in the *Eastern Daily Press* on Wednesday 2 September 1914:

*For several hours yesterday one beheld scenes showing clearly that Norfolk and Norwich will not allow any stigma to be cast upon its loyalty and patriotism. The young men of the city and county may have been a little slow in moving when the first appeal was made to their sense of national duty. They are now proving that this was not because of lack of courage or the disposition to shirk a common responsibility.*

*The real fact of importance is that the type of young man who is specially needed is coming forward eagerly now that he has awakened to the urgency of his country's call. From the homes of the well-to-do and from the homes of the poor, from the capital of the county and from the tiniest hamlet within its borders the young able-bodied manhood of Norfolk presented itself yesterday in greater force than had so far been experienced. The appeal of Monday's recruitment meeting sounded a clarion call. Its response was equally emphatic. Yesterday recruiting went on vigorously from early morning to late in the evening at the Britannia Barracks. In addition Black-friar's Hall had to be requisitioned from 2 o'clock in the afternoon. At both these centres men waited long and patiently for their turn to be medically examined. 'Are we downhearted because we have to wait?' shouted one of a crowd besieging the door of a medical ante-room at Black-friar's Hall. 'No' came a thunderous response. The only regretful look to be seen was when a man came away rejected. He carried the air of having been unfairly baulked of a good thing.*

*One middle-aged man walked briskly into the hall and almost demanded that he should be allowed to serve. The recruiting officer asked him 'How old are you?' 'Forty-nine' was the reply from the man, 'Sorry you are too old' said the Recruiting Officer. The man retorted 'I'm perfectly strong and healthy. I have served in the militia. Please give me a chance.' The regretful Recruiting Officer could only reply 'Sorry but it is impossible just yet. Anyway, go round and see Major Beck. He can perhaps put you on the Reserve.'*

*At Britannia Barracks if anything the scene was even more stirring. Amid a blazing sun at mid-day whole detachments of intending recruits hurried up the steep approaches as if the fate of the Empire depended upon their being enrolled before the day was out. Sturdy, fine limbed, with the glow of health in their cheeks and the sun of the harvest field on their necks, hands and faces – these were the men whom the country is more particularly wanting and here they were coming along in numbers that made one feel that the noblest traditions of the King's county would be worthily upheld. Many brought little parcels under their arms. These parcels spoke eloquently of their carrier's determination not to return until they had done their duty.*

*With men so strong and fit rejections were naturally comparatively few. 'They are the men' said an officer pointing to a line of them which had just passed the doctor. 'They are not particularly tall or big but they are jolly well knit and for endurance they'll take some beating.' Among them was a sprinkling of keen-eyed, wiry men, well on the sunny side of thirty. Their look and carriage pointed them out as coming from the counting house and not the land, 'Most of those boys' it was observed, are either London Stock Exchange clerks or clerks in London business houses. Some of them wished to enlist with the Norfolks and others have come here because the London corps are full. Jews and Gentiles were in the line. Class or creed have no place in Kitchener's Army except the place of common service for a common end.*

*It may be wondered how the recruit straight from the land and with no sort of previous military experience is likely to shape up in the comparatively short time he will have for training before he may be called upon to play the true soldier's part.*

*One learnt yesterday that there is a marked disposition to be less exacting in the medical test than was the case at the outset of recruiting. Nevertheless it is good physique and sound powers of endurance that are in demand. During just over three weeks there have been about 2000 applicants as recruits. The fishing villages on the East Coast are said to be showing a magnificent spirit. From Blakeney alone 36 men have applied to enlist. With the finish of the harvest work, the Norfolk labourers are rapidly making their way to the recruiting stations. The difficulty now arising is to get the services of those who are qualified to serve as non-commissioned officers.*

*The 7th (Service) Battalion of The Norfolk Regiment has been fully enlisted and is now complete, one thousand strong.*

*The number who came to enlist at Blackfriar's Hall yesterday was 200. Of them between 30 and 40 were medically rejected. Doctors and clerical staff were scarcely given breathing time in the transaction of their work. Today the task will be resumed. It is up to the flower of the city and county's manhood to see that that task is made continually harder for it will be cheerfully borne.*

Norfolk did not have 'pals' battalions as such, the nearest we had were the Norwich Businessmen's Company who presented themselves as a group in Kitchener's Army at St Andrew's Hall on Wednesday 2 September 1914, as reported in the *Eastern Daily Press*:

*There were just over 100 of them comprising clerks, bank clerks and the younger sons of business houses. Physically they were a very fine lot of young fellows, full of health and spirits and only too eager to do their duty for their King and country. They will, of course, train and fight together. They met Major Besant by appointment and have been informed they will have to parade at Britannia Barracks on Saturday morning and leave almost immediately for a selected locality to undergo a period of training before being sent to the field of battle. They have*

*New recruits proudly fall in for the photograph by Black-friar's Hall on Elm Hill, September 1914.*

**ENLISTMENT IN THE REGULAR ARMY.**

**HEIGHT NOW REDUCED TO NORMAL STANDARD FOR INFANTRY OF THE LINE.**

CONDITIONS TILL FURTHER ORDERS:
HEIGHT  -  5 ft. 3 ins. and upwards.
CHEST  -  -  34½ ins. at least.
AGE  -  -  -  19 to 38 years.

5th November, 1914.

*been told to bring with them their oldest clothes, shaving tackle, a tooth brush and a brush and comb. The rest of their outfit will be supplied. A slight percentage of their number were unable to pass the doctor and were grievously disappointed at their ill-luck. They deserved the fullest credit for offering themselves.*

In the countryside, once the harvest was over, recruitment was brisk in towns across Norfolk, the story of events at North Walsham which appeared in the *Eastern Daily Press* on 14 September 1914 is typical of events across the county at the time:

*The fruit of the war enthusiasm so far as it relates to the Kitchener's Armies was harvested at North Walsham on Saturday afternoon. A hundred and twenty young fellows of the kind which recruiting officers would call 'the right sort of stuff' paraded in the Market Place amid a scene of patriotic devotion that would have been remarkable in a far larger town and were sent off to Norwich amid the cheering of the crowd and the tuneful clatter of the band. Similar scenes have been or are about to be witnessed in other Norfolk towns. We are quoting the doings of North Walsham only as a typical case.*

*New recruits on the march in Norwich, September 1914.*

*New recruits on the march in Norwich, September 1914.*

The men aforesaid came from there and from Stalham and from a ring of parishes nearby and they constitute, so far as our present information goes, the first intact company – intact in the district sense – which has yet been formed anywhere in the county. They had been tested and attested at North Walsham so as to avoid delay and lighten such pressure as was experienced at Norwich last week. They were known personally to the whole countryside. Every man jack of them was in touch with his pals and knew himself destined to continue so. As applied to recruiting there is a wisdom in this area in this idea of localism. It is an excellent means of nullifying the sense of bewilderment bound otherwise to afflict a new recruit suddenly absorbed into a vast military machine whose parts and functions he can neither visualise nor comprehend. The mutual encouragement thus derived was commented on by Major Pearce at a send off dinner given to the men at the King's Arms Hotel. 'I have made a special request' he said, 'that you should be enrolled together and go to Norwich together and serve together and I know from a message I have received that Lord Kitchener will make short work of anybody who interferes to prevent this.'

Saturday started a great and sacred awakening to the North Walshamites, the flower of this countryside had risen heroically to the call the righteous war. The crowd saw in their men 'Whose God-like office is to draw the sword against oppression and to set free mankind.'

The recruits formed up in the Market Place with the bank behind them and the ancient pump in front. A gaze of unmistakable pride and affection radiated to them from a thousand or more of the townspeople and an equal throng of country folk from the villages round about. There were old men in the crowd with worn-ashen faces vaguely contemplative and void of all emotion, there were children terrified among the hubbub; there were toil stricken women whose

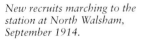

*New recruits marching to the station at North Walsham, September 1914.*

*More Norfolk men who answered Kitchener's call pictured during their early days of training.*

*tearful eyes and twitching mouths betoken a family interest in the scene. Among the recruits themselves were doctor's sons and farmer's sons, shopmen, carpenters, bricklayers, fisher-lads and field labourers. All but a very few wore cloth caps and overcoats and carried brown paper parcels under their arms. The prevailing mood was not uncheerful and there was in it a certain grim solemnity, as befits a man embarking on high and strange adventures. A gentleman in the throng who well knew most of the recruits reported that the war spirit in the villages whence they came was wonderfully deep and strong, much more than is imagined by a stranger – unused to the habitual reserve which in Norfolk masks the rural character. Many had thrown to the winds very weighty considerations of prudence. Probably quite ten per cent were married. One was father of eight children.*

*'Fall in' shouted an old volunteer sergeant who was helping Major Pearce to get all this raw material right minded. The band jostled its way to the head of the column. The crowd let up a hoarse cheer tinctured with the shrill chirrup of the girls. And so we went to the railway station affirming and re-affirming that considerable is the distance which separates us from Tipperary, 'Good-bye Piccadilly, Good-bye Leicester Square.' The band was blowing a blast of 'Auld Lang Syne' as the train drew up to the platform and the commotion of the last farewells began. A few babies were thrust up to be kissed, here and there a woman claimed yet one last embrace but in the main there were no tearful demonstrations, just a handshake and the mystic words 'So long.' At Norwich all the cheerfulness was gone out of the sky and the march to Britannia Barracks was made in a drizzling rain.*

To prevent soldiers returning home at every opportunity, and to begin fostering regimental *esprit de corps*, many of the freshly raised battalions were soon marched off, sent by the train load to training camps in other parts of the country; our Norfolk regiment Service Battalions were sent to Shorncliffe near Folkstone in Kent. Major H. P. Berney Ficklin of 8th (Service) Battalion, The Norfolk Regiment recalled the early days of the battalion at Shorncliffe: 'The conditions in England at this time were practically indescribable. The men appeared in thousands... all in civilian dress... and had to be found accommodation, food, cooking utensils and boots; and had at the same time to be taught the first principles of soldiering. England owes a very large debt to those ex-non-commission officers who came forward immediately, some of them after ten or fifteen years of civilian life, and placed their experience (rusty perhaps, but albeit of the utmost value) at the service of their country. Some idea of the difficulties experienced in these early days may be gleaned from the fact that there were sixteen men to a tent, and that there was an average of two plates and at the most half a dozen knives and forks to each sixteen men, that tobacco tins had to be used as cups, and that there was a shortage of ablution places and washing materials. The latter were compensated for by taking the whole battalion down to the sea at 5am every morning and making every man bathe.'

A shortage of uniforms could not stop basic military training, which focused on getting men to obey orders without question. Recruits wearing everyday clothes were put through their paces in drill, rifle training and physical exercise, with some demanding compensation for wear and tear, especially to boots. Even knives, forks and spoons had to be shared. A stop-gap measure to compensate for the

*Swedish drill for new recruits on Chapel Field Gardens, Norwich October 1914*

shortage of uniforms were armbands and regimental cap badges worn on the lapel of the jacket and, if promoted to NCO rank, stripes would be worn on the sleeves. Pending the issue of uniforms recruits had to send home for a pair of good boots and a greatcoats. Carriage was paid to the Depot or training centre and the considerable sum of 7s 6d was given to each man who produced greatcoat, suit and boots to wear until a uniform was issued.

The main drive, however, was to provide the recruits with some sort of uniform. In an act of sheer desperation, the War Office introduced 'Kitchener Blues', probably the most disliked uniform in the history of the British Army. The jackets and trousers were sourced from uniform stocks held for postmen, prison warders and

*Kitchener volunteers on parade upon the Carrow playing fields, Norwich 1914.*

*Kitchener volunteers Dining Hall, Carrow Club House, Norwich, 1914.*

*The 'Southrepps Boys' who had joined Kitchener's Army, November 1914. A number of them are wearing 'Kitchener Blues' uniforms.*

The 'Southrepps Boys' who had joined Kitchener's Army, November 1914. A number of them are wearing 'Kitchener Blues' uniforms.

prisoners, although the uniforms for prisoners tended to be grey and therefore had to be dyed for Army use! This motley collection of uniforms was crowned with a side cap of simple construction.

The Army also looked to its stores and found that its only stockpile of personal equipment for other ranks consisted of pre-1900 pattern whitened hide pouches, belts and cross straps, worn during the reign of the late Queen Victoria. Unfortunately Kitchener's men did not have the pipeclay to whiten this old equipment, not that there was sufficient go round; most men ended up wearing a belt and one ammunition pouch. Victorian webbing was accompanied by the issue of rifles of similar vintage, and when these ran out, men were issued with wooden 'rifles' and even broomsticks with which to learn arms drill.

The public didn't know what to make of the strange blue uniforms. Some thought that prison warders had been conscripted to maintain public order; others decided that those wearing blue must be Belgian soldiers, and therefore refugees. There were still not enough military buttons and regimental badges to go round, and when khaki uniforms became more plentiful men still ended up wearing collar badges or even buttons in place of a cap badge like the New Army recruit on our front cover. To cap it all, much of the cloth had been dyed in great haste, using inferior chemicals. This was partly due to the fact that Britain had relied upon the more advanced German chemical industry for many of its dyestuffs, and what was in stock soon ran out. The inferior dye ran if the uniform became wet or its wearer sweated too freely, turning the skin blue. With typical good humour, Kitchener's men sang a song about their tribulations, featuring Fred Karno the then 'King of the Comedians':

'We are Fred Karno's Army,
Fred Karno's infantry,
We cannot fight, we cannot shoot,
What blooming use are we?
But when we get to Berlin,
The Kaiser he will say,
Hoch, Hoch, Mein Gott!
What a bloody fine lot,
Fred Karno's sent today!

From May 1915 most of the 'Kitchener battalions' were sent to the Western Front. Training in trench warfare under simulated battle conditions began as soon as they arrived. Each unit spent about a month in training. Everyone became expert in digging trenches and latrine pits. Under the supervision of bawling Sergeant Instructors, the men fixed bayonets and ran to stab and skewer sacks filled with straw hung from gallows, practised firing at targets with the faces of German soldiers printed upon them, and threw both live and practice grenades to prepare them for 'bombing raids' across no man's land. Selected men were trained on machine guns, in sniping, advanced signalling, and firing trench mortars. They then marched off to the trenches and served with remarkable distinction, courage and determination but then, after all, they were for the most part, Norfolk men.

## A brief overview of the Battalions, major actions and fighting men of
## The Norfolk Regiment 1914-1918

## REGULAR ARMY BATTALIONS

### 1st Battalion

Mobilized for war from Holywood, Belfast and after being brought back up to war service strength by reservists formed part of the 15th Brigade, 5th Division British Expeditionary Force (BEF) they landed at Le Havre and entrained for the front on the night of 17 August 1914, arriving at Le Cateau the following day. The battalion fought at Mons (Elouges), Le Cateau, the Aisne, La Bassee and Ypres. Christmas 1914 the weather was vile, with bitter frosts and snow; the men were exposed to varying depths of water and mud and trench foot became prevalent. On Christmas Day the men of the 1st Battalion were present at the famous 'Christmas Truce.'

*Runners and Scouts of C Company, 1st Battalion The Norfolk Regiment pictured at Holywood, Belfast shortly before the outbreak of war 1914.*

*The men of 1st Battalion, The Norfolk Regiment in the trenches near 'Plug Street' Christmas 1914.*

## The Christmas Truce 1914

Christmas 1914 the men of 1st Battalion, The Norfolk Regiment (1 Norfolk) were serving in 15th Brigade, 5th Division as part of General Smith-Dorrien's II Corps holding a line on the Wulverghem–Messines Road, a short distance from Ploegsteert, Belgium. Facing them were members of the 133rd and 134th Infantry Regiments of the 89th Brigade, XIX (Saxon) Corps, part of the Imperial German Sixth Army led by Crown Prince Rupprecht of Bavaria.

*A soldat of the Imperial German Army 133rd Infantry Regiment, one of the regiments in the trenches opposite the men of 1st Battalion, The Norfolk Regiment at the time of the Christmas Truce.*

The men of 1 Norfolk had landed at Le Havre British Expeditionary Force (BEF) in August 1914 and had fought through Mons (Elouges), Le Cateau, the Aisne, La Bassee and Ypres. In December 1914 the weather was vile, freezing cold temperatures and snow combined with varying depths of water and mud with the result that trench foot to become prevalent among the men.

Pte Bertie Guymer of East Dereham had been called as a National Reservist and joined 1 Norfolk in October 1914. Returned home wounded in March 1915, he related his experiences of Christmas in the trenches to a reporter from the *Norwich Mercury*:

'At 10.00pm on Christmas Eve the Germans got up on top of their trenches. One man called out 'Don't fire, I want to talk.' He walked half way to our trench and 'Cock' Warminger, the heavy-weight boxer of Norwich left our trench and met him. The two men shook hands and exchanged presents of cigars and chocolates. The men returned to their respective trenches, and then the Germans came out, having left their rifles behind. We joined them and there was a sing along. We gave them 'Tipperary' and they responded with 'The Watch of the Rhine'. We buried some dead Frenchmen, Germans and Norfolks digging the graves, and a German officer read the prayers. After that we walked about as we liked and were glad to do so as there was a sharp frost. Our officers cut off their buttons and exchanged them for the German officers' buttons. The Germans told us they kept Christmas for three days and during that period not a shot was fired.' Bertie Guymer was killed in action on 25 June 1915.

continued overleaf

*Private Walter Allen of Cromer, one of those present at the Christmas Truce.*

Pte George Crisp of Cromer, was another National Reservist mobilised shortly after the outbreak of war. Despite being well over 40 he was anxious to 'have a cut at the Germans'. He volunteered for active service and after four weeks' training at Felixstowe, he joined 1 Norfolk in late December 1914. In the firing line he met old Cromer pals Walter Balls, Walter Allen and Walter Wright, all members of the National Reserve who had preceded him. When Pte Crisp was with his battalion they were entrenched but fifty yards from the Germans. Crisp found the men of the battalion full of the stories of the Christmas Truce:

*'The Germans came out of their trenches singing 'It's a Long way to Tipperary' and as they were without their rifles our boys wondered what it all meant. One of them, 'Cock' Warminger, the well-known Norwich boxer, volunteered to go and find out and he came back with them, apparently the best of friends. Then the rest of the Norfolks joined them and the German's said 'The Kaiser won't give us a holiday and we are taking one. We don't fire today, tomorrow and the next day.' Some of the Germans were very old men and some were boys who could not have been more than 15 years old. Our men mixed with them and they smoked, drank and talked together. The Germans fully believed they were winning, saying, 'We are still fighting you in France and Belgium and holding our own' but when they repeated what they had been told to the effect that our Navy was sunk and the Germans had taken Paris and London our men showed them papers from home to disillusion them. Tears rolled down the cheeks of some of the older men who had been showing the Norfolks photos of their loved ones at home when they began to realise that all was not so well with their cause as they had been told.*

*Walter Balls had a strange experience in this affair – one of the Germans, a young fellow, went up to him and said 'You come from Cromer. Don't you?' The German then told him that he had been a waiter at a hotel in Cromer during the last summer and had left when he was recalled to his regiment in Germany.*

*The Norfolk lads had plenty of tobacco out at the front. Crisp stated 'It's a waste for relatives to send more, but what our men really would appreciate are cocoa, sugar, candles and matches, Oxo cubes and such things as that. I've seen one match used for lighting eight or nine woodbines – the matches here as so expensive and difficult to get.'*

B Company Lance Corporal, Walter Balls, well known in the years before the First World War in his home town of Cromer as one of the local postmen, wrote of what happened next in a letter to his old friend Roy Read who sent it in for publication in the *Norfolk Chronicle*:

*On Christmas Day things were very quiet. I don't think there was a rifle shot on either side near us. At night we could hear them singing in the trenches quite plain, so we got a good fire up and did ditto – carols and songs, A1. I should have told you that every night we slip across the field to a farm and get enough water to last till the next night. On Boxing morning we could see the Germans on top of their trenches walking about. So we did ditto. Some of them came across so some of us went half way to meet them and shake hands with them. One could speak English well. He told us they did not want to fight. One of the officers snapped one of our chaps with a small camera. He told us they were the 45th and 49th Regiments and they fought with us at —— and ———; they were "driven to the firing line" to use his own words "death in front and death behind". They were going back to a concert. After that I had a look around the farm. It was tobacco on half of the field and potatoes the other half. About a dozen bullocks etc. laid about the field killed, we buried them later. On Christmas Day we had photos of the King and Queen from them and Princess Mary pipe tobacco and fags. I shall send them home if I can.'*

*Lance Corporal Walter Balls wrote home about his experiences of the Christmas Truce.*

At the end of February 1915, 15 Brigade was moved from the neighbourhood of Messines to the southern face of the Ypres salient and the notorious 'Hill 60'; it was a time to take stock. By this time, of the officers who had left Belfast in August 1914, only five remained in the battalion. Over the ensuing months of holding the lines, raids and attacks, the casualties were so severe the men of the battalion stoically became all too familiar with losing their comrades or seeing another pal removed to the aid post. In May 1915 the battalion experienced one of the first gas attacks on the Western Front and suffered 75 casualties from it on 5 May 1915. The battalion was relieved the following day after 26 days continuously in the trenches. After a brief time to recuperate and reinforce the 1st Battalion was returned to the lines of the Albert front. From September to December 1915 the battalion's frontal trench service was in the area between Carnoy and Mametz. The increasing challenge for the men, on top of the fighting, was the terrain which after a year of pounding by artillery, bombs and mines now more resembled the moon than Northern France. Liquid mud and water filled the craters and when a shell or mine blew nearby, if the blast did not injure or kill, men could easily become buried under the earth displaced by the explosion. There are numerous incidents involving officers, NCOs, men and particularly the stretcher bearers, digging out men who had become buried. Due to the urgent need to dig out these casualties before they suffocated, such rescues were often conducted under fire. Troops were also called upon to help those specialists involved in tunneling and mining operations.

In July 1916 the men of 1 Norfolk served with distinction in an action to capture Longueval, High Wood and Delville Wood but it was to cost them the lives of 17 officers and 412 other ranks in the space of a week. Over the ensuing months they fought again at Falfemont Farm, Morval and Givenchy. On October 1st 1916 the battalion left the Somme area, but not without a special battalion order from the Commanding Officer, Colonel Stone:

*'Before leaving the Somme and all it will mean to us and to the history of the Regiment, I wish to convey my most sincere thanks to all ranks for what they have done…You had everything against you, but you have been through the heaviest fighting of the war and come out of it with a name that will live forever. At Longueval, your first battle you were given your first and severest test, and no praise of mine can be too high for the extreme gallantry and endurance shown on that occasion. The severest test of discipline is for men to stand intense shell fire and to hold on to the ground they have won under it – and this you did. At Falfemont Farm you again had a difficult task and a severe fight, but you stuck to it and eventually captured it – a position whose importance cannot be over-estimated. Then, during the most trying weather conditions, you were in the open making trenches and at one time the limit of complete exhaustion had almost been reached, but when one final effort was asked of you at Morval, you carried out a brilliant assault. You came to the Somme battlefield with a very high reputation, which you had rightly earned during twenty-three months of strenuous warfare – you leave the Somme with the highest reputation in the British Army.'*

And so the men of the 1st Battalion fought on into 1917 through Vimy, Oppy Wood and back again to Ypres in the Battle of Cambrai. But then came the great Austro-German offensive on the Italian Front which saw seven French and five British divisions sent to reinvigorate the Italian Army. The men of the 1 Norfolk were despatched in November 1917 and were undoubtedly pleased to get out of the trenches of the Western Front. They were not unduly taxed by their role in the lines around Piave and their sojourn would not be for long as they returned to the Western Front in April 1918. Within days they were in the advance guard of the brigade at St Venant, south of the key battle area of Nieppe Forest, where again the men fought with distinction. In July the curtain was raised on the last 'Big Push' and by August 5th Division was attached to 4th Corps. These final battles of the war were hard won for the men of the 1st Battalion, many of the stalwarts of the battalion who had been with them through thick and thin over the last few years fell at this last hurdle, many to wounds sustained under the intense German shell fire. The CO, Lieut-Colonel Humphries, Captain G. C. Tyler the adjutant and Rev. R. W. Dugdale MC CF, the padre, were killed. But the battalion came through with laurels, the Divisional Commander formally asked their CO to inform all ranks 'how much he appreciated the extraordinary good work carried out by the battalion during the operations from August 21st to September 2nd.' The men of the 1st Battalion entered their last action of the war at 5.30am on 5 November when they led an attack on the forest of Mormal from Neuville. Withdrawn to Jolimetz on the west of Mormal Forest it was here news was received of the Armistice on 11 November 1918.

## 2nd Battalion

August 1914, in Belgaum, India, sent as part of 18th Indian Brigade, 6th (Poona) Division to Mesopotamia in November 1914. They did see action in 1914 and had experience of using their bayonets in the attack on Kurna. They saw out 1914 on the banks of the River Tigris but their first major action was to be one which was to be etched bold among the most notable in the history of the Regiment. On 14 April 1915 2 Norfolk received the order 'Push forward at all costs. Take the enemy's trench'. Colonel Peebles drew his sword and in the finest traditions of The Norfolk Regiment led the attack personally with the shout of 'Come on the 9th!' attacked an estimated enemy force of some 10,000 to 12,000 Turks in heavily wired trenches, redoubts and well made gun emplacements at Shaiba. As Tim Carew described it in *The Royal Norfolk Regiment*: '…they advanced over 500 yards of feature-less desert and never a man faltered – machine gun and rifle bullets zipped about their ears, but still they came on. They charged, heedless of fire and casualties, yelling as men will, to keep their hearts jumping out of their mouths; the Turks, shaken by the wildness of the charge, fled from them, and the mile long low ridge which was the Shaiba position became the property of the 2nd Battalion, The Norfolk Regiment.'

Such was this victory the men of the 2nd Battalion, and indeed the regiment have celebrated 'Shaiba Day' ever since. It was a decisive victory and one of the last occasions when British Army officers carried swords in action but many men fell on that desert soil. There were many wounded, and

sickness took its toll on the men too; by the following day Major de Grey estimated they were left with about 300 men.

As 1915 rolled on heatstroke and diseases like beri-beri and dysentery claimed many of the men. Their next major action was at the Battle of Ctesiphon in October 1915. The battalion fought with just 500 men after which just seven officers and 250 men were left on their feet. And then those left were sent to Kut-al-Amara; here they spent the Christmas of 1915 under siege in the stinking and oppressive environs of Kut. The rations were soon depleted and men were reduced to ten ounces of bread and one pound of horse or mule flesh. Amidst such depravation the men of 2 Norfolk did not waver, General Townsend wrote in his despatch 'It is my handful of Norfolks, Dorsets and Oxfords who are my sheet anchor here.' But despite their solid will their bodies were weakened through starvation and disease. On 29 April 1916, after 146 days of siege, Kut was surrendered and the remnants of the 2nd Battalion there became prisoners of war. But that was not to be the end of the 2nd Battalion – there were still available drafts and recovered sick or wounded of the Norfolk and Dorset Regiments. Neither regiment had enough men to raise a battalion in their own right so on 4 February 1916 it was decided to take two companies from each and raise a composite battalion, soon known to the men as 'Norsets.' They fought at Sannaiyat and, despite outbreaks of cholera, held their positions along the Tigris until the 2nd Battalion was reconstituted in July at Basra. Few of these men were 'old soldiers,' the majority of the new men coming equally from Kitchener and Derby recruit schemes. They returned to the Tigris and over the next two years, driving the Turks back along its course, transferring in February 1917 to 37th Indian Brigade, 14th Indian Division. When Lieut-General Sir R. G. Egerton relinquished command of the 3rd (Indian) Corps he communicated his appreciation of 2 Norfolk in these later actions: 'The great feat of arms performed by you in the clearance of the Dahra Bend was followed by the magnificent achievement at Shumran, when you forced the passage of the Tigris in full flood in the face of a determined enemy – a performance, which will, I believe, live in history as unique in the annals of any army in the world. And in connection with this I raise my hand to salute the gallant Norfolk Regiment in particular.'

## 3rd (Special Reserve) Battalion

Initially based at Britannia Barracks as a training and depot unit. On Saturday August 8 the battalion was despatched to Felixtowe forming part of the Harwich Garrison coastal defences where it remained for the rest of the war. In addition the 3rd Battalion acted as the conduit for many Militiamen, Reservists and unattached Officers before they joined battalions on 'Active Service' as well as training and despatching drafts overseas. A tragedy recalled by the Commanding Officer Colonel Tonge was the loss of the troop transport ship *Royal Edward* after being torpedoed in the Aegean Sea in August 1915. Of the 1,400 men she carried only 600 were saved. Out of these all but 18 of 300 men who had volunteered from the battalion to serve in The Essex Regiment survived. In July 1919 the battalion was despatched to Ireland on peacekeeping duties. The battalion was eventually absorbed by 1st Battalion.

## Territorial Force

When the winds of war blew in 1914 the War Office knew that Territorial soldiers were under no obligation to fight overseas but knowing the 'call may come' a general appeal was put out to the Territorial battalions for volunteers for overseas service. The response was very positive, with many

Territorial battalions sending in returns of around 90 per cent volunteering 'to do their bit overseas.' A white metal badge bearing the legend 'Imperial Service' surmounted by a crown was issued to those who so volunteered before 30 September 1914, and was worn with great pride above the right pocket on the tunic. Very few Territorial units were to see action in the opening battles of the First World War such as Mons or the Marne. In fact many were tasked with the duties for which they were originally raised – guarding the homeland but as the war progressed and widened the men of the 1/4th and 1/5th Battalions were sent to see active service in Gallipoli and on to Egypt and the Middle East.

*One of the platoons of B Company, 4th Battalion, The Norfolk Regiment, Colchester 1914.*

## 1/4th Battalion T.F.

Mobilized at the Drill Hall on Chapel Field, Norwich, part of the Norfolk and Suffolk Brigade, East Anglian Division, the battalion officially became part of the 163rd Brigade, 54th Division in May 1915.

*Officers and men of 4th Battalion, The Norfolk Regiment at a roadside halt in Watford, shortly before their departure to Gallipoli, 1915.*

*The men of the 4ᵗʰ Battalion (Reserve) on parade before they were all issued with full uniforms, 1914.*

They landed at Suvla Bay, on 10 August 1915 and served throughout the Gallipoli Campaign. In December 1915 their division was sent to the Middle East; landing at Alexandria the battalion spent the rest of war in Egypt and Palestine and served with distinction with the 5ᵗʰ Battalion at the Second Battle of Gaza in April 1917.

### 2/4ᵗʰ (Reserve) Battalion T.F.

Formed at the Chapel Field Drill Hall, Norwich in August 1914 as a second line battalion, its purpose was to supply drafts for overseas units and continue recruiting for the battalion to enable it to undertake Home Defence. On the formation of the East Anglian Division TF it was the first to complete its establishment and moved to divisional headquarters at Peterborough in November 1914. Moved to Lowestoft in January 1915 they undertook the construction of defences for the port, provided personnel for naval searchlights and helped man the No. 2 Armoured Train. They remained on duty at locations along the Suffolk coast until November 1916 when re-named 11ᵗʰ Battalion, Norfolk Regiment T.F. In December 1916 the battalion was transferred to the 212ᵗʰ Brigade, 71ˢᵗ Division and moved to Aldershot command, stationed at Guildford. Moved to Colchester in March 1917 the category A and B1 men were transferred to overseas unit, and the unit was gradually wound down and finally disbanded by order of the Army Council in July 1917.

### 1/5ᵗʰ Battalion T.F.

Mobilized at their HQ in East Dereham the battalion officially became part of the 163ʳᵈ Brigade 54ᵗʰ Division in May 1915. They landed at Suvla Bay, Gallipoli on 10 August 1915. On 12 August 1915 the battalion was involved in an attack at Kuchuk Annafarta Ova. The battalion pushed as far as they

could but became fragmented and the farthest forward soldiers penetrated enemy lines. The enemy closed in and the battalion suffered terrible casualties of 22 officers and 350 men (figures according to the battalion War Diary). The King had a personal interest in the battalion, men from his estate at Sandringham were serving in the officer corps, among the NCOs and in the ranks, and his friend and Estate Agent, Frank Beck, was a Company Commander. At the time the casualties from the forward troops of the battalion were now behind enemy lines and, not knowing if the men were killed or taken prisoner, many families were simply notified that their relative was 'Missing'. The King pressed for

*Band of 5th Battalion, The Norfolk Regiment c1914.*

information but specifics, at the time, could not be given. Sir Ian Hamilton's despatch, worded with his flowery prose, describes 'a very mysterious thing' where 'the colonel, sixteen officers and 250 men, still kept pushing on, driving the enemy before them... Nothing more was ever seen or heard of any of them. They charged into a forest and were lost to sight or sound. Not one of them ever came back.' The bodies of the 5th Battalion soldiers who fell on that day were discovered by the Graves Registration Unit in September 1919, sadly most were beyond individual identification but the damage was done and the 'mystery' of the disappearing Norfolks had entered into military myth, much in the style of the 'Angel of Mons' and has been discussed in serious and scurrilous publications ever since. In December 1915 their division was sent to the Middle East; landing at Alexandria the battalion spent the rest of war in Egypt and Palestine and served with distinction with the 4th Battalion at the Second Battle of Gaza in April 1917.

Sgt. Theo Randall, 5th Battalion, The Norfolk Regiment.

Sgt Theo Randall, 5th Battalion, The Norfolk Regiment, a well known and popular a figure in his native town of Cromer, wrote home with his personal and vivid account of the action of 12 August 1915 which was published in the *Cromer and North Norfolk News* on 17 September 1915:

'*It was a queer sensation the first time we came under fire, which was the morning after we landed, and 10 days after we left England. We had got out into the open and were starting to dig ourselves in when, bang, whistle, thud and shrapnel was bursting over our heads and plastering the ground with bullets. I am sure a spectator would have roared with laughter, you never saw a party of men fall down with one accord so quickly. And their faces when they got up were studies in expressions. My sensations were a sort of empty feeling in the tummy and a curiosity as to where the next one was coming. We shifted back from there pretty quickly and got behind a hedge in a dyke where they couldn't spot us and our casualties were four men in the company. The next day the fun commenced at 4p.m. The Brigade had to make an advance across a plain along a front of about 1½ miles and push on as far as possible. Off we started in long lines, one in front of the other, and as soon as we got going the enemy's guns opened fire on us. It was simply awful. I rushed my platoon on as fast as possible to get out of the area that was being shelled but we kept losing men fast. Once I lay panting for breath in a ditch with about eight men, a shell got us properly* and five of the party were wounded. I felt the bullets hitting the ground all round me but none touched. We got up again and off, just out of the artillery zone, thank goodness, and we lay down for a breather behind a fence. As we lay there small parties kept coming up and I got those near me into something like a line and off we went once more, over very deeply ploughed land now, and horrible going.*

*Very few of the fellows could do more than stagger along and here the enemy opened fire with rifles and machine guns. The noise was frightful and it seemed a miracle how anyone could get along at all without being hit. Luckily, there was plenty of cover till I had about a dozen men with me and then made a rush as far as I could run or until I came to another ditch or hedge. Still onward we went and now we came to the remains of a village built of stones, which was held pretty strongly. Into it we went and here I fired my first shot and saw the first of the enemy. They scurried away as soon as we got anywhere near them, though they laid out many a good man as we advanced...*

*At last I got into a ditch running diagonally across the front, with about a dozen men, and there we got stuck. We could see none of our fellows on either side and from the sound of the firing we were being enfiladed from one side and bullets were coming from all directions. Up we popped and blazed away to our front as hard as we could, but it was no good. Down went three or four poor chaps and the remainder crouched flat on our stomachs in the ditch. At last we could stick it no longer, no reinforcements reached us and the enemy were in force about 20 yards in front of us. So back we had to crawl about 200 yards until we came to some of our fellows holding a long lane. Here we stuck for about half an hour under fairly decent cover and then we got news that a party of our fellows were holding a line 100 yards in front, so we collected about 50 men and rushed forward to give them a hand. We found one of our lieutenants holding a short line of hedge and trying to get in touch with other small parties on either side of him. We were uncertain as to whether we had any of our own men in front of us and as it was now dark we were in a somewhat peculiar position. After a short consultation the officers decided to retire to our line 100 yards in the rear. This we managed all right and held on there for five days till we were relieved. The advance lasted about 4½ hours and we went forward about 2½ miles in all.*

## 2/5th Battalion

Under the expansion scheme of the Territorial Force a Reserve Battalion of 5 Norfolk was raised in East Dereham, at the HQ of the 1/5th Battalion in October 1914 initially known as 5th (Reserve) Battalion, The Norfolk Regiment (T.F)

Although they had no uniforms, rifle or equipment, their zeal in drill, exercise and training were

'remarkable' and their fine, uniformed band under Bandmaster Dines was a great asset. But the uniform situation for the men became critical to the development of the unit. Sir Aylwin Fellows, the Chairman of the Norfolk Territorial Force Association visited the HQ and upon seeing for himself gave leave for the OC to buy boots and what uniform could be procured for the troops – and the association would pay the bills. The only khaki uniform and most of the greatcoats which could be procured were second hand and even with this in hand when the battalion was ordered to proceed to Peterborough on 5 December 1914 a number of men still had to march with their comrades wearing their civilian clothes, coats and caps.

*Uniforms at last! Distributing hats to men of 5th Battalion, The Norfolk Regiment (Reserves) outside 5th Battalion Headquarters on Quebec Street, East Dereham, 1914.*

The Battalion was quartered in Peterborough until May 1915 when it proceeded to Cambridge and marched to Bury St Edmunds in late July 1915 and after five days there moved to camp at Thetford. In August 1915 the Battalion moved to undertake trench construction for the defence of London scheme at Brentwood in Essex. While in Brentwood many of the junior officers left the 2/5th to join the active service battalions shortly before they departed for Gallipoli. By winter the remainder of 2/5th had returned to Bury and were eventually absorbed into 4th (Reserve) Battalion.

## 3/4th and 3/5th Battalions T.F.

Formed in early 1915 at Norwich and East Dereham respectively. Both battalions were quartered in their 'Home' depot city and town until August 1915 when they were moved to Windsor Great Park. In the first week of October 1915 they moved again to Halton Camp near Tring in Hertfordshire and from there both battalions sent out many drafts to the 1/4th and 1/5th Battalions in the Middle East.

In February 1916 the battalions were formally designated 4th and 5th (Reserve) Battalions. On 1st September 1916 the 4th Battalion absorbed the 5th and joined East Anglian Reserve Brigade. By November 1917 the battalion was at Crowborough, Sussex and saw out the war in Hastings.

## 1/6th Battalion (Cyclists) T.F.

Attached to 1st Mounted Division, the battalion remained in UK on Home Defence duties along Norfolk Coast. During 1915 the entire establishment of the 1/6th Battalion consisted entirely of 'A1' foreign service men who had volunteered to go abroad as military cyclists, infantry, pioneers or in any other capacity but they were officially informed that the coastal duties entrusted to them were too important for them to be spared – quite a blow to these men filled with patriotic fervour. Towards the end of 1915, however, the 1/6th were relieved of the greater part of their coastal defence duties by a mobile brigade of the Royal Naval Air Service the battalion retired to become an inland mobile reserve training in drill and trench warfare. In early 1916 the 1/6th Battalion was ordered to furnish a platoon to take over from the London Cyclists at Kessingland, Suffolk. On relief, this platoon (comprising men recruited in Thetford), under the command of a young Brandon Officer, 22 year old Lieut. Frank Fison, rode back from Kessingland to North Walsham, a distance of some fifty miles and in the teeth of a bitter north-easterly snowstorm and over roads in shocking condition. The journey was accom-

*Robert Hilliard, the seven-year-old mascot of 2/5th Battalion, The Norfolk Regiment while they were billeted at Peterborough 1914-15.*

*Officers and men of a platoon of the 6th Battalion, The Norfolk Regiment (Cyclists) gather for a photograph around a senior coastguard who shared his seafront premises with them at Cromer 1914.*

plished at a uniform pace of seven mile an hour and with only one casualty. The feat was mentioned in the Regimental History concluding with the comment 'it speaks volumes for the condition and state of efficiency that battalion had attained as military cyclists'. Sadly, the gallant leader of this expedition, Lieut. Fison was later killed in action on the Western Front on 19 July 1916 while serving with The Gloucestershire Regiment.

By 1916 the need for men at the Front far outweighed the need for Home Front duties and men of all the cyclist battalions supplied 'an excellent stamp of men for service with the Regular and New Armies in the field' but it would always be a regret expressed by many veterans of the Battalion that they were never allowed to serve abroad together as a unit. By the time of the 'Big Push' of July 1916 practically the whole of the remainder of the original 1/6th had been drafted to overseas units. For those left in the 1/6th, with many new recruits and conscripts, they did eventually go overseas – to Ireland, on a stinking cattle boat where every man was sick from the stench alone. While undertaking these peacekeeping duties the battalion was stationed at a number of locations including Tralee, Castle Mayo and Randalstown.

## 2/6th *Battalion (Cyclists) T.F.*

On 30 September 1914 Lt-Col. Prior wrote to the *Eastern Daily Press* stating the Battalion, although previously having a waiting list for membership, due to 90 per cent of the Battalion signing up for overseas service there was an opportunity for men aged between 17 and 19 years to join both the first and a new reserve battalion. By 20 October 1914 it was proudly announced that the reserve battalion was now full and thus the 2/6th (Cyclist) Battalion was embodied and a new sobriquet born to a battalion of the regiment the 'Half Crown Holyboys' because of the 2/6 regimental designation and the time honoured nick-name of The Norfolk Regiment and 9th Foot – 'The Holy Boys'. After initial training at North Walsham the 2/6th was marched down to Brandon in Suffolk where they expected to be kitted out with full uniform and equipment and their training completed. This was not to be; in a rapid turn-around the War Office ordered the men of the 2/6th initially to Hornsea and then to Bridlington on the Yorkshire coast.

Telegrams were despatched to the Territorial Association in Norwich and War Office explaining the uniform and equipment crisis and the Commanding Officer was soon authorised to purchase additional clothing. Some four hundred rifles and bayonets arrived first. Uniforms did eventually arrive, but only piecemeal – a box of caps, a few tunics, a few trousers and puttees. Kit was a hotch-potch of Victorian Slade Wallace and Valise Pattern equipment, often a belt and only one pouch for ammunition and, if you were lucky enough to be issued a hat a collar badge or even a shoulder title, this would have to suffice for the time being in place of a cap badge.

The 2/6th supplied numerous cadres of men and officers to active service battalions of The Norfolk Regiment and other regiments, but the battalion itself remained in Yorkshire with brief sojourns in Filey and Hunmanby until its final return to Bridlington where it disbanded in 1918.

*Signals Section, 2/6th Battalion, The Norfolk Regiment (Cyclists) T.F., Bridlington 1915.*

*Motorcycle section 2/6th Battalion, The Norfolk Regiment (Cyclists) T.F., 1914.*

### 3/6<sup>th</sup> *Battalion (Cyclists) T.F.*

Raised at Norwich in May 1915 this battalion acted as a draft-finding unit with Home Defence Duties. It had one detachment at Worstead commanded by Lt-Col. Dewing where they had a bicycle riding school. This battalion was disbanded in March 1916.

### 7<sup>th</sup> *(Service) Battalion*

K1. Raised in Norwich from August 1914. Raising the Kitchener units was carried out at speed and it was imperative that the volunteers were

*Men of 2/6<sup>th</sup> Norfolk Regiment (Cyclists) T.F. in and around a Zeppelin bomb crater at Bridlington, 1915.*

formed into units as soon as possible and thus the men from Norfolk were despatched to Shorncliffe where the battalion was formally constituted using men from London, Lancashire and elsewhere; only about half the battalion were Norfolk men. Attached to 35<sup>th</sup> Brigade, 12<sup>th</sup> Eastern Division the battalion landed at Boulogne 31 May 1915 and joined the front line on July 4 1915 at Ploegsteert Wood. The first major action for 7<sup>th</sup> Norfolk came on 13 October from their line in front of the quarries at St Elie. The attack was covered by a barrage but the smoke that was to give them cover stopped before the attack and the men were exposed and many men were instantly cut down by the enfilading enemy machine gun fire. Reinforcements were impossible to send as they were mown down in the first twenty yards. After this action 71 officers and men lay dead, two hundred were wounded and 160 missing.

In March 1916 the battalion saw action at Hohenzollern Redoubt. On 1 July the battalion marched to Hennencourt Wood and entered reserve lines behind the embankment of the Albert–Arras railway. During the attack on Ovilliers the battalion was in reserve but suffered badly from heavy shelling. In the front line of the Ovilliers sector from 7 August they fought in the attack on Skyline Trench on 12 August where they not only established and held strong points, in each of which one Lewis gun, one machine gun and forty men were left, but also took a number of prisoners. In the attack on Bayonet and Scabbard Trench on 12 October 1916 the battalion ran into heavy enemy machine gun fire from both flanks, the advance continued but before their objective trench was reached the men of the battalion encountered uncut wire entanglements. After this action just eight officers and 350 men of the battalion were left in the trenches.

*16 Platoon, D Company, 7<sup>th</sup> (Service) Battalion, The Norfolk Regiment, Shorn-cliffe, November 1914.*

In April 1917, 7<sup>th</sup> Norfolk were on the Arras Front in the successful attack on Feuchy Chapel redoubt. On the night of 2–3 May the battalion repulsed a heavy attack upon them in 'Tool', 'Hook'

and 'Pick' trenches. Part of Pick Avenue communication trench was penetrated by the enemy and occupied before the men of 7th Norfolk successfully counter-attacked. It was soon clear the attack had been far more than a raid, the Germans had intended to occupy the trench, in fact the officers had even set up a mess table including a bottle of champagne – which was consumed with due appreciation by the men of 7th Norfolk. In November 1917 the battalion fought at Cambrai. In this confused and bloody battle over thirty officers and men were killed, almost a hundred wounded and 204 recorded as 'missing.' The final year of the war saw 7th Norfolk deployed on the right of the divisional front on the Lys where they countered the German spring offensive. In August 1918 the battalion was at the front of the autumn offensive starting at Treux on the lower Ancre; attacking, repulsing and counter-attacking. In that one month the battalion advanced eleven miles, took 13 enemy machine guns, three trench mortars, one 'granatenwerfer' and sixty prisoners. Over fifty officer and men had been killed and 313 wounded or gassed. In September the battalion was reorganised at Mountauban and fought its last battle on the Somme at Nurla, taking trenches near Epéhy and finally occupying a sunken road near the Quéant-Drocourt line on 10 October. When the armistice came they were far in the rear of the British front at Landas.

## 8th (Service) Battalion

K2. Raised at Norwich from September 1914. In its early days it acquired the nick-name of the Businessman's Battalion due to the large number of shopkeepers and workers from the city and county which made up its number. Formally organised and trained, despite initial chronic shortages of uniform and equipment, at Shorncliffe, later the battalion trained at Colchester and on Salisbury Plain before setting off to France from Folkestone on 25 July 1915, part of 53rd Brigade, 18th (Eastern) Division, entering forward lines upon relieving the 8th Suffolk trenches near the Mametz-Carnoy Road. Remaining in the neighbourhood of Albert into 1916 their baptism of fire was to come on 1 July 1916, the First Day of the Somme. The battalion's assembly trenches were just north of Carnoy, their objective, the enemy trenches south-west of Montauban. 8th Norfolk

*A Platoon of 8th (Service) Battalion, The Norfolk Regiment 'somewhere in Codford' during their training on Salisbury Plain, 1915.*

was one of the few battalions to take its objective on the day, but it had cost them 4 Officers and 104 other ranks killed on this day and over two hundred wounded. On 19 July the battalion was part of a counter attack on Delville Wood. Advancing from the south-western corner of the wood it was hard fighting but the enemy positions were taken, with no little thanks to 2nd Lieut Gundry White and his team of bombers. A brave day, but at the cost of almost 300 killed or wounded. Transferring to the Armentieres sector on 25 September the battalion moved to Wood Post, Authuille Wood in Brigade support for operations at Thiepval. The battle had been costly and the men of 'B' company were left at Crucifix Corner to carry the dead for burial. On 4 October 1916 the battalion was in the successful attack on the Schwaben redoubt. On October 21 the Battalion went in again with the attack on Regina Trench and held their gains until relief on 23 October. From 5–8 November 8th Norfolk was at Warloy where General Maxse, commander of the 18th Division presented decorations and medals for the battalion's actions on the Somme viz; one DSO, six MCs, six DCMs, thirty one MMs and 37 parchment certificates.

The next action for 8th Norfolk was on 17 February 1917 near Boom Ravine, on the left bank of the Ancre, an attack not only made challenging by the enemy shell fire but the slippery-sloped terrain

*Soldiers from 8th (Service) Battalion resting after having to fall out through sore feet during training at Hollesley, Suffolk.*

also led to sprained ankles and accidents. The battalion was back in the front line on 10 March for the attack on Grenvilliers trench and Irles, a little east of Poelcappelle. In truth, the Germans had been planning to evacuate Irles but the attackers chased them out. That achieved, the next objective was to capture Grenvilliers trench and push out certain strong points. It was no mean feat, but the battalion achieved the objective taking many prisoners and sixteen machine guns, with minimal casualties (34 all ranks) for such an action.

Poelcappelle was to prove to be the last major action of 8th Norfolk who held the line at there until they quit the forward trenches in December 1918. In January 1918, 8th Norfolk were in brigade reserve near Elverdinghe and it was here they learned the battalion was to be disbanded. Officers and men were distributed to the Regiments other service battalions, others went to reinforcement camps and entrenching battalions; to quote the Battalion war diary of 20 February 1918, 'The 8th Service Battalion The Norfolk Regiment ceased to exist from today.'

---

### KITCHENER'S ARMY POEM – IN FRANCE

*Composed by Pte B. Everett (of Castle Acre) and the men of the*
*Machine Gun Section, 9th Battalion, The Norfolk Regiment 1915*

Yes we have our Rum and Limejuice
And we get our Bully Beef
And for concrete biscuits
They break our bally teeth

We get no eggs for breakfast
But the Germans send the shells
And we dive into our dug-outs
And get laughed at by our pals

Just a tiny piece of bacon
Well! For short we call it ham
You are fighting! British soldiers
On a one pound tin of jam

Sometimes we get some ruty
Well you civvies call it bread
It isn't as light as feathers
And it isn't exactly lead

But we get it down us somehow
For we never send it back
Though its smothered with the whiskers
That get rubbed off the sack

The dirt blows in our dixies
There's dust upon our mits
So can you really wonder
Why soldiers are full of grit

But I'm not going to grumble
Because I am feeling well and fit
And I've one great consolation
That I'm here to do my bit

I've done a bit in Belgium
I've done a bit in France
And now my old Machine Gun
Is leading the Germans a dance.

*'At the Front' Lieut-Colonel Bernard Henry Leathes Prior (centre) and the band of the 9th (Service) Battalion, The Norfolk Regiment*

## 9th (Service) Battalion

K3. Raised at Norwich September 1914, sent to Shoreham and later moved to Blackdown Camp near Aldershot. Reviewed by Lord Kitchener in August, they proceeded to France on the 30th of that same month as part of 71st Brigade, 24th Division. Formed for the attack on Lonely Tree Hill, west of Hullach on 26 September, they were not engaged but received their baptism of fire late on that day when the enemy rained rifle fire on the trenches occupied by 9th Norfolk. Over 200 officers were killed or wounded. Transferred with their Brigade to 6th Division in October the battalion was reinforced and ready for action again. On 2 August 1916 the battalion entrained for the Somme front and saw its first major action of the year after taking up lines on the Ginchy-Leuze Wood Road for an attack on The Quadrilateral on 15 September. As 9th Norfolk advanced up the slippery slope (the barrage had stopped short leaving a gap of about 200 yards in front of the feature, to allow the advance of the tanks) they encountered uncut wire that stopped their progress, forcing them to retire to trenches which they held until relieved at midnight. The failed attack caused 431 casualties to the battalion.

By the time Lieut-Col Leathes Prior took over command of the battalion, after leaving 6th (Cyclist) Battalion in October 1916, he found it full of fresh drafts with only a small percentage of experienced officers and men left, but he was a great leader and one trusted and respected by his men. On 18 October 9th Norfolk attacked Mild trench. Their attack was delayed by the difficulties experienced by the men mounting greasy parapets and as a consequent much of the protection of the British barrage was lost and the battalion suffered an undue share of the German barrage. The men, however, managed to gain positions and consolidated them. Colonel Prior went forward to the position: 'There the garrison holding the trench, despite a good many casualties, were in the best of spirits. They had been heavily shelled, sniped at, and machine gunned, and withstood at least once counter attack but they had had a success, they had taken the trench, and before I left I felt quite satisfied that they would die to a man rather than lose it.' The first half of 1917 was spent, as the Regimental History describes it 'taking the usual turns of front line, support and reserve, and undergoing the usual enemy shelling in varying degrees.' The battalion was also exposed to gas attacks and men suffered from the constant wet, to the degree that trench foot became prevalent. They were not involved in major attacks but good officers and men were still being killed and wounded in minor actions, patrols, shell fire and picked off by sniper bullets.

On 20 November the battalion acquitted themselves well at the Battle of Cambrai where the battalion's attack culminated with the capture of Ribécourt. March 1918 saw 9th Norfolk face the German spring offensive, serving in front line trenches on the Ypres salient at Polybecke with head-quarters in what was left of Polygon Wood. They marched again in September and joined the final Allied offensive at St Omer and fought on to Le Cateau. On 11 November news of the Armistice was received by the battalion at Bohain. On 14 November, 9th Norfolk began its march to the Rhine and was the only battalion of the Regiment to enter German territory and form part of the Army of Occupation.

### 10th (Service) Battalion

Formed at Walton-on-the-Naze in October 1914 as a Service battalion, part of K4 based at Felixtowe and Colchester. In March 1915 it became a Reserve battalion to find drafts for the 7th, 8th and 9th (Service) Battalions. On 1 September 1916 it became 25th Battalion of 6th Reserve Brigade of Training Reserve.

### 11th Battalion T.F

Raised at Lowestoft in 1915 with Home Service personnel of Territorial Force Battalions. Based at Guildford and Colchester it was disbanded 20 December 1917. (Also see 2/4th Battalion).

### 12th (Norfolk Yeomanry) Battalion

The Norfolk Yeomanry had served in its own right as a unit in Gallipoli and Palestine within the 1st Eastern Mounted division. Men of the Norfolk Yeomanry have the distinction to be the last to leave land during the Gallipoli evacuation. The 12th (Norfolk Yeomanry) Battalion of The Norfolk Regiment was formed from the remaining men of the Yeomanry in Egypt on 11 February 1917. Joining 230th Brigade, 74th Division the battalion served with distinction in the battles of Gaza, Beersheba, Sheria and on the advance of their Division to Jerusalem. Sent to reinforce the Western Front, the battalion embarked at Alexandria on 1 May 1918 for Marseilles, landing there on 7 May, joining 94th Brigade, 31st Division and being deployed to Nieppe Forest. On 5 July the battalion CO Colonel Morse was wounded to the degree he did not return to the battalion before the end of the war.

The battalion fought through Nieppe Forest and on to Vieux Berquin and took part in further minor operations such as the attack they pressed home, despite considerable opposition, at Labis Farm on 19 August, killing many enemy and taking sixty prisoners to boot. Casualties were some of the heaviest experienced by the battalion – eight officers and 38 other ranks killed and over a hundred wounded, such was the cost of 'minor' operations.

On 31 October 1918, 12th Norfolk were covering the final advance in the Ploegsteert sector by patrolling the Lys and were involved in one of the last attacks on the north of the Scheldt towards Audenarde. After the end of October the battalion had no more fighting. On 10 November the battalion moved to Avelghem on the Schelt and was there when the Armistice was announced.

*A Squadron, The King's Own Royal Regiment, Norfolk Yeomanry, shortly before departure for Gallipoli 1915.*

### 1st Garrison Battalion

Formed at Seaford in Sept 1915 this battalion was stationed in India. Doing garrison duty in Indian stations from December 1915 until 1920 when the battalion finally returned to England and was disbanded.

## VC Heroes

### CSM HARRY DANIELS VC, MC

The county of Norfolk's first recipient of the VC during the First World War was CSM Harry Daniels, 2nd Battalion, The Rifle Brigade. In every way he is the 'Boy's Own' story book hero. He was born on Market Street, Wymondham, on 13 December 1884, the thirteenth child of a local baker. Tragically both his parents died while he was still a young boy. Put in the Norwich Boy's Home on St Faith's Lane had had a number of adventures running away and living in the countryside, and on one occasion he had even been out on a fishing trawler. He tried to join the army under age on several occasions until he just passed for old enough to be a boy soldier and enlisted into The Rifle Brigade. Always a fit, keen and daring man he shone at sports and gymnastics and spent time on a tour of duty in India before the war. He steadily rose up the ranks, by 12 March 1915 Harry was a Company Sergeant Major in the third day of the ill-fated offensive at the Battle of Neuve Chappelle, France. 'A' and 'B' Companies had been virtually annihilated. Just before 5.00pm 'C' and 'D' received the order 'Attack in fifteen minutes'. He could see his company faced a mass of wire entanglements that remained uncut just 15 yards from the trench, the men would get caught on this and with intense machine gun fire from the enemy it was nothing short of suicide. Calling to his pal Cpl Cecil Reginald 'Tom' Noble to 'Get some nippers' they both went over the top into a hail of bullets. They were both wounded almost imme-

*VC Hero CSM Harry Daniels stands to greet the crowds that lined the streets during his return to Norwich 1915.*

diately but they kept cutting until their job was done when 'Tom' took a fatal bullet in the chest. Harry, although badly wounded, managed to crawl back. For their gallant actions they were both awarded the Victoria Cross. Harry returned to Norwich to a hero's welcome, the streets were lined with cheering well-wishers and he was presented with the Freedom of the City, but did not forget to go and visit his old Boy's Home. 'Dan VC' was commissioned a few weeks later and he went on to be decorated again with the Military Cross for another action. After a distinguished military career, and an appearance on the British team at the 1920 Olympics, he retired as a Lieut-Colonel in 1942 and joined 'civvy street' as a manager at the Leeds Opera House. He died in Leeds on 13 December 1953, his last request being that his ashes should be scattered on Aldershot cricket pitch.

### SERGEANT HARRY CATOR VC, MM, CdeG

Sergeant Cator was Norfolk's most decorated soldier. Born on 24 January 1884 the son of a railway worker at Drayton, he was educated at Drayton School. He married on 2 September 1914 and enlisted the following day. He proceeded to France with 7th Battalion, East Surrey Regiment on 23 June 1915. He was given his first award, The Military Medal for Gallantry in the Field, in 1916 during the Battle of the Somme for helping to rescue thirty-six men who had become tangled in enemy barbed wire in no-man's-land he was also decorated with the Croix de Guerre avec Palme (France).

*Sergeant Harry Cator VC, MM, CdeG*

Harry's VC was awarded for action at Hangest Trench during the Battle of Arras. His citation states the award was: 'For most conspicuous bravery and devotion to duty. Whilst consolidating the first line captured system his platoon suffered severe casualties from hostile machine-gun and rifle fire. In full view of the enemy and under heavy fire Sergeant Cator, with one man, advanced to cross the open to attack the hostile machine gun. The man accompanying him was killed after going a short distance, but Sergeant Cator continued on and picking up a Lewis gun and some drums on his way succeeded in reaching the northern end of the hostile trench. Meanwhile, one of our bombing parties was seen to be held up by a machine gun. Sergeant Cator took up a position from which he sighted this gun and killed the entire team and the officer whose papers he brought in. He continued to hold that end of the trench with the Lewis gun and with such effect that the bombing squad was enabled to work along, the result being that one hundred prisoners and five machine guns were captured.' Three days later he was severely wounded by a bursting shell which shattered his jaw. He recovered from his wounds and was presented with his VC personally by HM King George V at Buckingham Palace on 21 July 1917.

After the war Harry worked for a time as a postman in Norwich and then with the Unemployment Assistance Board. During the Second World War he joined up again and became a Captain Quartermaster with 6th Battalion Norfolk Home Guard and later the Commandant of a prisoner-of-war camp in Cranwich. He passed away at the Norfolk & Norwich Hospital at the age of 72 on 7 April 1966 and is buried in Sprowston Cemetery, near Norwich.

*Cpl. Sidney James Day VC*

## PTE SIDNEY JAMES DAY VC

Sidney Day was born in Norwich on 3 July 1891 at 4 St Ann's Lane, St Julian, Norwich, this was one of the 'hard up' streets of Norwich, many good honest hard working folk lived here and these tenements were all many could afford. The property was demolished in the city slum clearances of the 1930s. Sidney's father, William, was a storekeeper for a local brewery and money was tight, with a number of other children's mouths to feed. There were four sisters called Ethel, Rosa, Edith, Alice and one brother, Harry. Three other siblings died when they were very young. Sidney was educated at St Mark's School, Lakenham and worked as a butcher when he left school. Day was seriously wounded in four places during the Battle of the Somme and was invalided back to England where he spent several months in hospital near his home in Norwich. When he was discharged, he returned to France as a Corporal serving with 11th Battalion, The Suffolk Regiment. He won his VC while in the line at Priel Wood, Malakoff Farm, east of Hargicourt, France on 26 August 1917. His citation published in the *London Gazette* 17 October 1917 reads:

> *'No. 15092 Cpl. Sidney James Day, Suffolk Regiment (Norwich). For most conspicuous bravery. Cpl. Day was in command of a bombing section detailed to clear a maze of trenches still held by the enemy. This he did, killing two machine gunners and taking four prisoners. On reaching a point where the trench had been levelled he went alone and bombed his way through to the left in order to gain touch with the neighbouring troops. Immediately on his return to his section a stick-bomb fell into the trench occupied by two officers (one badly wounded) and three other ranks. Cpl. Day seized the bomb and threw it over the trench, where it immediately exploded. This prompt action saved the lives of those in the trench. He afterwards completed the clearing of the trench and established himself in an advanced position, remaining for sixty-six hours at his post, which came under intense hostile shell, grenade, and rifle fire. Throughout the whole operations his conduct was an inspiration to all.'*

Day also returned to a hero's welcome in Norwich but on his return to France was wounded and taken prisoner. After the war and back on 'civvy street' Sidney Day did a variety of jobs. In the 1930s he ran his own tea rooms at Landport in East Sussex. The building was destroyed by bombing in 1941. Day then became a messenger in Portsmouth Dockyard but had to retire in 1948 after developing TB. Sidney Day died on 17 July 1959 and is buried in Milton Cemetery, Portsmouth.

## LIEUTENANT-COLONEL JOHN SHERWOOD-KELLY VC, CMG, DSO

*Lieutenant-Colonel John Sherwood-Kelly VC, CMG, DSO*

The Norfolk Regiment obtained its only Victoria Cross in The Great War at the Battle of Cambrai when John Sherwood-Kelly (37) an Acting Lieutenant-Colonel of The Norfolk Regiment, was on detachment Commanding 1st Battalion, Royal Inniskilling Fusiliers. On 20 November 1917 at Marcoing, when a party of men were held upon the near side of a canal by heavy rifle fire, Lieutenant Colonel Sherwood-Kelly at once ordered covering fire, personally led his leading company across the canal and then reconnoitred, under heavy fire, the high ground held by the enemy. He took a Lewis gun team, forced his way through obstacles and covered the advance of his battalion, enabling them to capture the position. Later he led a charge against some pits from which heavy fire was coming, capturing five machine-guns and 46 prisoners.

## LIEUTENANT GORDON MURIEL FLOWERDEW VC

*Lieutenent Gordon Muriel Flowerdew VC*

Gordon Flowerdew was born to Arthur and Hannah Flowerdew at Billingford Hall, near Scole in the Waveney valley, on 2 January 1885. After attending Framlingham College, at the age of seventeen, he emigrated to Canada and worked as a cowboy and later took up farming. He joined Lord Strathcona's Horse, a cavalry regiment, on the outbreak of the war and rapidly gained his commission and was soon serving in France with the Canadian Expeditionary Force.

On March 1918, an attack was planned for French troops to take the town of Moreuil to the south of a wood. While three mounted squadrons of the Royal Canadian Dragoons were to lead the initial attack, which was then to be followed up by men from Lord Strathcona's Horse, their object was to take an adjacent wood. The Canadian Brigade was to attack in three separate but converging thrusts. Two squadrons of Lord Strathcona's Horse were to attack the wood on foot, with 'C' Squadron, commanded by Lieutenant Flowerdew to make a mounted attack, one of the last of its kind to be staged on the Western Front.

They attacking force encountered strong resistance and there was a great deal of hand-to-hand fighting, but by late morning the northern section of the wood had been captured by the Canadians. It was at this moment that Lieutenant Flowerdew, his sword raised, led his men to almost certain death in a suicidal attack on two lines of the enemy, each with about sixty men and three machine-guns.

The *London Gazette* of 24 April 1918 published the citation that reveals what happed next:

*'For most conspicuous bravery and dash (NE of Bois de Moreuil, France) when in command of a squadron detailed for special service of a very important nature. On reaching the first objective, Lieutenant Flowerdew saw two lines of the enemy, each about sixty strong, with machine guns in the centre and flanks, one line being about two hundred yards behind the other.*

*Realising the critical nature of the operation and how much depended upon it, Lieutenant Flowerdew ordered a troop under Lieutenant Harvey VC, to dismount and carry out a special movement while he led the remaining three troops to the charge. The squadron (less one troop) passed over both lines, killing many of the enemy with the sword, and wheeling about galloped at them again.*

*Although the squadron had then lost about 70 per cent of its numbers, killed and wounded, from rifle and machine gun fire directed on it from the front and both flanks, the enemy broke and retired. The survivors of the squadron then established themselves in a position where they were joined, after much hand-to-hand fighting, by Lieutenant Harvey's party. Lieutenant Flowerdew was dangerously wounded through both thighs during the operation but continued to cheer on his men. There can be no doubt that this officer's great valour was the prime factor in the capture of the position.'*

He is buried in Namps-au-Val British Cemetery, Department of the Somme, France. Flowerdew's gallantry was immortalised further by Sir Alfred Munnings in his painting the 'Charge of the Canadian Horsemen'.

## CORPORAL ARTHUR HENRY CROSS VC MM

*Cpl Arthur Henry Cross VC, MM*

Born on 13 December 1884 at Shipdham, one of five children. When he was fifteen he moved to London, married at 17 and was a father by 19. He enlisted in the 21st Battalion (First Surrey Rifles), The London Regiment on 30 May 1916 and transferred to the Machine Gun Corps in 1917.

Promoted to Lance Corporal in the 40th Battalion, Machine Gun Corps, on 25 March 1918 at Ervillers, France he volunteered to make a reconnaissance of the position of two machine-guns which had been captured by the enemy. With the agreement of his sergeant he crept back alone with only a service revolver to what had been his section's trench that was now occupied by the enemy. He surprised seven soldiers who responded by throwing down their rifles. He then marched them carrying the machine guns complete with the tripods and ammunition to the British lines. He then handed over the prisoners and collected teams for his guns which he brought into action immediately, annihilating a very heavy attack by the enemy.

The following June he was awarded the Military Medal for another act of bravery. He later returned to visit Shipdham where more recently a road was named in his honour. For the making of the film 'Carrington V.C.' (1955) starring David Niven the producers felt it would be more realistic if Niven were wearing a real VC, and put out an appeal in newspapers, this was answered by Arthur Cross who brought his medal personally to the location. Cross died on 26 November 1965 and is buried at Streatham Vale Cemetery, London beside his second wife, Minnie and their children Terence and Mary, who were killed during the London blitz in 1941.

## L/CPL ERNEST SEAMAN VC, MM

Ernest 'Ernie' Seaman was born near Norwich in 1893 and grew up at Scole. When serving with 2nd Battalion, The Royal Inniskilling Fusiliers at Terhand, Belgium on 29 September 1918 the right flank of his company were being held up by enemy machine-guns. L/Cpl. Seaman went forward under heavy fire with his Lewis gun and engaged the position single-handed, capturing two machine-guns killing one officer and two men and capturing twelve prisoners. Later in the day he again rushed another enemy machine-gun post, capturing the gun under very heavy fire. Ernie was killed immediately afterwards, but it was due to his gallant conduct that his company was able to push forward to its objective. Ernie has no known grave but he is commemorated at Tyne Cot Memorial, Belgium.

## EDITH CAVELL – A Heroine in a League of her Own

*L/Cpl Ernest Seaman VC, MM.* Image courtesy of Norfolk County Council Library and Information Service

Britain's greatest heroine of the war was, Edith Louisa Cavell (1865-1915). Born at Swardeston in Norfolk at school she showed an aptitude for French and found her first employment as a governess in Brussels. Returning to England in 1895 to nurse her father she made the decision to make nursing her career. Accepted to become Assistant Nurse, Class II at the Fountains Fever Hospital in Lower Tooting to obtain her general hospital training, Edith progressed to the London Hospital as a probationer in 1896. The following year a typhoid epidemic occurred in Maidstone and Edith was one of six London Hospital nurses seconded to help; out of the 1,847 people who contracted the disease, only 132 died. Edith received the Maidstone Typhoid Medal for her work here; it was the only medal she was ever to receive from her country. Edith spent a number of years in private nursing but found her strongest calling was to those in dire need, such as those suffering from disease or among the sick and poor in London and Manchester. In 1907 she returned to Brussels and was soon appointed Matron of the École Belge d' Infirmières Diplômées – a new training school for nurses, often simply known as the Clinique. Although often described as stern and aloof of by some of her young trainees, Edith was a natural teacher and gave the girls the very finest training and instilled great humane values in her aspiring nurses.

When war was declared Edith was visiting friends and family in England and, even though the Germans were on the border of Belgium, she was determined to return to Brussels. The Clinique became a Red Cross Hospital. Edith impressed on the nurses that their first duty was to care for the wounded irrespective of nationality. She sent many of her nurses home but Edith, her chief assistant Elisabeth Wilkins, Sister Millicent White and a handful of other chose to remain, even after Brussels fell. Then, without discrimination they tended German soldiers as well as Belgians.

As the British retreated from Mons and the French were driven back, many from both armies ended up being stranded. In the Autumn of 1914, two bedraggled and wounded British soldiers, Colonel Dudley Boger and Sergeant Fred Meachin of 1st Battalion, The Cheshire Regiment found their way to the training school and were sheltered there for two weeks. More followed and soon an escape route to neutral territory in Holland was established. Her motives were simple; the protection, concealment and the smuggling away of hunted men was as much a humanitarian act as the tending of the sick and wounded. By the end of February 1915 an advanced escape route was established in conjunction with the Belgian underground, masterminded by the Prince and Princess de Croy. Guides were organised and about 200 allied soldiers were helped to escape. All of those involved knew the risk they were taking, that they could face a firing squad for harbouring allied soldiers. The secret escape organisation lasted for almost a year, until a Belgian collaborator betrayed some members of the Belgian underground escape group. Edith was arrested on 5 August 1915, interrogated and imprisoned, mostly in solitary confinement, there to await trial.

On 7 October 1915 thirty-five members of the escape group were tried. The proceedings were conducted in German and translated into French. Edith wore her civilian clothes and gave her evidence in French. On Monday 11 October she learnt that the sentence of death had been passed on her (and four others) for 'conducting soldiers to the Enemy'.

The trial and particularly the sentence passed upon Edith had drawn international concern; diplomats discussed whether or not to intervene. Hugh Gibson, First Secretary of the American Legation at Brussels, made clear to the German government that executing Cavell would further harm their nation's already damaged reputation, but no reprieve was granted; her execution was set for 12 October 1915 at The Tir Nationale (National Rifle Range). The night before her execution she was attended by Chaplain, Stirling Gahan. His account recalls Edith wished all her friends to know that she willingly gave her life for her country and said: 'I have seen death so often that it is not fearful or strange to me, and this I would say, standing as I do in view of God and Eternity. I realise patriotism is not enough. I must have no hatred or bitterness against anyone.'

Edith Cavell faced the firing squad with unflinching dignity and was buried at the range. There was international outcry to the 'Murder' of 'Nurse' Cavell (a forty-nine year old Matron clearly did not have the same media appeal as the younger and pretty sounding 'Nurse'). The propaganda

*Patriotic' 'In Memoriam' postcard sold all over Britain in memory of Edith Cavell: Christian, Patriot and Martyr.*

*Nurse Cavell's coffin, removed from the gun carriage and taken onto the shoulders of NCOs, a number of whom she had helped to escape, in front of the Erpingham Gate at Norwich Cathedral, 15 May 1919.*

machine went into full swing producing posters, papers, magazines, postcards, in memoriam cards and all sorts of paper souvenirs, some showing Edith's portrait but far more contained artists impressions of the execution depicting an angelic nurse in full uniform prostrate on the floor, firing squad in background, with a hulking German looming above her with pistol, still smoking from the *coup de grace*, in his hand.

After the Armistice Edith's body was exhumed and returned to England to be given a full honours funeral. The Belgian Army guarded the coffin across Flanders to Ostend, where it was handed over to the Royal Navy. The destroyer *Rowena* carried it across the sea and Royal Navy ratings bore it ashore at Dover. In London the coffin was drawn on a gun carriage to Westminster Abbey and then taken by train to Norwich where Edith Cavell, Christian, Patriot and Martyr was laid to rest in the soil of the county she born into, knew and loved so well at Life's Green outside Norwich Cathedral on 15 May 1919.

## Prisoners of War

In closing this chapter of those who served 'For King and Country' it is worthwhile remembering those who are often forgotten in history books – our boys who were taken prisoner of war. Treatment of our men in German hands was variable, in some camps they were treated well and the worst they had to deal with was the monotony and frustration caused by imprisonment. In some camps the men were allowed to have gardens, concert parties, pets and sports, many were used for manual labouring jobs. But there were also some horror stories such as those related by Pte L. Lawn of the R.A.M.C., who arrived back home at Wrenningham in September 1915 after ten months as a prisoner of war at Sennelager Camp, near Paderborn in Northern Germany. This his own account of his experiences, published in the *Eastern Daily Press* on 1 October 1915:

> 'I was taken prisoner by the Germans in the early stages of the war after being hard at it at Mons. I was captured in hospital with 140 more wounded at Landrecies, in the north of France. We were all thoroughly searched and everything taken from us. Some of our captors could speak good English and told us in half an hour's time we should be shot and I wish many a time after I got to Germany that they had carried it out. We were kept there three days and then were taken back to Mons. We were marched around the town three times just to dishearten the Belgians but it was a good turn they did us as the Belgians gave us food and tobacco. Next day we were put on the train, 'English Swine' was chalked on all the trucks we were put in. Three nights and two days we were in the train and they would not even give us a drop of water from one station to another. It was telegraphed that we were coming and the stations were packed with people who stoned us, kicked us and spat in our faces. I was very glad when we were taken out, cramped stiff and sore, hungry and thirsty. Some poor fellows dying.
>
> The place we were taken off at was a large town called Recklinghausen. I was kept in that hospital three days and I had a very decent time. From there I was sent to Sennelager where I found two or three thousand there already. We were all put in a big field and wired in. We had to keep in fours and we daren't move without an order. Every now and again they would shout 'Up, Englander.' Then we had to stand for an hour or two till they thought fit to shout 'Down, Englander.' We got very little food and not much to drink. For six weeks we were on this field without a bit of protection. A little straw to lie on was all that was allowed and it was mostly swimming with water before morning. We had no overcoats and the majority of us had no

A small prisoner of war camp orchestra, including a number of members of The Norfolk Regiment 'somewhere in Germany'.

boots. We were supplied with wooden clogs and pieces of rags to wrap around our feet in place of socks. We could never grumble about our breakfast biscuits because we never got any. We had to go to work as soon as it was light on a pint of coffee they called it. We never did know what they made it with. It was very black and had a peculiar taste as if it was made with some burnt stuff and there was no sugar or milk in it.

When we went to work we were counted through the gate like sheep and if we didn't go through quick enough we were helped through with a boot or bayonet. Most of our work was seven or eight miles off. It was bad enough to do the march without the work which was very hard. We had so much to do and it had to be done before we were marched back. We had to go out all weathers and we had nowhere to dry ourselves and many a poor fellow died of cold and starvation. We had a cruel winter to face and we had to sleep in rotten tents up to the week before Christmas when we moved into huts we had built.

We never had a chance of washing and we were nearly eaten up alive with vermin. It was no use refusing to work because we were driven out with the bayonet. If we wave them a black look of made a complaint of being hungry we were tied to a tree for two hours after we came from work. Our food for the day was a pint of coffee for breakfast with nothing to eat, dinner about a pint and a half of soup. We used to march round big coppers with a tin basin and got it ladled out as we went past. If we were caught going twice we got tied up or our bread stopped. For tea we got a slice of bread each or they gave us a loaf to cut up, ten men to a 4lb. loaf. Sometimes we got a raw herring or a piece of sausage to eat with it.

Our work was road making, railway making, farm work, felling trees, carrying corn up granaries and building huts. The only thing which kept us alive was the parcels from home, which I am very thankful to say we used to receive all right. The Germans were very sure of winning the war and were always telling us they had swept our Navy from the sea and that most of their troops were on the way for London. They used to print papers for us to read, but there was never any good news about England. I kept at work every day up till April when I had to be carried to hospital where I got a clean shirt – the first one for eight months. I was doubled up with the rheumatism and I had strained my heart badly. I was lucky to get home. I could not have lived another week, in fact, I wanted to die. When I got the news last week in June that the Red Cross were being exchanged [a prisoner of war exchange was being arranged] I cheered up a bit. I couldn't walk, in fact I could hardly move and the German doctor told me I would never live to reach England but home meant a lot to me and I landed in England 2 July and thanks to good treatment in a London Hospital and at Sutton in Surrey I am much better today. There are hundreds of Norfolk boys today prisoner in Germany and I thought if their friends saw this and knew how they are treated and that they get their parcels all right they would send them plenty of good food. It's food they want, not chocolates and sweets, especially in the Sennelager camp. Friends don't forget them, for every one of them 'did their bit' for old England at Mons.

*Returned prisoners of war from North Walsham and District with Canon Aubrey Aitken (centre) who did so much for local servicemen and their families during the First World War.*

## The First Published list of NCOs and Other Ranks Soldiers of 1st Battalion, The Norfolk Regiment reported as Prisoners of War and their places of Internment in Germany, where known 1914 -15 (published June 1915)

Aldous, Pte William – Wahn, Rhein

Archer, Pte Albert  – Soltau, Hanover

Bailey, Pte  John – Paderborn, Westphalia

Bailey, Pte Thomas – Gardelegen, Altmark

Barnes, Pte F.W. – Soltau, Hanover

Barnes, L/Cpl. William

Barber, Pte Frederick W. – Friedrichsfeld, Rhine

Barkaway Pte Edward

Barnard, Pte Edward (Died in captivity 27 December 1914)

Barnard, Pte William. – Darmstadt, Hesse

Beales Pte Charles  - Göttingen, Hanover

Beldom, Pte Herbert – Döberitz, Brandenburg

Biggs, Pte  John

Bishop, Sgt. T. – Giessen, Hesse

Bone, L/Cpl. Arthur  – Darmstadt, Hesse

Bowden, Pte  Edward C. – Wahn, Rhine

Brett, Bdsm. William – Soltau, Hanover

Brooks, Pte Edward

Brooks, Pte Robert

Bullock, L/Cpl. Lawrence

Burridge, Pte Charles – Cologne (Died in captivity 26 September 1914)

Butt, Pte W. A. – Münster, Westphalia

Bygrave, Pte William

Calver, Pte Percy

Chapman, Pte W. – Munster, Westphalia

Coates, L/Cpl. Arthur – Soltau, Hanover

Chenery, Pte S.

Chiverall, Dmr. Albert – Paderborn, Westphalia

Clarke, Sgt. Frank – Paderborn, Westphalia

Cobbin, L/Cpl. Ernest – Münster, Westphalia

Cooper, Pte Charles Walter – Friedrichsfeld, Rhine

Cooper, Pte Steven – Paderborn, Westphalia

Cooper, Pte William – Soltau, Hanover

Copeman, Pte Harold S. – Döberitz, Brandenburg

Cotterell, Pte J.

Crotch, Pte William – Soltau, Hanover

Crowe, Pte Stephen

Cushing, Pte Thomas – Paderborn, Westphalia

Dack, Pte Ralph – Morsburg

Dansie, Sgt. Charles – Güstrow, Mecklenburg

Davis, Dmr. Albert E. – Döberitz, Brandenburg

Davis, Pte T. – Altdamm, Pomerania

Deane, L/Cpl. Alfred W. – Paderborn, Westphalia

Devenport, Pte J. – Göttingen, Hanover

Dingles, Pte  John W. – Soltau, Hanover

Doraston, Pte W.

Downes, Pte James E.

Dugan, Pte  – Güstrow, Mecklenberg

Edge, L/Cpl. Edward – Döberitz, Brandenburg

Edmonds, Pte Arthur  – Wittenberg, Saxony

Edwards, Pte Thomas – Ohrdruf, Thuringia

Elvin, Pte Sidney – Wahn, Rhein

Fawkes, Pte Arthur – Döberitz, Brandenburg

Field, Sgt. Ambrose – Güstrow, Mecklenburg

Fish, Pte Walter

Ford, Pte A. – Niederzwehren, Hesse

Frewer, Sgt. Robert W. – Marsburg

Fulcher, Pte Samuel W. A. – Paderborn, Westphalia

Fuller, Pte Charles – Lubeck, Pomerania

Fuller, Pte Fred – Münster, Westphalia

Fuller, Pte Sidney – Soltau, Hanover

Funston, Pte Frederick George

Galey, CSM Samuel G.

Garnham, Pte  Frederick J.

Gathercole, Pte John – Paderborn, Westphalia

Gillman, L/Cpl. Frederick T. – Wittenberg, Saxony

Golden, Pte Victor J.

Golder, Pte Ben – Münster, Westphalia

Gowing, Pte  Frank B. – Döberitz, Brandenburg

Gowing, Pte Thomas – Döberitz, Brandenburg

Graves, Pte  Joseph – Hameln, Hanover

Green, Pte Leonard F.

Grigglestone, Pte Henry P. – Soltau, Hanover

Gunton, Pte Robert W. – Gardelegen, Altmark

Gurney, Pte Francis F. – Paderborn, Westphalia

Hardy, Pte James A. – Soltau, Hanover

Hart, Pte George

Harrison, Pte G. – Soltau, Hanover

Harrison, Pte William – Döberitz, Brandenburg

Harvey, Cpl. Ernest – Paderborn, Westphalia

Hawkins, Sgt. Arthur R. – Soltau, Hanover

Hensley, Pte Charles

Herbert, Pte G.

Heyhoe, Sgt. Sidney R.

Hill, Pte Henry – Ohrdruff, Thuringia

Hills, Pte  Thomas H.

Holland, Pte Harry

Holmes, Dmr. Sidney

Horton, Pte Edward – Munster, Westphalia

Humphreys, Pte Francis J.

Hurrell, Bdsm. Reginald – Soltau, Hanover

Hutchins, Pte C. – Merseburg, Saxony

Hudson, Pte Henry – Munster, Westphalia

Huggins, Pte William

Isbell, L/Cpl. William – Munster, Westphalia

Johnson, Pte Albert – Wahn, Rhein

Johnson, Cpl. Arthur – Döberitz, Brandenburg

Johnson, Pte Walter G. W. – Munster, Westphalia

Jolly, Pte Herbert – Paderborn, Westphalia

King, Pte Harry H. – Paderborn, Westphalia

Kinsman, Pte Herbert – Döberitz, Brandenburg

Landsdowne, Cpl. Frederick William – Döberitz, Brandenburg

Lawes, Pte  Joseph – Güstrow, Mecklenburg

Lister, Pte  Sidney G. – Niederzwehren, Hesse
Littleboy, Pte George F. – Friedrichsfeld, Rhein Lodge, Pte Arthur
    G. – Wittenberg, Saxony
Lloyd, Pte  James – Döberitz, Brandenburg
Lurkins, Pte  David – Soltau, Hanover

Mack, Pte Arthur J. – Paderborn, Westphalia
Manning, Pte Alfred E. – Limburg, Hesse
Martin, Pte Charles – Paderborn, Westphalia
Marshall, Pte W. – Berlin (Hospital)
Masterman, Pte R. – Soltau, Hanover
McManus, Cpl. Howard
Meadows, Pte H. – Döberitz, Brandenburg
Meeks, Pte Edward E.
Mills, Pte  Thomas W. – Soltau, Hanover
Missen, Pte Alfred R.
Mountain, Pte  Percy W. – Döberitz, Brandenburg

Nelson, Pte Philip H. – Soltau, Hanover
Norman, Pte Cecil – Munster, Westphalia

O'Driscoll, Pte Joseph

Palmer, Pte E. – Döberitz, Brandenburg
Palmer, Pte  F.
Pardon, L/Cpl. Sidney G. – Paderborn, Westphalia
Parker, Pte John
Payton, Cpl. George R.
Pellowe, Pte Harry
Pettit, Cpl. Charles – Paderborn, Westphalia
Pilgrim, L/Cpl. Leonard W.
Pitts, L/Cpl. Ernest F.
Pollard, Pte  James R. – Soltau, Hanover
Pond, Pte Benjamin – Soltau, Hanover
Porter, Pte Harry – Friedrichsfeld, Rhein
Pratt, Pte George
Price, Pte George – Münster, Westphalia
Punchard, Pte Ernest – Hanover

Quinton, Pte G.

Ramm, Pte Arthur H. – Friedrichsfeld, Rhein
Rice, Pte Walter – Güstrow, Mecklenburg
Riches, Pte W. – Wahn, Rhein
Roberts, Pte J. – Soltau, Hanover
Rolf, Pte  Arthur
Russell, Cpl. Wilfred C. – Soltau, Hanover
Rutledge, Pte Clinton – Burg

Sanders, Sgt. Alexander Edward  – Munster, Westphalia
Saunders, Pte Charles – Paderborn, Westphalia
Savory, Pte Arthur S. – Gardelegen, Altmark
Scotter, Pte William
Secker, Pte William B. – Döberitz, Brandenburg
Shaw, Pte A. – Döberitz, Brandenburg
Sheldrake, Cpl. Harry – Soltau, Hanover
Sheldrake, L/Cpl. Horace - Hamburg (Hospital), Pomerania
Sheldrake, Pte Robert – Zwickau (Hospital), Saxony
Sherwood, Pte  James
Shingfield, Pte Frederick  – Soltau, Hanover

Shorten, Pte Bertie J. – Munster, Westphalia
Siddle, Pte Alfred V.
Skipper, Herbert – Munster (Hospital), Westphalia
Smith, L/Cpl.
Smith, Pte F.
Smith, Pte H. – Cologne
Smith, Pte R. H.
Snell, Pte Archibald
Snelling, Pte Samuel J.. – Soltau, Hanover
Soames, Cpl.William – Paderborn, Westphalia
Spinks, Pte A – Soltau, Hanover
Springett, Pte Sidney
Stackwood, Pte Ernest – Munster, Westphalia
Starling, Pte Walter
Starr, Pte John – Wittenberg, Saxony
Stewart, Pte  James
Still, Pte Thomas – Ohrdruf, Thuringia
Sturgeon, Pte George

Tanmore, Pte W. J.
Taylor, Cpl. Frank – Soltau, Hanover
Thompson, Pte  Ernest W. – Döberitz, Brandenburg
Thurston, Pte A. – Munster, Westphalia
Tibbenham, CQMS Wallace S. – Soltau, Hanover
Tooley, Pte Montague – Salzwedal
Tungate Pte  – Friedrichsfeld, Rhein
Tubby, Pte Thomas G. – Soltau, Hanover
Turner, Pte H. – Paderborn, Westphalia
Twaite, Pte Robert
Tyrell, L/Cpl. C. – Soltau, Hanover

Underdown, Cpl. William B. – Soltau, Hanover

Vincent, Pte William – Wahn, Rhein

Wabling, Pte A. – Döberitz, Brandenburg
Wallis, Pte W. R. – Wahn, Rhein
Warren, Pte Sidney – Mons (Hospital)
Watling, Pte Albert  E. – Döberitz, Brandenburg
Watson, Pte  Benjamin – Soltau, Hanover
Webster Pte, Isaac
Webster, Pte William C. – Halle, Saxony
West, Pte Albert W. – Erfurt, Saxony
West, Pte Frederick C. – Soltau, Hanover
West, Pte P. – Paderborn, Westphalia
West, Pte W. – Cassel
White, Pte  A. – Cassel
White, Pte Herbert  – Munster, Westphalia
Whiting, L/Cpl. Charles
Wicks, Pte Bertie G.
Wilding, Pte Ernest R. – Soltau, Hanover
Wilkins, Pte Albert  – Neuhaus
Woodward, L/Sgt. P. – Munsterlager
Woods, L/Cpl. Sidney T.
Wright, Pte Joseph – Munster, Westphalia
Wyett, Pte Edward – Paderborn, Westphalia
Wynn, Pte E. – Soltau, Hanover

Yull, Pte Thomas - Soltau, Hanover

# 8 Keep the Home Fires Burning

The County of Norfolk answered 'the call' magnificently when war came. Local lads joined the armed forces by the thousand and the city, towns and villages from whence they came supported them throughout the war by holding an amazing array of events, socials and drives with such novel titles as 'Flag and Fag Week'. These aimed to raise money, make and donate items to send 'comforts' to the boys 'at the front,' the wounded and prisoners of war. A typical example of so many can be found at Diss where in December 1914 £24. 4s. 6d. was subscribed to their local fund for sending Christmas parcels to the 200 local men serving in the forces at that time. Each parcel contained a plum pudding, pair of warm gloves, boxes of matches packed in tins, ½lb. of peppermint balls and a slab of chocolate for those in the navy and Expeditionary Force and to all those in camps in England. The gift also included a khaki silk handkerchief and a card.

*Men of 4ᵗʰ Battalion, The Northamptonshire Regiment at the YMCA canteen at Thetford Town Hall, December 1914.*

Most towns and villages had an Auxiliary War Hospital nearby and there was never a shortage of young ladies who wanted become members of the Voluntary Aid Detachments. Many businesses released their eligible staff to serve for the duration, women took the places of these men and did their bit on the land and in factories, many of which turned their production entirely over to munitions.

There were also YMCA 'huts'; if in a town they tended to be in converted buildings and church rooms as in Thetford, Swaffham of North Walsham or, if near a village or on an army camp, in an actual wooden barrack hut such as 'Aline Hut' on Bulmer Road in Winterton. In Norwich the main YMCA centre for troops was in St Andrew's Hall. By 1918 the Association county headquarters in St Giles controlled twenty-five YMCA 'huts' across the county, many of them with the troops along the North Norfolk coast; all of them providing soldiers with food, drink and free writing paper and envelopes and requiring friendly Christian ladies and gentlemen run them.

## Belgian Refugees

One of the first and most selfless gestures of Norfolk people during the war was the way they offered homes to Belgian refugees. Between August 1914 and May 1915 some 250,000 thousand Belgians fled

*Some of the Belgian refugees given homes by Mr and Mrs Geoffrey Buxton at Stoke Holy Cross and Poringland.*

to England for sanctuary after the invasion of their home country by German forces. In early September Mrs Jane Locker Lampson of New Haven Court, Cromer launched an appeal to raise money for the support of 40 Belgian Refugees (among them were three Mexicans, Luis G. Ugalde, Francisco Larranaga and Francisco Orozco Munoz who had been resident for a number of years in Belgium). These refugees were taken in by some of the lodging-house keepers and cottages in Cromer, others were also housed at Hunstanton in holiday houses and apartments and at King's Lynn where the *Lynn News* included a column entitled 'Latest News in Flemish' with the request that 'readers please hand this report to Belgian visitors'. In Norwich the first Belgian refugees were provided accommodation under the agency of the Catholic Women's League in the city and at Poringland, Stoke Holy Cross, Hingham and Gillingham. As more refugees arrived, bringing a large number of children with them, many were found to have come from the poorer classes and were described as being in 'a very distressed condition.' Mr and Mrs Geoffrey Buxton assisted Canon Fitzgerald in sorting the new arrivals and finding them the most suitable places to stay. Members of the local gentry were prominent in their kind hospitality, including Mr Reginald Lawrence who took a family into a cottage on his estate at Felthorpe, the Hon. Mrs Gurney conducted some to Caister Old Hall, Mrs F. T. Miller and Mrs Ernest Bolingbroke provided for others in Norwich, while Mr and Mrs Geoffrey Buxton took more into the 'colony' they established for Belgian refugees at Stoke and Poringland.

*Alien Registration Order poster for Belgian refugees in Norfolk, December 1914.*

## ALIENS RESTRICTION (BELGIAN REFUGEES) ORDER.

### REGISTRATION.

NOTICE IS HEREBY GIVEN:—

1. All Belgian refugees are required to register with the Police.

2. Those who have not received a Certificate of Registration by the 21st December should apply to the Police

3. Proposed changes of address must be notified to the Police.

The expression "Belgian Refugee" means a person, who, being either a Belgian subject or an Alien recently residing in Belgium, has arrived in the United Kingdom since the commencement of the War.

Any person neglecting to observe these requirements is liable to proceedings.

### E. F. WINCH,

Guildhall, Norwich. CHIEF CONSTABLE·
9th December, 1914.

On Tuesday 20 October the Home Office issued instructions 'Owing to the danger that German spies may make their way into the country disguised as Belgian refugees' that no Belgian refugees were to be admitted anywhere on the East Coast. This resulted in confusion in the negotiations between the official relief authorities and the departmental authority as to the exact scope of the order and information was not available in the immediate aftermath to clarify whether the refuges already domiciled in the county would have to be removed. There was also doubt whether the Order was permanent or intended to be temporary only, enabling the authorities to sift the claims of all applicants. Most were allowed to stay although alternative accommodation was often found for them by the National War Refugees Committee.

*The prefabricated 'wards' erected outside the Norfolk and Norwich Hospital for returned wounded soldiers c.1915.*

## Hospitals

At the beginning of the war the only extant hospital for the reception of wounded in the county was the Norfolk & Norwich Hospital. On the outbreak of war, the hospital offered 50 beds, which the Admiralty gladly accepted, with a further 50 beds four days later. To free up these beds as many of the patients as possible were discharged, whilst the children were transferred to the Jenny Lind Hospital. In addition the Lakenham Hospital was set up by the Red Cross in the local schools to act as an overspill for The Norfolk & Norwich and a Royal Army Medical Corps Hospital was established in The Close.

The Norfolk & Norwich Hospital stood in about seven acres of its own grounds and on one of the tennis lawns at the back of the building, four tents, the gift of Mr R. E. Horsfall, were erected as further overspill wards. The tents were each 50ft by 20ft by 8ft to the eaves; the sides, ends and roof were of single canvas and the floors were boarded. There were 18 beds in each tent, making 72 beds in all. The nursing staffs, despite many discomforts worked with a will and there was much competition for the experience of nursing in the tents.

Convoys of 100 men at the rate of about one in ten days for two months were received. During October and November it became evident that, unless additional beds could be provided, the intervals between the convoys would have to be considerably lengthened, owing to the residuum of bad cases and this in spite of the fact that in addition to the 72 beds in the tents, Ward 2 with 26 beds, Ward 8 with 18 beds and the King Edward Wards with 26 beds, had been set aside for military patients. This

*Members of the No.15 Detachment, City of Norwich British Red Cross and members of the RAMC removing a soldier from the first train of wounded brought to the county at Thorpe Station, Norwich 29 September 1914.*

fact had only to be mentioned to the Norfolk public by the editor of the *Eastern Daily Press*, when a sum of £2600 was subscribed through its columns in less than a week for a new temporary building.

Each of the four tents were soon lengthened to accommodate 28 beds, so that the total number of military beds provided rose to 250. During the opening months of the war the number of casualties varied between 77 and 131 British troops and there was one Belgian (as the war progressed a number of troops from around the Empire including Australians and Canadians were nursed there). Between 17 October 1914 and 31 July 1915, 23 convoys were received, with an average interval of 12 ½ days, though on one occasion, early in the war, two convoys arrived within twenty-four hours.

A typical arrival of wounded soldiers, with a surprise addition was reported in the *Cromer and North Walsham Post*.

> At 11.30 on the night of Friday 16 October 1914 a hospital trainload of wounded soldiers arrived at Norwich Thorpe Station on their way to the Norfolk and Norwich Hospital. Awaiting their arrival at the station a large crowd assembled and a roped passage-way from the arrival platform was kept by a numerous body of special constables under the direction of Chief Constable Winch. On the platform the Hospital Board of Management were represented by Mr Horsfall, Sir Eustace Gurney, Mr R. Laurence and others.
>
> The Red Cross staff officers present were Mrs Burton-Fanning (Vice-President), Mr G. A Grieg (Commandant), Dr Marriott (Medical Officer) and Mr Steel (Secretary). There were altogether 215 bearers and nurses on parade, three sections of bearers being placed on duty at the hospital, under Mr F. C. Robb; the nurses at the station worked under the direction of Mrs Hales, Mrs Mahon, Mrs Robb, Miss Skipper and Miss Burton-Fanning.
>
> The wounded numbered a hundred. They belonged to a variety of regiments, including the North Staffordshire Regiment, the Warwicks, the West Yorks, the Durham Light Infantry, the Scottish Rifles and the Seaforth Highlanders. Besides British wounded, there was a Belgian artilleryman, who had with him a cross and rosary taken from a dead German; he accepted with gratitude the offer of Miss Burton-Fanning to acquaint his family of his safe arrival in Norwich. There was also a German soldier, who, it was said, had purposely severed the arteries of his right hand in order that he might have a chance of being removed among the British wounded from the battlefield. Things turned out as he hoped, but instead of remaining in hospital, he was removed to Britannia Barracks as a prisoner of war.
>
> The men had been travelling since 2.30pm but many of them were quite cheerful and expressed their gratitude to those who conducted them to the motor ambulances and motor-cars waiting in the station yard to convoy them to the hospital. Naturally, the first to be removed were those whose injuries permitted of their walking with little assistance. The removal of the worst cases was necessarily a more prolonged affair but it was carried out with tender care and efficiency, the men being borne on stretchers, first to the first-class waiting room, where Dr Burton-Fanning, Dr Cleveland, Mr Burfield and Dr Marriott were in attendance to afford what little medical attention might be required and where light refreshment was also provided. As the party passed out of the station to the motor ambulances and cars they were warmly cheered and a large number of people also watched their arrival at hospital.

Once the wounded started returning to Norfolk by the train load, and despite further prefabricated 'wards' being erected in the grounds for returned wounded soldiers, existing facilities were in danger

*The Norfolk War Hospital (the former Norfolk County Asylum), Thorpe 1915.*

*Centre section of a long roll out photograph of The Norfolk War Hospital staff in 1916. Seated at the centre of the group is Lieut-Col. D. G. Thompson MD, RAMC, the Officer in Command of the hospital.*

of being swamped. Even with 26 auxiliary war hospitals established across the county by the end of 1914 the pressure on the extant facilities became acute and, as a result, the County Asylum at Thorpe was taken over by the War Office under arrangement with Norfolk County Council who had its patients removed and it was turned over to become The Norfolk War Hospital on 1 April 1915.

The necessary structural alterations, such as the provision of operating theatres, X-ray rooms, hutments for the accommodation of the extra nurses required and other numerous additions and alterations were at once undertaken and completed during April and May and on 1 June the hospital was ready for its new purpose.

In its first 12 months of existence some 5000 sick and wounded were received, chiefly from France and Flanders; nearly 4000 of whom were subsequently discharged, either as convalescent to the fifty auxiliary hospitals in Norfolk, of which the Norfolk War Hospital stood as 'Central Hospital,' or were returned to their Regiments after furlough, or invalided out of the service. Thirty-three men died in hospital, less than one per cent of those admitted.

The hospital consisted of two sets of buildings, the main hospital and the annexe hospital. Each of these hospitals, which were one-third of a mile apart, was complete in itself, with the exception of the laundry, entertainment hall and chapel, which were at the main hospital and served both. Initially the two hospitals contained 500 beds each, 1000 beds in all . Temporary buildings for three hundred beds were also erected at each hospital. By the end of the war the hospital had expanded to a remarkable 2428 beds.

The Officer in Command of the Hospital was the indefatigable Lieut-Col. D. G. Thompson MD, RAMC, and the facility was regularly attended by a number of members of the honorary medical staff of the Norfolk & Norwich Hospital, chiefly in the capacity of consultants. The resident medical staff comprised six temporarily commissioned officers of the Royal Army Medical Corps, ten civilian medical officers and a female pathologist. The Matron and two Assistant Matrons controlled a body of nurses, numbering over two hundred, of whom thirty were Sisters, sixty were Staff Nurses and the rest probationers. The Sergeant Major, or Chief Orderly, was in command of about one hundred orderlies, all of whom were enlisted men in the RAMC nd most of whom had been declared medically unfit for general service.

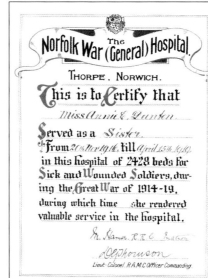

*Norfolk War Hospital service certificate presented to Sister Annie Dunton. Praised for her nursing and ward management, she had charge of a surgical ward of 70 beds between 1916-1919.*

The General Clerk and the Steward managed the financial and supply departments of the hospital, respectively, with the necessary number of clerks and assistants. The pack store, usually managed by men in a military hospital, was here 'most successfully and economically' run by women. A large number of female domestics were also employed in the kitchens, laundry and household departments. The Wayland Infirmary near Attleborough was also taken over as a military hospital in April 1917.

### Auxiliary War Hospitals

The story of the auxiliary war hospitals began a year after the creation of the Territorial Force when, the War Office issued its *Scheme for the Organisation of Voluntary Aid in England and Wales* in 1909. The War Office had recognised that in the event of a major European war, which seemed ever more likely, existing medical arrangements for its armed forces would be wholly inadequate. Some form of supplementary aid would be required, in addition to the Territorial Force Medical Service, to provide transport and care for the thousands of casualties returned from a British Expeditionary Force on the Continent.

*Attleborough Auxiliary War Hospital opened in the town's Corn Hall, November 1914.*

In Norfolk a total of 64 male and female Voluntary Aid Detachments (VADs) had been registered in locations all over the county between October 1910 and July 1914. There were no mixed detachments. Male detachments were the most difficult to recruit as they required 56 volunteers, headed by a Commandant, with a Medical Officer, Quartermaster and Honorary Secretary, Pharmacist and four sections, each comprising a Section Leader and 12 men.

On the outbreak of war, public meetings were held in Norwich and in towns and villages to ascertain which public buildings and houses were available for conversion to Auxiliary War Hospitals. Many families offered a spare bedroom, and municipal buildings such as schools and concert halls were made available. However, the need to concentrate convalescent servicemen in one place made their dispersal in ones and twos a nonsense, while many municipal buildings were required for their original purpose, even in time of war. In most cases a large local house or the rectory proved to be the most practical place in which to open a hospital, although hospital 'annexes' were opened in public buildings or other houses when returning casualties overwhelmed the bed space available. Nationally, to avoid duplication of effort, the Red Cross and Order of St John also agreed to join forces for the duration of the war.

The first Auxiliary War Hospital to be established in Norfolk was opened at the request of the Admiralty for the treatment of wounded sailors at Great Yarmouth. The local branch of the British Red Cross Society issued a placard on Wednesday 5 August stating that they proposed to equip a hospital of 50 beds ready for immediate use by midday on Thursday. It was intimated that all offers either of gifts of money, of articles or personal service would be received from 10.00am to 10.00pm during Wednesday and Thursday at the Supper Room, Town Hall, which had been kindly made available by the Mayor. The following list of articles would be required:

*Bedsteads, single and preferably high, with one mattress, two pillows, three blankets, four sheets, two draw sheets and four pillow cases. This is an 'equipped bed.' It is hoped bedsteads will be promised with this equipment to save confusion. Extra mattresses, pillows and cases, blankets, sheets and draw sheets; chairs, easy chairs and carrying chairs; tables various; handkerchiefs; table cloths; dusters; waterproof sheeting; hot water bottles, stone, metal and rubber; cushions, air, feather or vegetable down; sofas, sponges, combs, sanitary bins for soiled linen, bedpans and urinals, water buckets and pails, scrubbing brushes, water beds, thermometers, medicine glasses, feeding cups, old linen and old blankets, towels, various enamel basins, cans and jugs, trays of various sizes, tea urns, teapots, including small ones to be used as feeding cups, mugs, plates and dishes of various sizes, knives, forks and spoons, pudding and mixing basins, jugs, kettles, small tin fish kettles, saucepans, frying pans, self cookers, frying pans, self cookers, stew pans, funnels, mincing machines, scales, lemon squeezers, whisks, washing-up tubs, Primus or Beatrice oil stoves, tea clothes.*

Mr C. S. Orde promised a supply of articles for use in the hospital and fully equipped beds were given by Palmers, Arnolds and Bonings. The result was that in 48 hours the Red Cross had their fifty beds with sufficient nurses and cooks to run the hospital.

On the evening of Friday 7 August the Mayor of Yarmouth opened a special meeting speaking of the gravity of the crisis. Dr A. C. Mayo then rose and announced the Admiralty had instructed him as Admiralty Surgeon to prepare for the reception of wounded men to be landed at Yarmouth. A Red Cross hospital had been formed and was ready for service. Sir Savile Crossley, 1st Baron Somerleyton had also nobly offered to equip and maintain an additional hospital as long as it should be needed (this became known as Lady Crossley's Hospital after his wife's keen interested and involvement). They had also had an offer of 12–18 properly staffed beds at the Nurses Home and 20 more at the Sailor's Home. The General Hospital would also be available for 20 to 60 patients, and at Gorleston they were promised up to 22 beds. Initially the Red Cross had the use of the Sailor's Home on Marine Parade and the Drill Hall on York Road for hospital purposes, before a more permanent hospital was opened at 47 Marine Parade in November 1914. By that same month Lady Crossley's Hospital had opened on the South Denes and a temporary hospital for a party of 30 wounded Belgian soldiers at the Mariners' Chapel as the result of the British and Foreign Sailors' Society having already offered the Naval authorities the use of all their buildings for hospital purposes.

A number of convalescent hospitals were turned over for the use of returned wounded such as the Fletcher Convalescent Hospital in Cromer, some were sponsored by wealthy individuals like Saville Crossley or were established in religious houses including The Convent of the Little Sisters of the Assumption, but the greatest number of Auxiliary War Hospitals in the county were run under the auspices of The British Red Cross Society and Order of St John. Often simply referred to as 'Red Cross Hospitals' the first of these to officially open its doors for the treatment of returned wounded soldiers in Norfolk was at Woodbastwick on 28 September 1914 and it was here that the first convalescent wounded were brought after their arrival on an ambulance train at Thorpe Station, Norwich on 29 September 1914. The readiness of the VADs was well evinced by the fact that another 26 fully staffed and equipped Auxiliary War Hospitals from across the county had opened their doors to convalescent troops by the end of 1914.

The British Red Cross Society and Order of St John (although at that time working as separate Voluntary Aid Societies) immediately began to establish so-called Voluntary Aid Detachments (VADs) to recruit and train local volunteers for the task. Wartime recruitment of VADs was never a problem, as most were inspired by patriotism and a sense of doing their bit, while soon the 'Romance of the Red Cross' became a term which featured heavily in newspapers, books and magazines.

*Loading returned wounded soldiers into ambulances and transport bound for Woodbastwick after the arrival of the first ambulance train at Thorpe Station, 29 September 1914.*

*Convalescent soldiers at The Convent of the Little Sisters of the Assumption, Grapes Hill, Norwich 1914.*

*Mrs Sarah Gamzu Gurney and the Voluntary Aid Detachment nurses of Ingham Auxiliary War Hospital 1914.*

Girls wishing to nurse had to be 'presentable,' and were to provide a reference or recommendation from a local doctor, priest or magistrate. They also had to be able to give time to their duties on a regular basis. In 1915, with the introduction of the 'General Service' section of the VAD, there were a wide variety of duties for girls of most abilities, so the majority could find a place: as a cook or laundresss, a clerk, typist, telephonist, driver, chauffeur – or VAD nurse.

The premier position of the VAD nurse was often the preserve of the young ladies from local middle-class families who could afford to give the time, pay for the lectures and had £1 19s 2½d to buy a uniform (although later in the war local VAD units did have funds to issue uniforms, or at least replace worn out aprons, collars and cuffs). Officially, VAD nursing members had to be 23 to 38 years old to serve in military hospitals, but if girls looked old enough and were keen enough they would get in. Girls as young as 17 became VADs, especially in the more rural Auxiliary War Hospitals. They were appointed on two weeks' probation. If found to be suitable, they would be expected to serve for up to three months, and many served for much longer. The engagement of VAD members could be terminated if 'at any time they were found unfit in any respect for service'.

By 1916 most of the hospitals in Norfolk were equipped with all the basic necessities but many were able to boast advanced equipment such as minor surgery theatres, 'apparatus for massage and elec-

trical treatment' and x-ray machines. The most outstanding evidence for the standards and efficiency of the Auxiliary Hospitals in Norfolk are the recovery statistics. It is estimated that the number of deaths of troops in Norfolk Auxiliary hospitals was about one in every three hundred and the average stay of patients in the hospitals to recovery and discharge was almost a whole day below the national average.

By 1918 Norfolk had provided over sixty fully equipped Auxiliary Hospitals for convalescent troops through the duration of the war but the achievements of the British Red Cross Society and Order of St John working groups, which backed up or were allied to the Auxiliary Hospitals are no less significant. The Lazar House Auxiliary Hospital Supply Depot handled 102,339 items throughout the duration of the war. The Rest Room or 'Soldiers and Sailors Rest Home' in the yard of Thorpe station was described in the *British Red Cross Society Norfolk Branch Report* of 1918 as 'consistently full.' Even more remarkable was the service provided by the B.R.C.S. Norwich Transport Company. Their

*Nurses and convalescent soldiers at the East Dereham Auxiliary War Hospital 1915.*

*Afternoon tea for convalescent soldiers at The Close, Norwich c.1916.*

*Convalescent troops in wheel-chairs are taken out for 'an airing' by their more able comrades, Brundall Auxiliary War Hospital 1914.*

job was to collect the wounded and convalescent soldiers from Thorpe Station, Norwich and to run them to The Norfolk & Norwich, Lakenham Military or Norfolk War Hospitals for assessment and treatment (if necessary) before despatch to an Auxiliary Hospital that dealt with 317 convoys and 40,498 patients between 1914-1918.

Out of the 61 counties with Auxiliary Hospitals in them Norfolk was one of only 19 with more than 1,000 beds available between 1915 and 1918. Out of those 19 Norfolk was one of the 15 who were able to run their hospitals at a cost of less than 4s. per patient, per day. Norfolk was below the national average for the amount of time patients occupied their beds or convalesced and was below the national average for deaths in convalescence. It is also notable that, with net receipts from donations to the Norfolk VAS of almost £15,000 a year since 1914, a third of the total running costs of the Auxiliary War Hospitals in Norfolk were met by public donations and subscriptions.

Between 1918 and early 1919 the last of the convalescent soldiers were discharged from the Auxiliary Hospitals across Norfolk and the Hospitals were gradually closed, decommissioned and returned to the private use of their owners. A total of 62 Auxiliary Hospitals in the county had provided some 1377 beds, through which passed 27,446 convalescent soldiers who had been cared for by a total of 35,736 VAD Nurses, orderlies, drivers and volunteers drawn from both Voluntary Aid Societies in the county. The last Red Cross and Order of St John Auxiliary Hospitals run under the VAD system in the county closed in April 1919. The last of the convalescent soldiers aided by VAD Nurses was the Wayland Military Hospital, which finally closed on 26 April 1919.

*The 1ˢᵗ Norfolk Voluntary Aid Detachment ambulance bringing wounded to the Great Yarmouth Auxiliary War Hospital c.1915.*

## The Auxiliary War Hospitals of The British Red Cross Society & Order of St John, Norfolk, 1914–1919

| PLACE | OPERATIONAL DATES | PATIENTS ADMITTED |
| --- | --- | --- |
| Attleborough | | |
| *Corn Hall* | 26 November 1914 – 22 November 1917 | 656 |
| Brancaster | 11 December 1914 – 14 February 1915 | 31 |
| Brundall | 12 October 1914 – 1 October 1916 | 712 |
| Buckenham Tofts | 1 January 1916 – 25 May 1916 | 52 |
| Catton | 2 September 1915 – 4 February 1919 | 687 |
| Cawston | 12 November 1914 – 21 February 1918 | 2884 |
| Cromer | | |
| *Red House* | 1 October 1914 – 10 December 1917 | 734 |
| *Colne House* | 11 March 1915 – 31 January 1919 | 634 |
| Diss | 9 September 1914 – 24 January 1919 | 1651 |
| Ditchingham | 1 November 1914 – 26 April 1919 | 240 |
| Downham Market | 19 February 1915 – 14 April 1919 | 1274 |
| East Dereham | 16 November 1914 – 5 April 1919 | 2067 |
| Fakenham | 1 June 1915 – 21 January 1919 | 480 |
| Felthorpe | 11 November 1914 – 14 January 1919 | 432 |
| Garboldisham | 7 November 1914 – 19 January 1919 | 324 |
| Hardingham | 1 May 1917 – 20 November 1917 | 305 |
| Harleston | 5 May 1917 – 7 April 1918 | 136 |
| Hedenham | 3 April 1915 – 23 December 1918 | 771 |
| Hingham | 2 October 1915 – 23 December 1918 | 200 |
| Holkham | 1915/16 | 30 |
| Hoveton & Wroxham | | |
| *St Gregory's* | 6 May 1915 – 22 January 1919 | 810 |
| *Hoveton Hall* | 29 October 1914 – 13 August 1917 | 284 |
| Hunstanton | | |
| *Cliff House* | 5 February 1915 – 31 January 1919 | 440 |
| *Prince Edward Home* | 1 July 1916 – 31 January 1919 | 869 |
| *Convalescent Home* | 19 June 1915 – 28 February 1916 | 190 |
| Ingham | 29 October 1914 – 28 January 1919 | 1082 |
| Kirstead | 7 November 1914 – 30 December 1918 | 391 |
| Letheringsett | 9 December 1915 – 25 January 1919 | 1082 |
| Loddon | 19 November 1914 – 23 November 1918 | 474 |

| | | |
|---|---|---|
| Lynford Hall | 22 June 1918 – 28 January 1919 | 49 |
| Matlaske | 16 October 1914 – 7 October 1915 | 144 |
| Melton Constable | 18 December 1915 – 31 January 1919 | 399 |
| North Walsham | | |
| *Lower House* | 11 November 1914 – 20 March 1919 | 714 |
| *Wellingtonia* | 25 January 1915 – 31 January 1919 | 475 |
| Norwich | | |
| *Bracondale* | 25 November 1915 – 28 March 1919 | 956 |
| *Town Close* | 26 November 1914 – 1 August 1915 | 600 |
| *Town Close Lodge* | 10 August 1915 – 19 February 1919 | 2087 |
| *The Convent of the Little* | | |
| *Sisters of the Assumption* | 9 November 1914 – 17 December 1918 | 361 |
| *The Palace* | 23 April 1918 – 4 March 1919 | 276 |
| Overstrand | 3 November 1914 – 6 April 1916 | 65 |
| Reepham | 26 November 1914 – 5 April 1919 | 1158 |
| Saxlingham | 8 July 1915 – 28 September 1915 | 22 |
| Sheringham | | |
| *Knowelside* | 29 October 1914 – 31 January 1919 | 957 |
| *The Dales* | 1 July 1918 – 10 January 1919 | 71 |
| Swainsthorpe | 2 October 1915 – 3 February 1919 | 663 |
| Thetford | 19 January 1915 – 28 April 1915 | 102 |
| Thorpe St Andrew | | |
| *Coonor* | 30 November 1914 – 9 December 1918 | 608 |
| *Sunny Hill* | 2 January 1915 – 30 November 1918 | 1152 |
| Thornham | 5 January 1915 – 31 January 1919 | 617 |
| Walsingham | | |
| *Berry Hall* | 20 October 1914 – 7 September 1915 | 110 |
| *Oddfellows Hall and* | | |
| *Lower Farm* | 22 February 1915 – 31 December 1918 | 384 |
| Weasenham | 19 October 1914 – 19 October 1915 | 102 |
| West Bilney Manor and Narborough Hall | 26 March 1915 – 8 June 1918 | 607 |
| West Harling | 7 November 1914 – 31 December 1918 | 130 |
| Woodbastwick | 28 September 1914 – 1918 | 1113 |
| Wymondham | 26 November 1914 – 31 January 1919 | 803 |
| Yarmouth | 29 November 1914 – 17 January 1919 | 815 |

## Women and the War

From early on in the war many women took over simple clerking and shop work in local businesses that had a 'vacancy' left by a man gone to war but, that said, most employers took on female staff on the strict understanding that it was only a stop gap measure and that when the man returned he would be able to have his job back. Most women were quite happy with the arrangement – it was the patriotic thing to do. However, there was a potential army of women who wanted to do *something* for the war effort but were simply not being utilised. The Women's Suffrage Movement had suspended its militant action to allow a concentration on the war effort so when they felt they were not being used effectively the country could expect the women would soon find a way of voicing their desire. It took a combination of events in 1915 to really get women mobilized into munitions work.

The sea change began with what became known as the 'Shells Scandal' of 1915, after the publication of the startling revelation that in the opinion of Sir John French the British Commander-in-Chief, a shortage of munitions led directly to the failure of the British offensive at Neuve Chapelle in March 1915. The Liberal Chancellor, David Lloyd George fervently believed radical improvements were required in the munitions industry if the nation was to carry on what was now appearing to be a prolonged war against Germany. The 'Shells Scandal' became a key factor in the fall of the Liberal Government in May 1915 and the establishment of a new coalition in which the new Ministry of Munitions was created under Lloyd George.

On 21 July 1915 numerous women from the county had travelled down to the capital for the 'Women's March Through London' where some 30,000 women marched through the capital under the banner of 'We Demand the Right to Serve.' The pressure was on and as a direct result of the scandal munitions work was expanded. Women were going to do their bit too!

At this juncture it is worthwhile pointing out that in the First World War the term 'munitions' did not just refer to the manufacture of shells but a whole host of operations from pulling flax crops (used for industrial purposes and in textile manufacture) to manufacturing wooden boxes for military purposes and even working in the various stages of aircraft manufacture. Broadly speaking, if it involved 'feeding the guns' of the war effort it could be considered 'munitions' work – so a girl could have been involved in munitions throughout the war and never touched a gun shell!

Several local lasses went off to serve in the National Explosives Factories, National Filling Factories and major industries employed in the manufacture of explosives and gun shells around the country. The women working in munitions tended to have been predominantly from domestic service backgrounds with a liberal smattering of shop assistants, laundry workers and clerks and similar working/lower middle class occupations. Requirements were similar to any other occupation in this employment sector, basic education and physical fitness to do the job was enough. The days were long, many factories working flat out 24 hours a day with women working 12 hour shifts, typically 6am to 6pm and vice versa for the next shift. Although there were great disputes over the inequality of wages – men were paid an average of £4 6s. 6d. whereas women only received £2 2s. 4d, but most women were quite happy because the wages were higher than they were accustomed to before the war. One is recorded as saying 'I thought I was very well off earning over two pounds a week.'

Because of the nature of work and requirement of mobility their overalls were soon supplemented with trousers – something no young lady would have been seen wearing on the street before the war. This additional item of clothing was worn as a badge of honour on the street by the munitions girls, who soon acquired the nickname of 'munitionettes'. Although the eyebrows of many of those who still held Victorian values many have been raised, they could hardly complain because these women were 'doing their bit' and any criticism could be seen as unpatriotic. It is certain that many of the munitions 'girls' took brave steps forward in public behaviour and through the war years, not only in wearing trousers, but having short hair cuts (the girls were told to keep their hair short as long hair, even if braided, could get caught in the factory machinery and metal hair grips, combs etc were all considered contraband), going to the cinema unaccompanied by a man, smoking cigarettes and drinking in public houses. The women soon got into their stride organizing entertainments, pantomimes, theatrical productions and even (shock-horror to the blue stockings) playing organised games of football! They were also known for getting up to mischief – woe betide any kilted Scottish soldier passing the gates of the Norwich vinegar works at knocking off time!

The times were changing and the labour exchanges across the county displayed the poster 'War Service for Women' calling for women to enter their names 'at once' on the Special Register of Women for War Service, indicating that in particular women were required locally for 'farm work, dairy work, leather stitching, brush making, clothing machining and light machining for armament' with the advice 'But even if you have no special experience in any of this work, you should register. It may

*A young female billposter who carried on her father's work as official billposter and town crier while he was away at war, Thetford 1915.*

*Advertising card for the Norfolk and Norwich Branch of the Voluntary War Work Association c1917.*

## The East Anglian Munitions Committee

In May 1915 a meeting was called by Mr. P. A. Sanders of Davey, Paxman & Co. Ltd, Essex at the Great Eastern Hotel, Liverpool Street, London at which 19 representatives of East Anglian manufacturers were present. The meeting was convened to hear from a representative of the War Office what was expected of the area in the manufacture of munitions of war and how these results were to be obtained. Two proposals were made: one for a National Factory and the other on the basis of co-operative production, and it was decided to adopt the latter. In order to discover the resources of the area Mr Wilfred Stokes of Ransomes and Rapier Ltd and Mr. Francis H. Crittall of The Crittall Manufacturing Co. Ltd. undertook to make a week's tour through the three counties to make such arrangements with the War Office as they found practicable.

A contract for 60 pdr shells was undertaken by Messrs Laurence, Scott & Co. Ltd of Norwich who not only designed the machines for making this shell but also manufactured them. In addition to the H.E., shrapnel shells were made in large quantities by Messrs R. Garrett & Sons Ltd (Leiston, Suffolk), Messrs Charles Burrell & Sons Ltd (Thetford, Norfolk) and at Laurence & Scott from forgings made by Messrs Ransomes, Sims & Jeffries Ltd (Ipswich); the total number came to over 882,000.

In 1916 the war effort badly needed fuses and a contract was undertaken by four firms – J. W. Brooke & Co. Ltd. (Lowestoft, Suffolk), Messrs Lake & Elliott Ltd (Braintree, Essex), Messrs Reavell & Co. Ltd (Ipswich, Suffolk) and the specially created Norwich Components Ltd in the city – to produce 100, 101 and 103 fuses for use with H.E. shells. Special tools had to be made or bought for the purpose, buildings put up, organisation got together and girls trained. This

*A fine line up of Norwich 'Munitionettes' 1916*

entailed an immense amount of work but resulted in a total of over 4,700,000 fuses being produced by the four companies. This number would have been considerably increased had it not been for the shortage of brass, which led up to the adoption of a cast iron body, with all the delays and difficulties making it rustproof.

In the production of flying machines Boulton & Paul took a leading part and built entirely new works for the purpose, so that 45 complete machines were turned out per week towards the end of the war and flown over France from their testing grounds. Their total output of aeroplanes was 2,525. Beside this they made 70 flying boats and 7,835 propellers.

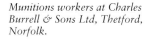

*Munitions workers at Charles Burrell & Sons Ltd, Thetford, Norfolk.*

Left: *Female clerk at the Great Eastern Railway Station, King's Lynn, 1917.*

Right: *Violet Jackson the Trunch postwoman, 'for the duration'.*

be possible to train you. It is certain that as more men join the forces, more women will be wanted to work while they are away. Even if you can work only half of each day, you may be useful.'

Even more women were taken on to the workforce in 1916 as the introduction of conscription saw thousands more men leave their places of work to serve in the forces. Women were working in jobs for which female labour would have been taboo in the years before the war. Across Norfolk women were employed in such diverse occupations as 'clippies' on buses and trams, working on the railways, as postwomen and working the 'rounds' driving horses and carts for local businesses as diverse as the butcher, the dairy and the general dealer. Extant factories were often given new, but allied items to produce for the war effort, many expanded their premises as their workforce was supplemented by women at various levels along the production line. Hobbies of Dereham produced munitions, Savage of Lynn, previously an agricultural and fairground machinery maker went into aircraft wing manufacture, Mann Egerton made a number of different aircraft including Short bomber and seaplanes. Also in the city, Barnards Ltd Engineers supplied over 6,994 miles of wire netting for the War Office and Admiralty and hundreds of prefabricated wooden barrack buildings. The ready-made clothing department of Chamberlins was dedicated to the manufacture of khaki clothing supplying the War Office and Norfolk Territorial units and volunteer battalions as well as serving contracts for oilskins, the GPO and Government munitions factories. F. W. Harmer supplied two tons of clothing a day to assist the war effort from its St Andrew's Street factory. Caleys made thousands of bars of their famous 'marching' chocolate and Jarrold's printed the letterheaded paper for YMCA, Church Army and Navy & Army Canteen Board as well as making thousands of pocket wallets and stationery designed for Christmas gifts for the fighting men at the front. Above all, at this time Norwich was a city of shoe manufacture; Howlett & White Ltd, just one of a number of large scale boots and shoe making businesses in Norwich made 453,000 pairs of boots and shoes for the British Army, 32,000 for the Allies and 21,000 British Aviation Boots. Some factories were entirely passed over to war work and proudly displayed the sign 'His Majesty's Factory' above the door.

In the early years of the war Queen Alexandra's Imperial Military Nursing Service (QAIMNS), First Aid Nursing Yeomanry, Women's Forage Corps (1915) and The Women's Legion (1916) were the main women's units serving with or with close attachment to the military or War Office. The year 1917 heralded the creation of two more uniformed military services for women. Many local women saw their chance to get out of the county, seek adventure and do their bit in uniform by volunteering for service in the new women's forces of the Women's Auxiliary Army Corps (later re-titled Queen Mary's Auxiliary Army Corps), Women's Royal Naval Service (WRNS; popularly and officially known as the 'Wrens') both formed in 1917, and the Women's Auxiliary Air Force formed in 1918 for the express purpose of substituting women for men in non-combatant roles.

Earlier in the war such units would have been looked at askance but such had been the revolution in the role of women in the war great pride was shown in the girls joining up. They often went in small groups like those from Edwards & Holmes Ltd boot and shoe factory (early in the war they had made thousands of uppers for Cossack boots for the Russians) on Drayton Road who proudly sent their girls off under the banner of 'They are doing their bit.'

A Wren officer, Women's Auxiliary Army Corps and war workers at Pulham airship station 1918. Each woman holds an item representing the type of work she was doing.

## On the Land

The County War Agricultural Committee had existed since the outbreak of war when all County Councils had been requested by the President of the Board of Agriculture and Fisheries to set them up to ascertain the needs of farmers and the best means of assisting them in cultivating their land, training women for farm work and to develop the agricultural resources within each county. Further District sub-committees were established across the county. Their duties included the survey of uncultivated land, the registration of all holdings over 5 acres, co-ordination of supply and distribution of manure, and of cultivation of crops and vegetables and allocating temporary labour. Sub-committees also monitored what happened to the land in their area and questions would be formally put to land owners who reduced their productive land – even the clergy did not escape as one Norfolk vicar received a roasting for erecting a tennis court on land that could have been used for growing food. Even the army got involved when in March 1918 the Army Council urged that 'every opportunity should be taken to cultivate lands in and adjacent to barracks'. To encourage this the Commander-in-Chief in each command was to appoint a Command Agricultural Committee of Officers – I bet they were delighted!

By 1917 the cold wet winters began take their toll on the country. In Norfolk the Brandon River had burst its banks and caused serious flooding at Southery Fen and Hockwold in 1915; the spring of 1916 was wet and snowy affecting spring sowing and hours of sunshine through the year were markedly

An Army Service Corps (Forage Corps) Sergeant and both male and female workers join local agricultural labourers working a bailer at Martham 1916.

reduced, hardly the best recipe for a good harvest to support a country in wartime. The year 1917 did not start much better, the cold winter having dragged on, with frost experienced in Norwich up to the 18 April. In the Channel, far from clear in February 1917, the German Navy sank 230 ships bringing food and other supplies to Britain. The following month a record 507,001 tons of shipping was lost as a result of the U-Boat campaign. Britain feared a war of attrition and in direct response to this the Board of Agriculture set up the Food Production Department (FPD) to organise and distribute agricultural inputs, such as labour, feed, fertiliser and machinery, and increase output of crops. The FPD officials had a wide range of emergency powers to enforce proper cultivation to the degree they could cross private property, dispossess inefficient tenant farmers and order new land to be ploughed up. New, streamlined, seven man Agricultural Food Executive Committees were established that drove on the land work and reinforced the policies of the FPD.

Although women had worked on farms in dairies, butter making, poultry keeping and at harvest time for generations before the war, many more joined them as the men went away to war. Women were recruited to help meet the massive demand for horse fodder and the Women's Forage Corps was formed by a government initiative, administered by the Army Service Corps in 1915.

*Three members of the Women's National Land Service Corps.*

There were also new voluntary organisations in operation such as the Women's National Land Service Corps (later known simply as Women's Land Corps), The Women's Farm and Garden Union and The Land Service Corps that had made one of its most important objectives the organisation of village women into working gangs. But it was not until 1917 that the Women's Land Army was formed. Initially there was scepticism from farmers and from the public generally about the ability of women 'taking the place of a man' in agriculture. Then there was the question of billeting, and a consideration of 'the loneliness of farm work' and wages. To address these matters and recruit the women the Board of had had in place Women's Agriculture Committees in each county, headed in Norfolk by Sir Ailwyn and Lady Fellowes. County offices were opened and organising Secretaries appointed. In Norfolk it was the energetic Miss Burgess but in such a large agricultural county her work would have been a lot harder without the keen assistance from Honorary Secretaries Mrs Parish and Miss Burton. Then followed the appointment of the Travelling Inspector for Norfolk and Suffolk, Mrs Harvey, who supervised the work in each area, and of Group Leaders in the villages. Recruitment campaigns were carried through the press and at open air rallies.

On 24 July 1917 the Norfolk Women's War Agricultural Committee met at the Shirehall. In her opening remarks The Hon. Lady Fellowes pointed out, with some pride and aware of the drive behind them, that all the WWAC Committees in the county now belonged to the Board of Agriculture Food Production Department. Lady Fellowes reported that 'according to actual returns they had over 5000 women now working on the land in Norfolk'. She also announced: 'Under the National Service Scheme, centres for training girls for work on the land had been opened as follows: Mr W. Case, Gateley, with accommodation for 15 girls; Mr G. Overman, Weasenham, 4; Mr W R Harvey, Illington, 6; Miss Godfrey, New Buckenham, 1; Mrs Oswald Ames, Thornham and Mrs Betts, Thornham each with accommodation for 2.' These girls were trained for four weeks, after which situations were found for them for various work on the land. They were provided with an outfit, and their railway fares were also paid. Though it did include breeches Lady Fellowes thought there was nothing in the outfit 'to which the most particular person could take exception'.

*A smartly turned out member of the Women's Land Army 1917.*

The complete uniform issued to each woman consisted of breeches, a knee length tunic with a button-fastening integral belt, boots and gaiters or puttees, soft hat and breeches which were cut to measure for each girl. After three months' proficient service (of not less than 240 hours) each girl would receive her official armlet – a loden green band with a bright red crown upon it. A circular cloth badge was also awarded for passing efficiency tests in such skills as milking, horse work, tractor driving, stacking corn, hoeing and manure spreading. Red cloth chevrons were also awarded, each chevron representing six months work of not less than 1440 hours; there was also a red diamond with an outline green diamond in the centre that represented two years' work. The girls started on a minimum wage of 18s. a week, steadily increased to 20s and finally 22s 6d in 1919. Despite initial scepticism the efficient organisation and training of the Land Army girls amply proved their worth to the farmers.

*Miss C. M. Spencer leads the Norfolk Forage Company of the Forage Corps as part of a recruiting parade, seen here on Prince of Wales Road, Norwich 1917.*

The Women's Land Army inherited The Forage Corps in 1917. Women in this section would often be working in a team or 'gang' of about eight, usually containing three soldiers, who would travel from farm to farm with a steam baling machine baling hay or straw. Many also worked in chaffing depots chopping the hay or straw into short lengths for horse fodder at a forage store. Land Girls working within the Forage Section had to sign up for a minimum of one year's service. If she showed suitable ability a girl could be promoted to 'Corporal' in charge of her work gang and would also act as a supervisor of labour and intermediary. Another promotion could be to Conductress; this woman was responsible for the issue of food to her team, the wire and the oil required by the balers, and accompanying the loads of hay from the farm to the railway or nearest chaffing depot. There are examples of this woman wearing three military style 'Sergeant's' stripes on her overall. Further promotion could come in the form Forwarding Supervisor. Her job had the responsibility of receiving the cart loads of hay, organising their despatch and filing a report to the Department for accounting purposes. This role was usually carried out by a female officer, many of whom had large areas to regulate and can be seen in photographs of the period wearing hats with goggles and storm flaps, gauntlets and breeches under their skirts so they could ride a motorbike.

Many of the Forage Corps Officers continued to wear their old uniforms until the end of the war, as did many women members who continued to wear their old hats bearing the brass letters 'FC'. All in all, the new Women's Land Army was quickly established, the weather improved, food production was up and the wheat harvest of 1917 was the best in our history.

Despite this great achievement there was still a fear among many people that the country was running out of food. Panic buying and hoarding food had manifested to varying degrees since war was declared. A Ministry of Food was established in December 1916 but throughout 1917 the Government had been concerned about the nation's food stocks and the particular shortages in sugar, flour and potatoes but had been reluctant to impose rationing. It was suggested instead that people may wish to adopt 'The National Scale of Voluntary Rations' of 4lbs of bread or 3lbs of flour, 2 ½ lbs of meat and ¾ lb of sugar per week. This became a matter of patriotic pride and many families signed pledges and placed red white and blue pledge cards headed 'In Honour Bound' in their windows to show their support. To help the situation the County War Agricultural Committee organised food economy lectures across the region particularly extolling the virtues of pickling vegetables and bottling fruit. Special economy recipes appeared in the newspapers and books like *Our War-Time Kitchen Garden* by Tom Jerrold (1917) informed us about not only what we can grow in our garden but also our dietary needs emphasising that we can still remain 'the bull-dog breed without the roast beef of old England'.

## Tanks and War Bonds

*Soldiers and members of the Norfolk Forage Corps at the chaffing store, East Dereham, July 1918.*

It is a little known fact that when the tank was in development as a top secret new weapon of war they were put through their paces in a secret training area on Lord Iveagh's estate on the Norfolk and Suffolk borders at Elvedon near Thetford. To ensure no prying eyes could see, long hoardings covered in hessian were put along the boundaries of the estate near public roads – the excuse being these were to protect passing traffic from gun shell explosions. When these landships were finally removed to

*Tank manoeuvring under armed guard by the Guildhall in Norwich Market Place during Tank Week, April 1918.*

the front line their secret was maintained by any reference in their shipment being referred to as 'tanks,' as in *water* tanks, and the name stuck.

In the latter years of the war drives for War Savings and War Bonds to keep up the supply of weapons and equipment were held across the country, mostly in the guise of 'Tank Week'. The idea was that you bought the certificates or bonds, which would be used for the duration and then would be paid back 'eventually – with a high rate of interest'. Adverts were explicit and demanded the attention of every patriotic citizen; such as this one that appeared in the *Eastern Daily Press* on 25 March 1918:

> *Every inhabitant of Norwich and District should buy National War Bonds or War Savings Certificates from the tank next week. You can buy a War Savings Certificate for 15/6 or a National War Bond for £5 or £5000 or any amount in between. Ask your friends to go with you to the tank. Go early and often. Beat every town in the Kingdom! It will be a matter of pride to you and your town. It will be acclaimed by the men on the Sea and at the Front. It will be an historic week for your town.*

Norwich's Tank Week was held between Monday 1st and 6th April 1918. Each day the press covered the events, speeches and rallies around the tank and published a running total and notable donations. With a magnificent effort from the people of the city and help from sizable purchases of War Bonds by the City Corporation and Norwich Union Life Insurance Society, Norwich raised over a million pounds – the final figure being the phenomenal sum of £1,057,382.

*Almost £60,000 was raised by Thetford during their 'Tank Week.'.*

*Great Yarmouth had a Submarine Week, but because the phenomena of the Tank was so thoroughly associated with War Savings the media referred to it as 'Tank Week' and they improvised their own – by cutting and fixing hoardings to a tram. Yarmouth raised £183,000.*

# 9 The Armistice and After

The Armistice was declared at the eleventh hour of the eleventh day of the eleventh month 1918. Public announcements were made and impromptu celebrations were held across the county but no proper celebration could be held until 'the boys came home'. A date of 19 July 1919 was set for what was to be the national grand celebration of Peace Day.

On Peace Day in Norwich the bells of the churches rang out, a great Thanksgiving Service was held in the Cathedral followed by a procession to the Market Place where representative detachments from all the military and civilian forces in the county lined and filled a square and were given a fine address and tribute by the Lord Mayor. There were then great festivities, luncheons for returned servicemen and organised sports, fancy dress parades and special events held across the parks; it seemed like 'the whole of Norwich and his wife' turned out for the proceedings. Events mirroring these grand celebrations were held in every town and village across the county.

*One almighty cheer goes up from the Officers and Men of 51st and 52nd (Graduated) Battalion, The Bedfordshire Regiment on the announcement of the Armistice in Norwich Market Place on the eleventh hour, of the eleventh day of the eleventh month 1918.*

Tragically, the county was also counting the cost of the war. Thousands of families had lost loved ones although some still held out hope for their boy who had been posted 'missing'. But as the weeks, months and years passed by after the Armistice each had to come to terms with the realisation that their lost love was never to return. Some mothers, wives and sweethearts never accepted it; many of those who did wore mourning black for the rest of their lives.

In 1920 the *Norfolk Roll of Honour* was published with returns from 626 of the 700 Norfolk parishes; it showed some 11,771 Norfolk men and women lost their lives in the war, over 2200 of them from Norwich. In its statistical summary it was estimated out of the total number of Norfolk people who served the proportion of them missing or killed was about 1 in 9. In the United Kingdom one man out of every 57 inhabitants was killed or reported missing. In Norfolk the proportion was even greater – one in 42. Out of the 20,000 or so English and Welsh parishes that saw its young men and women

*The parents and widows of some of the Norfolk fallen gather for the photographer on Thorpe Station platform, Norwich, before leaving for France to visit the graves of their loved ones c.1919.*

serve in the First World War, only fifty-three saw them all return, they became known as 'Thankful Villages' – Ovington was one of them. Twelve boys marched away to war and all twelve returned. It is believed Ovington is the only village or town in Norfolk to have this claim.

The published figures could not include those who died in the ensuing years from wounds received or sickness contracted on active service, neither do they include the thousands of local men disabled in body, mind and soul during The Great War.

The genteel world of Victorian and Edwardian life had been shattered during the carnage of First World War, everybody lost somebody they knew, loved and cared for. Soon there was talk of 'the loss of a generation'. Thousands of those young men had innocently walked arm-in-arm with their sweethearts and fiancées among the summer fields across our county, along our coastal pathways, dotted and spread with poppies, perhaps lingering at the spiritual heartland of Poppyland, the Garden of Sleep at Sidestrand.

Many of them already lay dead on the fields of France and Flanders by 1916, when on 26 February that year, as the plans for a 'Big Push' on the Somme were being formulated, the church tower of the Garden of Sleep, the focal point and so emblematical of that magical world slipped, unwitnessed, over the edge of the cliff and was smashed to pieces on the beach below. On just the First Day of the Battle of the Somme on 1 July 1916 the British Army suffered over 57,000 casualties. Many had said in the years before that Poppyland would end when the tower fell. Like the tower, a generation fell and was lost forever. The irony was not lost when poppies flowered 'between the crosses, row on row' in Flanders fields. Nothing was ever to be the same again.

Every Norfolk man and woman who served in the Great War has now passed away. Many of us can still remember them on Armistice Day parade, the one day a year most of them wore their medals and marched again with their old comrades. One of the last of them wrote: 'There can never be another war like the Great War, nor the comradeship and endurance we knew then. I think, perhaps, men are not like that now.'

*The dedication of East Harling War Memorial. Such scenes were repeated across Norfolk throughout the 1920s.*

# Select Bibliography

Christopher Andrew, *Secret Service: The Making of the British Intelligence Community* (London 1985)

G. Balfour, *The Armoured Train; Its Development and Usage* (London 1981)

Jeremy Bastin, *The Norfolk Yeomanry in Peace and War* (Fakenham 1986)

Christopher Bird, *Silent Sentinels* (Dereham 1999)

J.P. Blake (ed.) *The Official regulations for Volunteer Training Corps and for County Volunteer Organisations (England and Wales)* (London 1916)

Thekla Bowser, *The Story of British VAD Work in the Great War,* (London 1925)

John Canning, *1914* (London 1967)

James Cantlie, *First Aid to the Injured* (London 1910)

James Cantlie, *Red Cross Training Manual No.3* (London 1914)

Tim Carew, *The Royal Norfolk Regiment* (London 1967)

H G Castle, *Fire Over England* (London 1982)

Winston S.Churchill, *His Father's Son: The Life of Randolph Churchill* (London 1996)

Randolph Churchill, *Twenty-One Years* (London 1964)

A. E. Clark-Kennedy, *Edith Cavell: Pioneer and Patriot* (London 1965)

Terry Davy, *Dereham in the Great War* (Dereham 1990)

A. Campbell Erroll, *A History of Sheringham and Beeston Regis* (Sheringham 1970)

Val Fiddian (ed.), *Salthouse: The Story of a Norfolk Village* (Salthouse 2003)

Helen Fraser, *Women and War Work* (New York 1918)

Harold Hood, *Illustrated Memorial of the East Coast Raids by the German Navy and Airships* (Middlesborough 1915)

C. B. Hawkins, *Norwich: A Social Study* (London 1910)

Lt Col Ronnie Cole Mackintosh, *A Century of Service to Mankind* (London 1994)

L L Gore, *The History of Hunstanton* (Bognor Regis 1983)

Gerald Gliddon (ed.), *Norfolk & Suffolk in the Great War* (Norwich 1988)

Jane Hales, *A Tale of the Norfolk Red Cross* Watton 1970

Holcombe Ingleby, *The Zeppelin Raid in West Norfolk* (London 1915)

Brigadier E A James, *British Regiments 1914-18* (fourth edition) (London 1993)

Tom Jerrold, *Our War-Time Kitchen Garden* (London 1917)

Major J H Kennedy, *Attleborough in War Time* (London c1920)

Peter Kent, *Fortifications of East Anglia* (Lavenham 1988)

P.S. King, *The Volunteer Force and the Volunteer Training Corps during the Great War: Official record of the Central Association Volunteer Regiments –* (London 1920)

Colonel C E Knight MBE, *The Auxiliary Hospitals The British Red Cross Society and St John Ambulance in Norfolk 1914-1919* (Norwich 1989)

Herbert Leeds (ed.) *Norwich Peace Souvenir* (Norwich 1920)

Dan McCaffery, *Air Aces: The Lives and Times of Twelve Canadian Fighter Pilots* (Toronto, Canada 1990)

Lyn MacDonald, *1914* (London 1987)

Arthur Mee, *The King's England: Norfolk* (London 1940)

Captain Joseph Morris, *The German Air Raids on Great Britain* (London 1969)

Maurice Morson, *A Force Remembered* (Derby 2000)

H. Newhouse (Recruiting Officer), *A Little Chat about The 1st (City of Norwich) Battalion, Norfolk Volunteers* (Norwich 1916)

Bob Ogley, Mark Davison, Ian Currie, *The Norfolk and Suffolk Weather Book* (Westerham 1993)

Peter Parker, *The Old Lie* (London 1987)

F. Loraine Petre, *The History of the Norfolk Regiment* vol.II (Norwich 1924

Dr Eric Puddy, *A History of the Order of St John of Jerusalem in Norfolk* (Dereham 1961)

W J Reader, *At Duty's Call: A Study in Obsolete Patriotism* (Manchester 1988)

A V Sellwood, *The Saturday Night Soldiers* (London 1966)

W. E. Shewell-Cooper, *Land Girl: A Manual for Volunteers in the Women's Land Army* (London 1941)

Sue Smart, *When Heroes Die* (Derby 2001)

Jonathan Riley-Smith, *Hospitallers: The History of The Order of St John* (London 1999)

Rowland Ryder, *Edith Cavell* (London 1975)

C.F. Snowden Gamble, *The Story of a North Sea Air Station* (London 1928)

Neil R. Storey, *A Century of Norwich* (Stroud 2000)

Neil R. Storey, *A Norfolk Century* (Stroud 1999)

Neil R. Storey, *Norfolk at War* (Stroud 1995)

Neil R. Storey, *Norfolk in the Great War* (Wellington 2008)

Neil R. Storey,*The Pride of Norfolk – A History of the Norfolk Territorial Battalions in Two World Wars* (Wellington 2009)

Neil R. Storey, *The Royal Norfolk Regiment* (Stroud 1997)

Warner, Philip *Field-Marshal Earl Haig* (London 1991)

A Rawlinson, *The Defence of London 1915-18* (London 1923)

Peter M. Walker, *Norfolk Military Airfields* (Norwich 1997)

Ray Westlake, *The Territorial Battalions* (London 1986)

Ray Westlake, *British Battalions in France & Belgium 1914* (Barnsley 1997)

Henry Wills, *Pillboxes* (Leo Cooper 1985)

Emily Wood, *The Red Cross* (London 1995)

R J Wyatt, *Death from the Skies* (Norwich 1990)

## Reference Books and Government Publications

*Kelly's Directory of Cambridgeshire, Norfolk and Suffolk* (London 1912)

*A Pictorial and Descriptive Record of the Red Cross Hospitals of Norwich and Norfolk* (Norwich 1917)

St John Ambulance Association, *Annals of the Ambulance Department* (London 1929)

Norfolk News Company, *Norfolk Roll of Honour 1914 -18* (Norwich 1920)

City of Norwich, Public Library Committee, *Norwich Roll of Honour 1914-19* (Norwich 1920)

War Office, *Scheme for the Organisation of Voluntary Aid in England and Wales* (HMSO 1909)

War Office, *Scheme for the Organisation of Voluntary Aid in England and Wales* (December 1910 Revision)(HMSO 1910)

## Reports

British Red Cross Society & Order of St John of Jerusalem, *Financial Statement of The Joint War Committee* (London 1918)

British Red Cross Society & Order of St John of Jerusalem, *Final Reports by the Joint War Committee and the Joint War Finance Committee of the British Red Cross Society and Order of St John of Jerusalem in England on Voluntary Aid Rendered to the Sick and Wounded at Home and Abroad and to British Prisoners of War 1914-19* (HMSO 1921)

British Red Cross Society, *Norfolk Branch Report 1918* (Norwich 1918)

British Red Cross Society, *Norfolk Branch Report 1919* (Norwich 1920)

St John Ambulance, *X District Reports* 1909–1919

## Newspapers & Journals

*Aeroplane Monthly*

*First Aid, Journal of The St John Ambulance Brigade*

*The Red Cross, Journal of The British Red Cross Society*

*Carrow Works Magazine*

*Dereham & Fakenham Times*

*East Anglian Daily Times*

*Eastern Daily Press*

*Lynn News*

*Norfolk Fair*

*Norfolk Chronicle*

*Norwich Mercury*

*The War Illustrated*

*The Volunteer Training Corps Gazette*

*The Times*

*The Daily Express*

*The Daily Mirror*

*Punch Magazine*

*Yarmouth Mercury*

## Sources

### National Archives

WO 33/779 Distribution of Home Defence Troops (1916)

WO 33/828 Approved armaments and Anti-Aircraft guns (1917)

WO 372 Service Medal and Award Rolls Index, First World War

WO 372/23 Women's Services, Distinguished Conduct Medals and Military Medals

AIR 1/2123/207/73/2 Intelligence Section report on enemy airship raids on Britain (January-June 1915)

AIR 1/2123/207/73/3 Intelligence Section report on enemy airship raids on Britain (August-September 1915)

AIR 1/2123/207/73/12 Intelligence Section report on enemy airship raids on Britain (September-October 1916)

AIR 1/2123/207/73/28 Intelligence Section report on enemy airship raids on Britain on enemy airship raids on Britain (June-August 1918)

### Norfolk Record Office

For Smith-Dorrien's General Line of evacuation of the civil population see: NRO, MC 947/1

Deposit made by Colonel C E Knight MBE: Material relating to Voluntary Aid Societies: St John Ambulance Brigade and British Red Cross Society: NRO, SO161/1-37

### Internet Sources

Commonwealth War Graves Commission
www.cwgc.org/debt_of_honour.asp

Royal Navy Submarine Museum
www.rnsubmus.co.uk
(Submarine Losses 1904 To Present Day)

The Aerodrome: Aces and Aircraft of World War One
www.theaerodrome.com

The Story of Edith Cavell
www.edithcavell.org.uk

U Boat Net (German OB 3/11/14 and loss of Yorck)
www.uboat.net